Last Days in Cloud Cuckooland

Last Days in Cloud Cuckooland

Dispatches from White Africa

GRAHAM BOYNTON

RANDOM HOUSE NEW YORK

Several names have been changed in this book in order to protect the privacy of the real characters. Dion in the Prologue and Vince in Chapter 12 are pseudonyms, as are Barry, Bloat, Fivey, Lofty, Andrew Hastings MacGregor, and Stretch in Chapter 9.

Library of Congress Cataloging-in-Publication Data
Boynton, Graham. Last days in cloud cuckooland/Graham Boynton.
p. cm.
ISBN 0-679-43204-3
1. Boynton, Graham.   2. Apartheid—South Africa.   3. Antiapartheid movements—South Africa.   4. South Africa—Race relations.
5. Zimbabwe—Social life and customs.   6. Zimbabwe—Race relations.
7. Journalists—South Africa—Biography.   I. Title.
DT1957.B68   1997
968.05—dc21   97-894

Random House website address: http://www.randomhouse.com/

Printed in the United States of America on acid-free paper

2 4 6 8 9 7 5 3

First Edition

Book design by Lilly Langotsky

For Adriaane
and for Barnet William,
wherever he may be

Contents

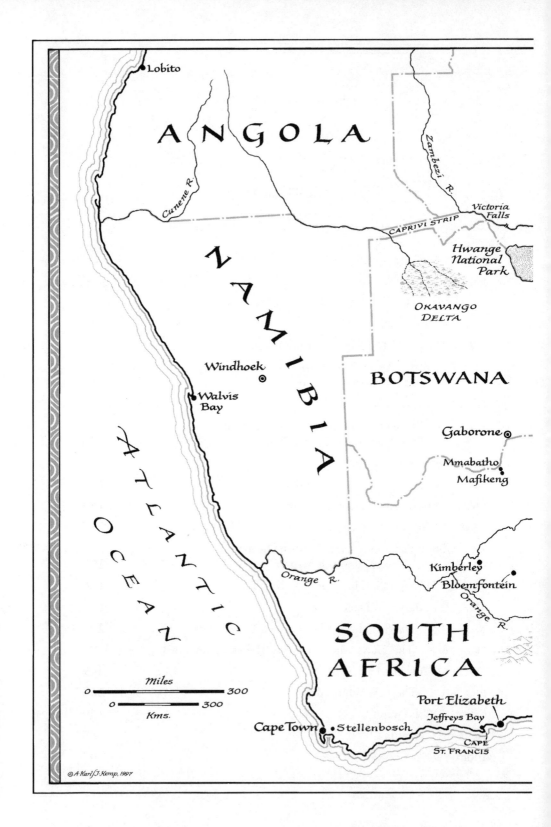

Lobito

ANGOLA

Cunene R.

Zambezi R.

Victoria
Falls

CAPRIVI STRIP

Hwange
National
Park

NAMIBIA

OKAVANGO
DELTA

Windhoek

BOTSWANA

Walvis
Bay

ATLANTIC

Gaborone

OCEAN

Mmabatho
Mafikeng

Orange R.

Kimberley
Bloemfontein

Orange R.

SOUTH
AFRICA

Miles

0   300

0   300

Kms.

Port Elizabeth

Jeffreys Bay

Cape Town   Stellenbosch

CAPE
St. Francis

© A. Karl/J. Kemp, 1997

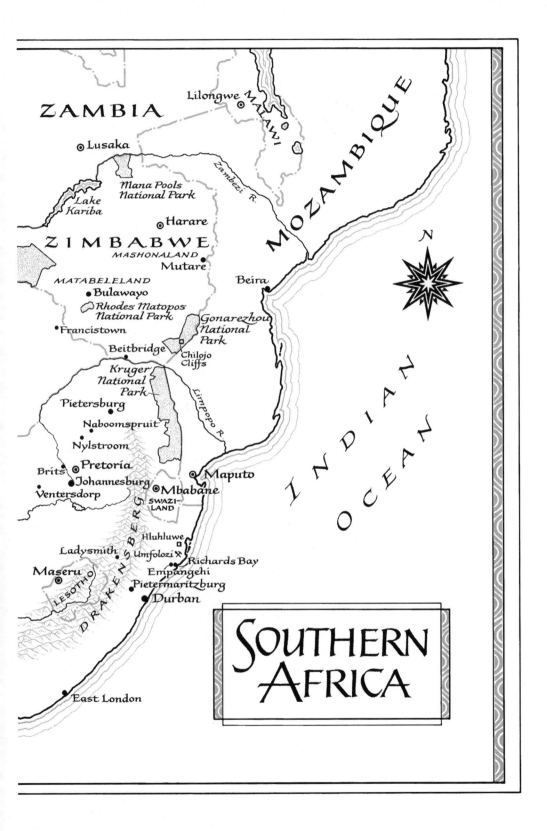

ZAMBIA

• Lusaka

MALAWI
Lilongwe ◎

MOZAMBIQUE

Zambezi R.

Mana Pools
National Park

Lake
Kariba

• Harare

ZIMBABWE
MASHONALAND
Mutare

MATABELELAND

• Bulawayo

Rhodes Matopos
National Park

Beira

Gonarezhou
National
Park

• Francistown

Beitbridge

Chilojo
Cliffs

Kruger
National
Park

Limpopo R.

• Pietersburg

• Naboomspruit

• Nylstroom

INDIAN

OCEAN

Brits • Pretoria

• Johannesburg

• Maputo

Ventersdorp

◎ Mbabane

SWAZI-
LAND

DRAKENSBERG

Hluhluwe

Ladysmith
Umfolozi

Richards Bay

Maseru ◎

Empangehi

Pietermaritzburg

LESOTHO

• Durban

N

SOUTHERN
AFRICA

• East London

Chronology

1652   Jan van Riebeeck arrives at the Cape of Good Hope and establishes a European presence in southern Africa; he and his Dutch countrymen form the nucleus of the Afrikaner nation.

1795   Britain takes over the Cape Colony from the Dutch East India Company.

1820   British settlers arrive at the Cape of Good Hope.

1828   The Zulu king Shaka is assassinated.

1833   Slavery is abolished throughout the British Empire.

1834   To get away from the British colonial rulers at the Cape, Afrikaner farmers, the Boers, begin trekking into the southern African interior and eventually form the Transvaal and Orange Free State republics.

1838   Shaka's successor, Dingane, leads a force that murders the Boer Piet Retief and seventy-nine of his men.

On December 16, the Boers take revenge and defeat the Zulus at the Battle of Blood River.

1886   Johannesburg is founded.

1888   Chief Lobengula signs the Rudd Concession, which gives Cecil Rhodes's company access to Matabele lands.

1890   Cecil Rhodes becomes prime minister of the Cape Colony.

1894   The town of Bulawayo, in what is to become Southern Rhodesia, is formally inaugurated.

        The slaughter of the Shangani Patrol by Lobengula's warriors gives Rhodesia its first white martyrs.

1899–
1902   The Boer War. The defeat of the Boers by the British army leads to a period of British dominance in South Africa.

1910   The Union of South Africa is formed from the former British colonies of the Cape and Natal and from the Boer republics of Transvaal and the Orange Free State.

1912   The South African Native Congress is founded; it is later renamed the African National Congress (ANC).

1914   Afrikaners form the National Party.

1948   South Africa's National Party wins its first election and begins introducing apartheid legislation.

1953   Southern Rhodesia joins Nyasaland and Northern Rhodesia to form the Central African Federation.

        The liberal missionary Garfield Todd becomes prime minister of Southern Rhodesia.

1958   Todd is ousted by his own cabinet in Southern Rhodesia.

        Hendrik Verwoerd becomes prime minister of South Africa.

1960   South African police shoot down sixty-eight black demonstrators at Sharpeville.

        The African National Congress is banned.

        Whites flee the Congo.

British prime minister Harold Macmillan delivers his end-of-empire Wind of Change speech to the South African parliament.

1961   South Africa declares itself a republic.

1964   The Central African Federation is dissolved.

Ian Smith becomes Southern Rhodesia's first native-born prime minister.

In June, Nelson Mandela and seven fellow members of the ANC are sentenced to life imprisonment for treason.

1965   The Southern Rhodesian government makes a Unilateral Declaration of Independence (UDI) on November 11. Britain imposes sanctions on the rebel colony.

1966   Prime Minister Verwoerd is assassinated in the South African parliament; John Vorster succeeds him.

1970   Southern Rhodesia declares itself a republic.

1972   A guerrilla attack on a Southern Rhodesian farm called Altena marks the start of the bush war.

An Air Rhodesia Viscount carrying fifty-two Rhodesian vacationers is brought down by a SAM-7 missile.

1973   Right-wing Afrikaners form the Afrikaner Weerstandsbeweging (AWB).

1974   A coup in Portugal leads to the almost immediate independence of its African colonies, including Angola and Mozambique; civil wars break out in both countries.

1976   In South Africa, the Soweto schoolchildren's uprising takes place.

Henry Kissinger and Prime Minister Vorster persuade Ian Smith to accept the principle of majority rule for Southern Rhodesia.

1977   Black activist Steve Biko dies in police custody in South Africa.

1978   P.W. Botha becomes prime minister of South Africa.

1979   A Rhodesian settlement is reached, legality is restored, sanctions are lifted, and the first democratic elections are set, for February 1980.

         Black trade unions are legalized in South Africa.

1980   In March, Southern Rhodesia becomes Zimbabwe, and Robert Mugabe becomes the country's first black head of state.

1985   South Africa's Mixed Marriages Act, one of the cornerstones of apartheid legislation, is repealed.

1989   F. W. de Klerk becomes president of South Africa.

1990   The ban on the ANC is lifted, and Nelson Mandela is released from prison; President de Klerk calls for "a new South Africa."

1992   In a referendum, South Africa's whites approve reform.

1993   Chris Hani, one of the leaders of the ANC, is assassinated by white extremists.

1994   South Africa's first democratic elections take place.

         White rule ends in Africa, and Nelson Mandela is invested as president of South Africa.

Last Days in Cloud Cuckooland

PROLOGUE

The Storming of Paradise

Johannesburg is at its most relaxed and pleasant on Sunday mornings. Through the week it is all hustle and noise, the cacophony of commerce one would expect in Africa's business capital. But on Sunday nothing stirs in the city, and in the affluent northern suburbs the only sound is the soft padding of Nike trainers on asphalt as joggers make their way through tree-lined streets.

The northern suburbs is a privileged world of large houses with manicured gardens, regulation swimming pools, tennis courts, and phalanxes of servants to keep things ticking over. Nadine Gordimer lives here, so does Helen Suzman. The cars—BMWs, Mercedes, Porsches, designer four-by-fours—are always glistening clean, and the cellars are stocked with the best Cape wines. The residents are served by Dallas-type shopping malls, islands of conspicuous consumption where you can buy everything from a Ferrari Testarossa to a million-rand diamond ring.

In striking contrast to the pretty suburbs, the city itself is plain and ugly—an agglomeration of monolithic, colorless 1950s skyscrapers. It is encircled by threads of asphalt highway and surrounded by the mine dumps that created its wealth. Only the marvelous Diamond House, designed by Helmut Jahn, breaks the monotony of an architectural landscape that owes more in spirit to '50s functionalism than colonial optimism.

At one time the center of the white business community, downtown Johannesburg has belonged to the blacks since the 1980s. Even before Nelson Mandela came out of prison and before the democratization process began, potent socioeconomic forces had drawn a million blacks into the center of the city and had the whites retreating to suburbs that grew like kudzu almost all the way to Pretoria. The city became the noisy, dirty, vivid, exhilarating heart of the new Third World South Africa, and the northern suburbs— the Beverly Hills of the bushveld—became one of the last refuges of the privileged lifestyle that was the old South Africa.

In 1994, during the first heady months of democracy, when South Africa took to calling itself the Rainbow Nation, wealthy blacks began moving into the northern suburbs. This was part of the new dispensation, with former bastions of white exclusivity and privilege falling one after the other. Previously elitist sports like rugby and cricket now boasted black heroes; international artists like the Rolling Stones and the Three Tenors clamored to tour a country they had all shunned during the apartheid years; and everyone was hoping Cape Town would succeed in its bid to host the 2004 Olympic Games. Indeed, the Rainbow Nation had become so fashionable that the appropriately polymorphous Michael Jackson had expressed an interest in immigrating.

For all that, things were not entirely right. Beneath the surface there was a slow rumbling, and the epicenters of the rumbling were the black townships beyond the polite suburbs. Upwards of twenty million unemployed black South Africans in the townships were waiting for the Rainbow Nation to come to them, to give them houses and jobs and a new life. I remember on election day in 1994 coming across an old woman on a plot of bare land on the outskirts of Soweto. She had swept a large rectangle of space in the dirt and told me she was preparing for the new house the African National Congress had promised. When Mandela is president, she said, I will have my house.

But the benefits of the Rainbow Nation were slow to come. Although Mandela had promised that a million houses would be built in the first five years of his presidency, barely a thousand had been constructed in the first year. There was the usual political finger-pointing about who was responsible—inefficient black bureaucrats from the new order who couldn't make a decision, or spiteful white bureaucrats from the old order who were intent on sabotaging progress. It did not matter. The point was that little was being done for the twenty million unemployed blacks. There were no jobs. The economy was reasonably healthy but was growing at nowhere near the 5 or 6 percent needed to begin drawing these people into the workplace. So the political violence of the apartheid years was replaced by criminal violence. Gangs of armed bandits poured out of the townships and laid siege to their prosperous fellow countrymen, black and white. The Rainbow Nation was filled with a new generation of brutal and nihilistic criminals.

DAVID DODDS IS A TYPICAL WHITE SUBURBANITE, AND ON ONE OF those tranquil Johannesburg Sunday mornings a few months into the second year of the new democracy in South Africa he found himself pacing the grounds of his comfortable home, thinking the unthinkable. He was thinking that the time had come to emigrate. David Dodds is tall, blond, rugged looking, a commercial photographer of some repute in South Africa. His journey through Africa had been similar to my own. He was born in Kenya, where his father worked as an industrial-relations expert. In 1963, when Kenya gained independence and began to be Africanized, Dodds senior lost his job. He packed up his family and headed south, to Rhodesia, where he became the country's director of family planning, building an international reputation and making a significant contribution to his adopted country. But then Rhodesia became independent, and in 1980 Dodds packed up his family again and headed farther south, first to Swaziland and then to South Africa. Finally, after the sons, John, David, and Anthony, had left home, he and his wife retired to Simonstown, at the southern tip of the African continent. They could go no far-ther south.

The Dodds' retreat is the story of white colonial life in Africa in microcosm. Since 1960, the white settlers who brought the twenti-eth century to Africa have been on the run. When independence swept through the continent from north to south, the new African leaders made conciliatory statements about their former oppressors, but they really didn't want too many whites around. Just enough to keep some of the essential services going. You could see their point. We had stolen their land, and we had hardly been benevolent land-lords. So, like the Dodds family, most of us retreated, bit by bit, until we reached South Africa or abandoned the continent entirely.

The Dodds boys put down their roots in Johannesburg. John moved into the computer business and started the Desk-Top Pub-lishing Association; with his wife, Kathy, and their two children he settled into a large house in the prosperous white suburb of Park-town. David, a die-hard bachelor who serial-dated Johannesburg's most beautiful models, bought a large bungalow with two acres in the nearby suburb of Bryanston. They were both concerned about the future under a black government—they said they'd seen it all before in Kenya and Rhodesia—but they were determined to re-treat no farther. They had been born Africans, and they believed they belonged in Africa.

I had just finished working on an assignment with David Dodds early in December 1993 when the news came through that John had been shot. We had been in Cape Town for a week, soaking up the optimism of that beautiful city and feeling good about the end of apartheid, and David had returned to Johannesburg to process his photographs. As soon as he got the call, he leaped into his car. He was at his brother's house within twelve minutes, running every red light along the way. John was still alive when the paramedics drove him away, but he died in the operating room an hour later.

It had been a typical armed robbery gone wrong. Five young black men had forced the maid at gunpoint to stand outside the back door and shout for help. When John came out to see what was wrong, they burst in, and he tried to hold them off, shouting for

Kathy to get their gun from the bedroom. In the scuffle, a shot had gone off and a bullet entered John's left side and tore open his arteries.

David and John had shared a passion for sport shooting, and within six weeks of John's funeral, David had won the long-range target-shooting competition at the South African championships, had been selected to shoot for South Africa at the Commonwealth Games, and had come in fourth, just outside the medals. He'd also begun fortifying his home, erecting an eight-foot-high wall strung with coils of razor wire and putting up electronic security gates. The house was fitted with an alarm system that was connected to Security Centre, a private armed-response company. For all that, in the last months of 1994 and into the following year, armed gangs broke in four times, always while David was out. He installed more security equipment and bought a flock of geese to patrol the grounds with his two golden retrievers. There were now coils of razor wire running along the lawn beside the wall.

On Wednesday, August 23, 1995, David had some clients around for a drink, and after they left, at seven, he drove across to the nearby shopping mall to buy a takeout dinner. When he returned to his fortress home, the electronic gates swung shut behind him, and he peered out across the garden, making sure all his traps were in place. It was still. The geese were silent, and the dogs were asleep inside the house. Even so, he thought, he should have had his nine-millimeter Tanfoglio revolver with him. It was in the safe.

Once inside, David took a beer from the fridge and carried his plate of spaghetti into the living room, a large, open-plan lounge and dining area with subdued lighting supplied by scattered lamps. As he was placing the tray on a wooden stool in front of the couch, he realized that there was a strange shadow in the dark far corner of the room. Then he looked up and saw two young black men standing behind him against the fireplace. One was pointing a revolver at his head.

His weight was still on the balls of his feet, and he leaped up with the heavy stool in his hands, scattering containers of food. Shouting "Fuck!" and then "No! No! No!" he careered across the room, feeling as if he were plowing his way through quicksand. Everything seemed to be happening in slow motion, and as he was closing the gap between him and the men, he even had time to wonder why the one with the gun hadn't already pulled the trigger.

When he did shoot, he was way off line. The next second, Dodds hit him with the stool, and another shot was fired, this one ricocheting off the wall and thumping into Dodds's stomach, winding him. As he rose up once more to attack the gunman, a third shot went off. That bullet grazed Dodds's skull, leaving a neat furrow.

He pinned the gunman to the floor and tried to wrestle the revolver from his hand, but the second man jumped into the fray, grabbing an ornamental ax from the wall and rushing toward him. The man brought the ax down on Dodds's wrist, striking the steel wristband of his watch. The impact broke the wooden ax handle. An inch either way, and it would have taken Dodds's hand off.

It was at that moment the maid responded to the gunshots and pressed the alarm linking the Dodds home to Security Centre, setting off a siren. The two assailants paused and then fled into the bedroom and out the window they had broken in through.

Even as Dodds was getting to his feet, taking in gulps of air, he heard the Security Centre vehicle squealing to a halt at his gates. It had arrived so promptly because the guards were already in the area, responding to a carjacking at the shopping center and another armed robbery a few streets away.

That night, Dodds began to think the unthinkable. As his father had said, they could go no farther south and the choice was either to stand up to the bastards or leave Africa forever. He thought of Australia, but it seemed so remote. Canada was too cold. Europe was overcrowded and dirty. . . .

Then on Sunday, Dodds made his decision. He was going to stand his ground. He would resist with appropriate force. The next day he laid down more razor wire and planted a series of trip wires on the front lawn that were connected to homemade guns. He began carrying his nine-millimeter revolver everywhere he went, to photography sessions and client meetings, even when he got up to answer the phone. If his clients expressed dismay, he'd tell them that pretty soon every white would be carrying a weapon. His entrances to and exits from his fortress were conducted with military precision, as if he were anticipating an armed attack.

When we talked on the phone a few months after the incident, Dodds tapped his Tanfoglio revolver against the receiver and said, "So far, so good." There had been no further attacks, although the house had been burglarized once while he was away. He laughed and said, "Welcome to the new South Africa."

IF DAVID DODDS WAS ADAMANT THAT HE WOULD NOT BE MOVED, there were thousands of his peers who were no longer so certain. Dinner-party chatter in the plush suburban homes was almost exclusively of violence and emigration. This latter subject has been popular at other crucial moments in South Africa's history, most notably in 1960, after the Sharpeville massacre; in 1976, after the Soweto schoolchildren's uprising; and in the mid-1980s, during the state of emergency. With each crisis large numbers of educated professional white South Africans have shaken themselves free of Africa and have retreated to the security of the West. Now the crime wave was threatening to dislodge another group.

The statistics made grim reading. The country's crime rate was twice the international average. A serious crime was being committed in South Africa every seventeen seconds. There was a robbery every six minutes. More than 50 people were murdered every day. The murder rate of 45 per 100,000 people soared above the international average of 5.5 per 100,000. The crime *de jour* was carjacking: in the first six months of 1995, there were 5,033 of them nationwide, 4,060 in the Johannesburg-Soweto area alone. Since 1990, rape had increased by 80 percent, serious assault by 38 percent, vehicle theft by 43 percent.

The dinner parties resonated with stories of terrifying encounters with armed criminals. A few years back these were infrequent enough to be related with relish and carefree braggadocio, confirmations of white Africans' hard-arsed self-image. But no longer. The confrontations between the haves and the have-nots had turned very nasty, and at one northern-suburb party not long after Dodds's encounter, I heard my fellow diners rattle off half a dozen chilling tales, one after the other, of incidents that had taken place during the previous week. One advertising executive described how just two days earlier a young doctor, driving with his ten-year-old daughter in the passenger seat, had been shot dead by carjackers because he'd been slow to get out of the car. "I just can't help wondering how long it will be before it's me," the executive said. Which was precisely what everyone else at the table was thinking at that moment.

The new black government officials rightly blamed apartheid for having created a society of unequals, but they knew that if the crime wave was not checked, it would have a profound effect on foreign investment and the now booming tourism industry. Since they appeared incapable of taking the firm action that the beleaguered citizens in the northern suburbs believed was necessary, however, their intentions were met with skepticism. After the young doctor had been shot dead in front of his daughter, President Mandela telephoned the family to offer his sympathies. The call was met with polite hostility, and the president was told that it was too late for condolences. He then contacted the region's prime minister, Tokyo Sexwale, and instructed him to pay his respects to the family in person. Sexwale's reception was equally chilly.

The nervous whites in post-democracy Johannesburg were the skilled, professionals who had chosen not to join the exoduses of the mid-1970s and mid-1980s because they could not have matched their lavish lifestyles abroad and because they clung to that most basic of pioneer tenets—optimism. *"Alles sal reg kom,"* the Afrikaners say—"everything will come right."

Now these whites were having to measure their privileged lifestyles against the high costs of maintaining and protecting them. Several friends of mine were diagnosed as suffering from something called low-level depression, apparently brought on by constant proximity to violence. They no longer dared to drive their cars straight onto their property and circled the block a few times to ensure that no bandits were waiting to pounce the moment the electronic gates swung open. Nor did they stop for red traffic lights at night or take shortcuts along unlit streets.

One weekday afternoon I was sitting in a friend's garden, tranquilly reading and working, when the silence was broken by urgent cries beyond the stone wall. A neighbor was shouting, "Help. Help. I've got burglars in my house. Call the police." I ran inside, grabbed a couple of knobkerries (African fighting sticks similar to shillelaghs), and hurried across the street to find a white businessman in his late thirties circling his house, pointing at the drawn curtains. "They're in there. They're in there," he was repeating somewhat hysterically.

He said he'd returned early from watching a cricket match and had found a station wagon, a *bakkie,* parked in his driveway. The driver had hit the accelerator and wheeled off the grounds into the street and was probably halfway to Soweto by now. His accomplices must still be in the house, trapped, and the neighbor wanted me to circle the building with him to make sure they didn't flee before the cops arrived. Around back we found the smashed window they'd gone through. We had no idea how many were in there or whether they were armed.

It occurred to me that if the thieves were carrying AK-47s, which are commonplace in South Africa now, and chose to blast their way out, my two knobkerries would provide little protection. I was circling the house with mounting trepidation when the police arrived in a cloud of dust. We followed four heavily armed men in through the front door. Two trembling black boys were found hiding behind the shower stall in the bathroom. They were unarmed, and the cops gave them a couple of open-handed clouts on the head, then slapped cuffs on them. They were taken out to the lawn in front of the swimming pool and pushed roughly to the ground. There they lay, facedown, their arms locked behind their backs, looking like two black fish just pulled from the water. While the cops were taking the neighbor's statement, I sat on the grass beside the boys and asked them how old they were. One said he was twelve.

A knot of black women had formed on the far side of the street. They were chattering and clucking and clapping their hands, and when the boys were bundled into the police van, they pointed and shouted. I recognized several of them as maids who worked and lived in the neighborhood, and I crossed the road to talk to them.

I explained what had happened and added somewhat self-consciously that I felt terribly sorry for the two young boys, who were no more than children. Without pause, in spontaneous unison, the maids rounded on me. "You call them children," sneered one. "We call them murderers. If they come to our houses and find us there, they beat us and they kill us. They are not children, they are criminals."

Having poured scorn on my white liberal conscience, they proceeded to catalog various atrocities that had been visited on their friends and colleagues in recent months. One said that her sister had been bound and gagged and thrown into a bath of scalding water before a gang ransacked the house. She had survived but was a nervous wreck. Another described how the maid from the corner house had been beaten unconscious by armed robbers; the gang cleaned the house out, and when she came to, the leader was standing over her, pointing an assault rifle at her head. He told her he would have to kill her because she could identify his gang. Then without a word he turned on his heels and followed the others out of the house. She still did not understand why he hadn't shot her.

AFRICA'S WHITE RULERS HAD ALWAYS ARGUED THAT AN EROSION of law and order would come with black majority rule. Afrikaners have a name for it—*swart gevaar,* which means "black danger." It was one of the principal justifications for apartheid. Take away the constraints imposed by European civilization, they had said, and the continent would be plunged into the darkness of pre-colonial times; into the savagery and desolation of Conrad's Congo where, like Kurtz, we would all sink to the lowest level of degradation.

All my life I instinctively resisted such thinking, but on those harrowing first days and nights in the new South Africa, I began to find myself haunted by the specter of *swart gevaar.* I'd lie awake in the dark in my suburban Johannesburg bedroom, sweating the white man's sweat, listening to the sirens and the squealing tires of the security vehicles speeding from this crime to that, waiting for the inevitable crackle of gunfire. In the intermittent silences I strained to hear rustling in the bushes and the soft footfalls of an armed gang coming over the wall.

I am not particularly proud of this, but on those threatening, ink-black Johannesburg nights, waiting wide-eyed for my executioners to arrive, I began to hanker for the old days of colonial rule. Not the harsh oppression of apartheid, but the more benign paternalism of British colonies like Rhodesia and Kenya. These were reactionary thoughts, I know, but I could not resist them. I remembered the Rhodesia of my youth, when people didn't bother to lock their houses at night or their cars ever. Guns were seldom used for crimes, and the victims of the occasional robbery were never physically attacked. As kids we walked the suburban streets at night without fear, and as teenagers we hitchhiked around the country without a qualm.

Suddenly, vividly, the white African's inglorious past appeared to me as a glorious memory.

MY FAMILY ARRIVED IN AFRICA ON AUGUST 8, 1951. LIKE MOST OF our fellow British immigrants, we were escaping the gloom of post-war Europe. My father, the dashing eldest son of a well-to-do Midlands family, had lived a full life before the war playing jazz piano in nightclubs and racing motorcycles during the day. The war took the dash out of him. For five years he'd served king and country with distinction, first in North Africa and then in Burma, but when he returned to Britain, drained of his youth and his exuberance, he found nothing to revive him. Soon after marrying my mother, he began casting around, looking for somewhere far-off, a place where he could recharge his soul.

He liked the idea of Australia—a young, dynamic country populated mainly by fellow Brits, a familiar culture set against a huge landscape, no native problem to speak of. My mother, however, was more drawn to Africa, her enthusiasm fueled by a former business partner who'd immigrated to South Africa two years before and who sent back fervently optimistic reports. It was my mother who prevailed.

The author's father in Rhodesia in the 1950s.

My parents must have been thrilled that fine spring day when they looked upon Table Mountain for the first time and saw the rows of whitewashed, gabled houses nestled against it and heard the crashing of the surf on blinding-white beaches. Here were sunshine and cobalt-blue skies instead of overcast, damp-to-the-marrow old Britain. Here was a land of opportunity instead of a land of lost causes. Here was the promise of a new life, of something to work for. I was three years old, so for me this might as well have been Minsk.

We were now formal participants in the second scramble for Africa. The first scramble had taken place during Queen Victoria's reign. It had been led by explorers like David Livingstone and Henry Morton Stanley, adventurers like Frederick Courteney Selous, missionaries from rival churches, and empire builders representing fiercely competitive empires. They had been brave and resilient people who in the space of fifty years had probed and penetrated their way into the heart of a threatening and primitive land and established beachheads of Western civilization from the Cape to Kenya and beyond. The second scramble, which unfolded in the two decades following World War II, was significantly less heroic—an invasion of people like my parents, lured to the colonies by cheap assisted passages. Boatload upon boatload of pale, undernourished Brits packed onto the Union Castle mail ships like refugees. Then they swept along the routes carved out by the pioneers, turning dirt tracks into blacktop highways, villages into towns, towns into cities.

During the first scramble, the native populations had been subdued by the combined force of the Bible, the Martini Henry rifle, and a bagful of phony land agreements the tribal chiefs were tricked into signing. By the time the scramblers of my parents' generation arrived, the indigenous people had become the indentured laborers of white masters, banished to squalid shantytowns on the far borders of the white cities and rendered voiceless in the Western-style parliaments they found themselves ruled by.

The reign of the white man in Africa lasted a little more than a century. At its peak only two countries—Liberia and Ethiopia—

were not under European colonial rule. Then, in April 1994, all that ended. The final white edifice came down in South Africa, and black nationalists reclaimed their country. The whites who had not already fled to the European countries from whence their forebears had come argued that they were by then full-blooded Africans and for them to leave would be as difficult as it would be for a Zulu or a Xhosa. This was certainly true of the one genuine white tribe, the Afrikaners, three million white South Africans of varying political hues from fascist to Marxist, but how true it is for the rest is a subject of soul searching for people like me and David Dodds.

I find Dodd's claim hard to dispute. He was born in Africa. I was not, but my claim is no less passionately held. Whatever my birthplace, it was in Africa that my identity was forged; somewhere amid the rapid dismemberment of colonial rule, the wars and the triumph of black nationalism I became a white African, and will remain so for the rest of my life, wherever I live. The transformation began in the fifties. My family had barely settled into our new country when the promises of a prosperous, secure future for British settlers began to evaporate. We had been there only ten years when my father died suddenly, after being operated on in an African hospital with inadequately sterilized surgical equipment, and my mother's grand dream of a better life became a nightmare of self-recrimination. Africa's primitive conditions had claimed her husband, and Africa's anarchic collision with modernity would surely claim her sons. "Why had we come?" She asked herself over and over again.

But we gritted our teeth and survived the setbacks and hacked a comfortable life out of the bushveld. As our roots went deeper and the stakes got higher, so our transformation from immigrants to Africans began. I became a sun-tanned Rhodesian teenager in short shorts, playing rugby every Saturday afternoon, and doing quarter jacks of brandy and heavy petting at the drive-in movie on Saturday night. This carefree period ended rather quickly, however, when it became apparent that my country was about to go to war to preserve white rule and that I would be expected to fight.

If I had been a staunch Rhodesian, I would have fought. I did not, and that decision represented my first conscious moral choice as a bona fide African. As rough-hewn as my political perceptions were, instinct told me where to stand, instinct born out of deep affection for and familiarity with this place.

WESTERN LIBERALS HAVE TENDED TO PERCEIVE WHITE AFRICANS as a single breed of oafish oppressors. I remember in London in the 1970s being rather frowned upon simply because I'd had the bad taste to have grown up in racist southern Africa. The assumption, I suppose, was that white Africans were inherently racist, that some genetic factor automatically linked us to the national grid and made us as culpable as the architects and enforcers of apartheid.

I could sense people thinking that whatever I said, at heart I had to be a white racist. I once tried to explain to a young Trotskyite that I had been deported from South Africa because of my opposition to apartheid, and he just sneered and said, "I'm sure you could apologize and go back." Twenty years later I found myself accused on American television of being paid to write white racist propaganda. I had published an article on Winnie Mandela, the first detailed exposé of her involvement in the murder of children, and a prominent civil rights lawyer said he had evidence that I had accepted money from the South African government to discredit Mrs. Mandela. I was a white African, and what else could you expect? Of course it was a preposterous allegation, and Mrs. Mandela's subsequent trial bore out my story, but at the time I felt a little like a German after World War II.

The truth is that the whites of Africa were never a unified gang of coldhearted supremacists any more than the blacks of Africa have been a saintly group of idealists and altruists. In the still unfolding drama of modern Africa, the players, black and white, are more complex than that. They are wildly diverse characters who defy glib characterization. At times they even offer glimpses of the nobility of the human spirit.

There is a story here.

ONE

Vote the Beloved Country

"Anyone who thinks that the ANC is going to run the government of South Africa," Margaret Thatcher pronounced firmly in 1987, "is living in Cloud Cuckooland."

Seven years later, on Sunday, April 24, 1994, I was bivouacked in Johannesburg, the heart of Cloud Cuckooland, watching the clock run down on white rule. The country's first democratic elections were about to take place, and the ANC was going to rule the country after all. To be fair to Mrs. Thatcher, any kind of negotiated settlement in South Africa had seemed far-fetched in the mid-1980s, and the idea that the Afrikaners would release Nelson Mandela from prison had been too ludicrous to contemplate. But now, four days away from the election, even the white extremists seemed becalmed. Their humiliation five weeks before, in the Battle of Mafikeng, had finally persuaded the Afrikaner separatist leader General Constand Viljoen to register his party in the election. The dwindling *bittereinders* (bitter-enders), led by Eugene Terre Blanche of the Afrikaner Weerstandsbeweging (Afrikaner Resistance Movement, or AWB), held rallies and issued press statements denouncing the situation, but nobody was listening. I had been at an AWB rally in the western Transvaal a few days earlier, where Terre Blanche had thundered on about General Viljoen betraying the Boers and about Boers rising up

Manie Maritz, a descendant of great Boer leaders.

and taking the country by force—all the usual stuff—but he had sounded rather like a playground bully mouthing off long after everyone else had returned to class. There were no more than 200 ragged Boers in attendance on a day when Nelson Mandela had drawn a crowd of 150,000 in Durban.

The morning newspapers were filled with stories of hope and reconciliation. Under the banner headline FINAL STEP TO FREEDOM was a photograph of Walter Sisulu, the ANC vice president, beaming and pointing to a ballot. Alongside him was a young white secretary named Kim. For a few precious heartbeats of history, South Africa seemed to be carrying the hopes and dreams of the world.

A LITTLE BEFORE TEN THAT SUNDAY MORNING THE BOMB WENT off. I was standing barefoot in a suburban garden, paging through the Johannesburg *Sunday Times,* when there was a deep boom, then a pause, and then the windows rattled, and I felt shock waves ripple across my body. For a moment I thought that maybe a building was being demolished, but then I realized that the boom was an explosion, not an implosion. I grabbed my shoes and ran for my car, fearing the worst.

I drove in the direction of the sound, along Jan Smuts Avenue, up over the hill past Witwatersrand University, down Queen Elizabeth Drive, into the high-rise canyons of the inner city. On Bree Street, I pulled over just as the first ambulances arrived and the police began cordoning off the area. Two blocks away a pall of black smoke hung over buildings. Glass and twisted metal were strewn across the pavement. I began walking toward the mess and saw bodies lying among the debris.

Half an hour earlier this neighborhood had just begun to stir. The vegetable sellers had set up their tables on the sidewalk; early risers from nearby apartment houses had drifted into the Gold Coin Café to buy the papers and a cup of coffee; shopkeepers had unlocked their security gates. The only car traveling along Bree Street was a Volkswagen carrying Joan Fubbs and Susan Keane, two young white ANC candidates, toward party headquarters, where they were hoping to get an early start on the day's work.

At around nine forty-seven, one of the neighborhood characters, a hustler called Ice, noticed a white man running away from an Audi parked opposite the Gold Coin Café. As Ice passed the car, he peered inside and thought he could see something burning on the backseat. There was a yellow South African Police van parked outside the café, and Ice sprinted across the street to tell the cops what he had seen. As he entered the café and approached the two policemen, the bomb went off, and he was blown across the room.

Ice was just dazed. As he got to his feet, he peered out the shattered windows, through the clouds of smoke, and saw that the Audi was no longer there. Where it had stood was a six-foot-deep crater. Bodies were strewn across the street in various states of dismemberment. One of the vegetable sellers, a woman in her thirties, lay dead, facedown in the gutter. A naked woman ran into the street screaming and howling. Her three children had been crushed when a wall collapsed onto the bed where they were sleeping.

Reporters began to gather around a man who had been standing behind one of the vegetable sellers when the bomb went off. He said he had served in the South African Army and had always taken pride in his ability to remain calm in the face of brutality. Now he trembled as he stared down at the woman's body. He said he was talking to her, asking her the price of these apples and those bananas. "Next thing I was picking myself off the ground," he said. "I turned to ask her if she was all right, . . . and she looked up at me and tried to reply, but she couldn't because half her face had been blown away. . . . That was a bit heavy for me."

As he was talking, I noticed a white policeman standing to one side with his arm around the shoulders of a young black boy. He was the dead woman's son, and as he sobbed, the policeman talked gently to him and hugged him. Then he led the little boy away, all the time hugging him to his side.

The bomb had killed nine people, injured ninety-two more, and caused millions of rands worth of damage. Among the dead was Susan Keane, who had stopped her Volkswagen at the traffic light at Bree and van Willig just as the bomb exploded. Her passenger, Joan Fubbs, was unscathed.

Ice had seen a white man running away from the Audi.

The Bree Street bomb reminded the country that violent resistance was still a real possibility and that the line it was treading between peace and civil war was a thin one indeed. For all the talk of black tribal rivalries or constitutional impasses derailing the elections, everyone knew in their hearts that the one group with the will and the firepower to do it was the extremist wing of the last white tribe—the Boers. They were by this time a dwindling band, probably no more than a few thousand, but if they were able to sow the seeds of chaos, create enough havoc to cause the postponement of the election, then perhaps they could persuade the other nervous whites—particularly the army and the police—to abandon their flirtation with black rule.

If this seems fanciful in retrospect, one only has to recall the zealotry and a grim determination that brought the Boers to power. At the turn of the century, they were the poor and the dispossessed of South Africa, defeated in battle by the British army and treated like second-class citizens by their English-speaking rulers. But fifty years later they took political power, and during the next forty years they transformed the Afrikaner Republic of South Africa into the wealthiest country on the continent. This was a formidable tribe.

THE MORNING AFTER THE BOMBING I DROVE TO THE NORTH-western Transvaal, through the rolling farmlands that sprawl out to the Magaliesburg Mountains. This was white farming territory, and the word was out that hundreds of Afrikaner families were fleeing the urban centers and setting up camps on farms around conservative towns like Brits and Rustenberg. One of the farmers was Manie Maritz, a genial little Boer whose impossibly bowed legs make him roll along rather than walk. At a recent AWB rally Manie had told me that he had twenty families set up at his farm and that an armed AWB commando unit was guarding them. He had shaken his head vigorously when I asked him whether the commandos included any of the European skinhead mercenaries thought to have slipped into the country in the past few weeks, but he'd invited me to come and have a look for myself.

Just before I left Johannesburg, news came through of another massive car bombing—at a taxi stand in the nearby town of Germiston, during the morning rush hour. It seemed that the white right was now fully engaged in a final attempt to sabotage the election. Manie and his people had assured me their operation was purely defensive, a refugee center for scared whites, but if the radical Boers were rising up, as it was beginning to appear, I was driving into a war zone.

As I pulled up to the gates of Manie Maritz's farm, two young men in combat fatigues approached the car. They both had shaved heads and were carrying hunting rifles. One was an Afrikaner, and the other, I later discovered, was German. They searched the car carefully and then, with matching Elvis sneers, waved me toward the farmhouse. I noticed in my rearview mirror that one of them raised his rifle at me when I drove off. He was playing soldier.

A rutted dirt road took me to a cluster of oak trees that encircled a two-story house. Manie rolled across the lawn toward me on bowed and creaking legs. A horse-riding accident the previous year had added to his perambulation problems, and as he picked up speed, I was sure he would keel right over. "Welcome to the old South Africa," he said, half-grinning, half-grimacing.

As Manie led me across the lawn, I counted a dozen men dressed in fatigues. The large expanse of grass in front of the house was dotted with bell tents. Lines of wash were splayed out in front of them, and children and dogs and chickens chased one another in and out of the wet clothes while an elderly woman stood shouting at them all to *voetsak,* bugger off. It looked like a blue-collar holiday camp. At the far end of the lawn was a large, open-sided shed with a forty-foot-long table at the center. In one corner a group of women were preparing lunch in a makeshift kitchen.

The refugees had little money, so Manie was paying for everything, feeding some fifty people three meals a day and allowing them the run of his property. He had no choice. He was a Boer, and his people, his *volk,* were as threatened now as they had ever been in their 350-year history. It was self-preservation, and it was in his blood. His ancestors had been among the first Europeans to arrive in the Cape, in the middle of the seventeenth century. His great-great-great-grandfather, Gerrit Maritz, had led one of the Boer treks into the Transvaal. And his father was General Salomon Gerhardus Maritz, the Boer war hero who had led the 1914 rebellion against the British and had lived and breathed Afrikaner nationalism.

Even before we sat down at the long table, Manie began waving his arms around, expressing righteous indignation at the suggestion that anyone would think he had had anything to do with the bombings. He jabbed his finger in the direction of his motley visitors and said, "These people here wouldn't know how a bomb works.

"I have never planted a bomb," Manie went on. "You harm innocent people, ruin lives. I'll never stand for that. It makes sense if we strike certain targets, but that's another thing." What Manie and his guests wanted was their own homeland, a so-called *volkstaat,* where they could govern themselves. They insisted that this was not about race but about the preservation of the Afrikaner culture.

Unfortunately, most of South Africa's Afrikaners and all but one of the political parties contesting the election had long rejected this idea, and very soon a black government would rule over the Boers for the first time since they landed at the Cape, in 1652. This appalling and seemingly inevitable prospect was, according to Manie, driving large numbers of urban Afrikaners onto these northern Transvaal farms and creating de facto mini-*volkstaats.* There were already more than a hundred refugees on Manie's land and the two adjoining farms, and another influx was expected the following day.

"It's like when the whites fled the Congo," he said. "Do you remember that?"

I did. In the winter of 1960, when I was a boy in Rhodesia, they had come pouring into town, all their worldly possessions tied in precarious bundles onto car roofs, their children huddled in the backseats, some still shocked into silence by the terrible things they had seen.

The Congo—the very words struck terror in white people throughout Africa. The Congo was the setting for Conrad's journey into the heart of darkness, and when the Belgians lost power and the country gained independence, it came as no surprise that the indigenous forces of evil prevailed over Christian civilization.

Manie was right. There was a compelling symmetry in that first flight of European colonials and this ragtag retreat of Africa's last white tribe three decades later. They were bookends, matched pieces separated by white Africa's long and painful struggle to cling to power. Soon after the Belgians came the Tanganyikans and the Kenyans, then the Northern Rhodesians and eventually the Southern Rhodesians, a constant migration from the north as colonialism was rolled back and Africanization made them unwelcome. Only now they had reached the southern tip of the continent, and there was nowhere else to go.

To drive his point home, Manie called over a couple of his refugees and asked them to explain to me why they were here. One by one they repeated stories of civil disorder and white baiting. Once-law-abiding white neighborhoods had been overrun by blacks and turned into crime-ridden ghettos; the women could no longer go shopping alone because young black men sat outside the supermarket calling them abusive names and threatening to rape them; the blacks had moved into empty houses thirty at a time and turned them into slum tenements. One man said he had decided to flee his home the previous week after a group of black men had stood at his front gate and shouted, "Eat all of your meat tonight, white man, because we are coming to kill you tomorrow."

Manie's refugees, like the Belgians, Kenyans, and Rhodesians before them, were on the run from black Africa. For three centuries, their ancestors had successfully staved off black hegemony, but now even Manie was beginning to concede that the tide of history was turning against them. And it was one hell of a concession to make, particularly for someone like Manie, whose forefathers were present at every major event in Boer history.

Manie's people were there on the most famous day in Afrikaner history, December 16, 1838, when 350 Boers made the covenant that sustained the hopes and aspirations of the white tribe until the dark days at the end of the twentieth century. On the night of the sixteenth, the Boers camped on the banks of the Ncome River in Zululand and pledged solemn allegiance to their God in exchange for victory over the black army gathering behind the nearby hills. At dawn, what appeared to be the whole Zulu kingdom stood before them—there were at least 10,000 warriors—and for six hours the battle raged. When it was over, the Ncome River ran with Zulu blood: 3,000 of the nation's finest soldiers lay dead, and the Boers had not suffered a single fatality.

The Boers made the assumption, which seemed quite reasonable under the circumstances, that they had been delivered by a higher force, and everything they would do in the years to follow—from the great treks and the wars against the British to the creation of apartheid—would be founded on the belief that they had the blessing of the Almighty and that they had been charged with a divine mission.

Now, 150 years after Blood River, it seemed their God had chosen to desert them.

As the uniformed commandos assembled for lunch, I recognized their leader, a "General" (AWB appelation) Chris van der Heever. I had met him at an AWB weapons-training camp some months before, and he greeted me with the AWB handshake, a vigorous forearm clasp. A group of particularly nasty-looking skinheads had been glaring at me with unwavering hostility, so when the general clasped my forearm, I thought they would lay off. They didn't.

Manie noticed my edginess, and when the general moved away, he leaned toward me and admitted sotto voce that "one or two" of the men in fatigues were foreigners. He said that the AWB high command had assigned the commandos to his farm, and he didn't ask too many questions. He knew there were two Germans and an Englishman, "and there's another German and an English-speaking South African who have just come from fighting in Serbia." Then he shook his head and said ruefully, "They're very hard men." I wanted him to admit that they were just fascist bovver boys looking for a fight, but he didn't. Instead he said, "Don't forget that there were French sympathizers who fought with the Boers against the British in 1900." But he said it without conviction.

Just then there was a stirring in the mess. A squat leather-clad biker had arrived, and he walked across the lawn toward Manie and greeted him like an old friend. "Remember me, Oom Manie," he said in Afrikaans. "I'm Deon. It's good to be with my own people." Manie smiled vaguely and told Deon to help himself to the food. Deon took a plate of stew and sat at the far end of the table, away from the commandos, and they shifted their collective gaze away from me for the first time. Then van der Heever detached himself from his soldiers and came over to Manie. He said he had seen this guy Deon around before and he thought he might be a government spy. Manie shook his head sadly. It was the same old story: Boer betraying Boer betraying Boer until the *volk* collapsed in disarray.

A few minutes later a police helicopter passed over the farm, and just as the noise of its engine faded into the veld, we heard General van der Heever shouting at us from the house. He came running across the lawn and said that Charles Nelson, the AWB commandant on the neighoring farm, had phoned to warn that the police were about to raid Manie's place. They had just finished searching Nelson's farm and had said they were looking for weapons, explosives, and illegal aliens. Manie sat silent as van der Heever barked orders at the AWB commandos, who began disappearing into the tall grasses of the surrounding bushveld.

Manie stood up and placed a hand on my shoulder. He said he wanted me to leave before the police arrived. This was a private matter, he said, between the Boers here and the Boers who were coming in the police uniforms. He said, "Keep in touch," and he meant it. I said, "*Vasbeit,* Manie," using an Afrikaans word meaning "stand firm," and although I felt slightly silly saying it, I meant it. As I walked toward my car, the skinhead commandos began reappearing from the long grasses, now dressed as vacationing civilians in swimming costumes and T-shirts.

I drove out along the dirt road and turned south onto the tarmac strip that would take me back to the new South Africa. Manie's illustrious ancestors, those brave generals who fought and died for Afrikanerdom, were surely turning in their graves.

THE FOLLOWING NIGHT, THE NIGHT BEFORE THE ELECTION, I AT-tended one of the last formal send-offs for Manie's South Africa. At twenty civic centers through the land, the old flag was to be lowered for the last time. Fear of bombers striking again kept the crowd at Johannesburg's Braamfontein Civic Centre down to five hundred, but a massive police cordon surrounding the floodlit building provided comfort enough for the brave few. White liberals in denim jeans and tatty cardigans, black students and academics, Indian doctors and lawyers—all swayed gently to the rhythms of the venerable old African Jazz Pioneers and waited for the historic moment.

At a minute to midnight, the orange, white, and blue flag began to descend as the choir sang the dirgelike Afrikaner anthem "Die Stem"; then as the flag of the new South Africa was raised—the green, black, white, red, yellow, and blue one that looks as if it had been lifted from in front of a gas station—the choir sang the achingly beautiful liberation anthem "Nkosi Sikelel' iAfrika" ("God Bless South Africa"), and tears filled the eyes of everyone there. At two minutes past twelve, the choir embarked on the national anthem of the new South Africa, which is "Die Stem" followed by "Nkosi Sikelel' iAfrika," a six-minute-long testament to the prevailing spirit of compromise.

Undaunted by their negotiated, elongated new anthem, the spectators popped champagne corks, kissed and hugged everyone within reach, and toasted the new democracy. It was now unlawful to discriminate against anyone on the grounds of race or sex. It felt good just to say that.

I would not have predicted this. I could not. Throughout my childhood in Rhodesia, during what was still the heyday of the whites, I took it for granted that we would rule forever. Years later, in the 1970s, when apartheid was at its most oppressive, I believed the Afrikaners when they said they would go to war rather than hand the country over to the blacks. And by the '80s, I was certain that Mandela, Sisulu, and the other political prisoners would die of old age behind bars and that a low-level civil war would be led by the new generation of ANC leaders. It was impossible to imagine a black president of South Africa in my lifetime.

This confession of consistent wrongheadedness is offered as an illustration of the speed, capriciousness, and magnitude of the changes that swept through the continent in the last three decades of the twentieth century and brought us to that night in Johannesburg. The scramble for Africa had been a leisurely business compared with this retreat, and the confusion and upheavals accompanying it have misled many observers. From a feudal agricultural society to colonization, Westernization, and the industrial age and then independence in little more than a century—such profound and sudden changes are hard for anyone raised in the orderly, evolving democracies of the West to imagine. It had been a hell of a journey. And as Manie said, it all started in the Congo. I remember the exact day. Monday, July 11, 1960. Only yesterday.

TWO

Them and Us: Heyday of the Whites

MONDAY, JULY 11, 1960.

"The Belgians are coming!" May Batchelor yelled across the garden fence.

Her neighbor, Nora Hodgson, looked puzzled.

"The Belgians are coming," May repeated.

"What do you mean?"

"The Afs in the Congo have gone mad. They're shooting each other, and they're killing and raping all the whites. The Belgians are on the run. They're coming here," May explained.

Nora still wasn't sure what May meant. She'd heard on the news that there was trouble in the Congo. But she tried not to listen to the news. It was so depressing. Besides, she had her own problems to sort out. Eunice, her maid, had been stabbed the previous night, and the police were looking for her boyfriend. Eunice would be OK, but she'd be off work for a couple of weeks, and Nora had to find a replacement.

May persisted. "There's a meeting at the club tonight. We're setting up a refugee committee. The Belgians are expected to start arriving tomorrow."

"I'll come if I can find a girl," said Nora. "But whatever's needed, count me in."

The author as a boy in Durban in the 1950s.

. . .

I WAS WATCHING MAY AND NORA FROM BEHIND MY OWN GARDEN fence. Good old Rhodesians. The mere hint of a crisis, and we were forming committees and marshaling resources and pulling together, doing the right thing. It was the Dunkirk spirit. You could almost hear Vera Lynn's voice crooning over the dry winter veld. Nora didn't need to know the precise details—better not to know, really. But if there was a crisis, she was in there with the others. If you were going to get into trouble in Africa, there was no better place to do it than in Rhodesia. Particularly Bulawayo.

That July the poinsettias were in bloom and the winter gardens were in full color—daffodils, freesia, narcissus, delphiniums—great swathes of yellow, magenta, and purple, all tended diligently by platoons of garden boys under the direction of the ladies of Bulawayo. In November the rains would come and clear the way for the summer colors, the blue jacaranda, the scarlet flowers of the Australian flame tree, and the magenta parabarachi, the orchid tree. Bulawayo was one of the prettiest places in Africa. The wide avenues were lined with majestic gum trees interspersed with silver oaks and mimosa and kigelia trees; behind them miniature poinsettias formed creamy white carpets that ran up to great hedges of purple bougainvillea.

The suburbs where we lived had large brick houses and tile bungalows with conspicuous verandas, swimming pools, and tennis courts set on one-acre plots. We were ten minutes by Morris Minor from the city center, and at night the only sounds you could hear were the *claaaaaking* of the crickets and the resonant snorting of bullfrogs down by the river.

Amos and Winston, May's two garden boys, were carrying huge stones from the driveway to the new rock garden she was creating in the far corner of the property. May was up to her elbows in dirt, and her hands were caked in thick, reddish brown soil. She'd have to cancel bridge tonight, which was a shame. Still, nothing else for it. Poor bloody Belgians.

That Monday night May attended the crisis meeting as promised. Nora didn't find a replacement maid, so she couldn't make it. It was clearly a crisis because no less a figure than the mayor of Bulawayo, Syd Miller, had convened the meeting. The news from the Congo was grave. Independence celebrations had lasted barely a week when Congolese troops began to mutiny. Now rioting and looting had spread throughout the country, and Moise Chombe's Katanga Province had announced it was seceding. On the previous Friday boatloads of European women and children had fled across the Congo River and were holed up in Brazzaville, which was being described as a refugee camp. By that evening a third of Léopoldville's twenty thousand whites had been evacuated, and Belgian reinforcements were being flown in from West Germany to get the rest out. At one point a train carrying eight hundred refugees on the Katanga rail line was stopped by rebel troops and eight white men were taken off as hostages. Their fate was unknown.

Twenty-four hours later the Rhodesian federal government (which ruled the three British territories—Southern Rhodesia, Northern Rhodesia, and Nyasaland) called out the territorial troops in the towns along the border with the Congo, and the first refugees began pouring in to the Copperbelt towns, tattered and terrified. They were in shock. Some had watched black soldiers round up six white shopkeepers in Elizabethville and hang them in the street. Others told of random shootings and gang rapes of white women. One Belgian army officer described how he and his wife had stopped in the middle of their flight and held a roadside service before burying their seven-year-old son in a makeshift grave. He had been shot through the lung and had died in his mother's arms as the car was jolting over dirt roads toward Rhodesia.

As the stories went around the crisis meetings, old Rhodesians began growling into their beards. Someone said that Communist China's official news agency had described the Congo uprising as "anti-colonialist and patriotic demonstrations" by the indigenous people, and the growling turned into howls of rage. Bloody Commies, they roared. This is what they had been trying to tell the British for years. The Communists were behind the whole thing. The blacks were easy meat for them. Hand the country over to the blacks, and there will be chaos. Insist on majority rule, and there will be mob rule. It's the Belgians today, it may well be us tomorrow.

What appalled Rhodesians most about the Congo crisis was the way the colonial government—Belgium—had just thrown in the towel. At a constitutional conference in Brussels on January 27, 1960, fearing they would be drawn into another Algeria, the Belgians had announced the Congo's first ever political elections and set the date for independence six months thence. No country could have been less prepared. Everything in the Congo had been run by the Belgians. No native Congolese had experience in national government, and very few even in regional government. Of the fourteen hundred senior civil service posts, only three were held by locals. In a country of more that fourteen million people, there were only sixteen university graduates; the previous year only 136 children had completed secondary school.

The Bulawayo meeting was a great success. The mayor formally announced the launch of the Congo Fund and said that the entire proceeds from the concerts of the contralto Miss Maud Weyhaussen that week would go to the fund. Offers of food, clothing, and accommodation were overwhelming. A trainload of 350 refugees—mainly children—was due to arrive on Wednesday. They would be met by doctors and nurses of the Red Cross and then taken to the City Hall, which would be transformed into a refugee registration center. From there the women and children would be sent to homes in the suburbs.

By the time the refugees began arriving in Bulawayo, everything was in place. The Bulawayo *Chronicle* started running a daily column in French: "*Nouvelles pour les réfugiés.*" Macdonald Club invited unattached refugee women to its Bastille Day Ball and appealed to male escorts with a knowlege of French to join them. The city library announced it would allow subscribers to take out two extra French books without charge for refugees staying with them.

Bulawayo radio hams set up a station—code-named ZE1JBY—to connect with the refugee dispersal centers on the Copperbelt and to try to pick up news from the Congo. One evening at around seven, a faint but clear signal came through. It was a man's voice, pleading for help. He said he was with thirty Europeans holed up in an agricultural station sixty miles outside Stanleyville. His voice seemed to drift through the ether, a distorted and desperate cry to white Africa. "We are surrounded by ten thousand Africans. . . . We are surrounded by ten thousand Africans." His last words were "We anticipate mass murder within the hour." Then the radio went dead.

Those words echoed through Bulawayo's subconscious. Under the comaraderie and calm efficiency of the refugee program, there was fear and horror. The good citizens of Bulawayo could see their own lovely manicured suburban homesteads surrounded by bloodthirsty black mobs. They imagined their wives raped and their children disemboweled. After living for sixty years in splendid peace and tranquillity, the whites of Rhodesia were beginning to confront the reality of black Africa.

That Saturday, a further 350 refugees arrived, and Nora's husband booked a flight for Toronto. He was a doctor, and he'd been offered a job there. It seemed a good time to go and have a look.

In my family there was also talk of emigration. It was probably the first time I'd heard the subject discussed in earnest, a subject, I might add, that would become a constant companion over the next thirty-five years. Was there a future for the kids here? Would our black servants rise up and attack us, as servants had in Kenya during the Mau Mau years? Would we wind up like the Belgians five years down the road? I was mortified. It seemed to me that we had only just arrived and settled in. For a little over a year, we had been living in the sprawling bungalow my father had designed, and now the lawns had taken and the rock gardens had started to bloom. And I had finally shaken off my tag as a whey-faced, rosy-cheeked Pommie. My skin had turned brown under the African sun, and my accent was suitably corrupted by the flat vowels and clipped consonants of white Rhodesian-speak. I fitted in for the first time.

But the subject would not go away. From the moment the Belgians arrived, you could not escape it. History is against us, my mother would sniff. This was particularly irritating to my father, who hadn't wanted to come to Africa in the first place, far preferring Australia, and had capitulated only in the face of incessant exhortations from the person who was now exhorting him to pack up and return to Britain.

IT WAS IRONIC THAT IN THE VERY MONTH THAT THOSE HARBINgers of doom arrived in Bulawayo, with their dire warnings for the white settlers, Benjamin "Matabele" Wilson died. He had been one of the first white men to arrive here, and some said he had hung on just long enough to see the end of the whites' heyday. Matabele Wilson had always believed the blacks would take their land back. That was because he had seen them in their awesome splendor, proud and fearless, before the whites had crushed them, displaced them, and built a colony where they had once had a kingdom.

Matabele Wilson was born in Scotland in 1861. He landed in the Cape at the age of twenty and struck out for Kimberley and then the gold mines of the Rand to seek his fortune. By 1887, he had given up the idea of prospecting for gold on the Rand because licenses had become too expensive and it cost too much to live there. He formed a partnership with two Englishmen, John Cooper-Chadwick and Alexander Boggie, and began organizing an expedition to cross the Limpopo River into the unchartered land of the Matabele tribe.

Wilson's ox wagons rumbled out of Johannesburg in March, and it took seventy-two days to cover the three hundred miles between Johannesburg and South Africa's border at the Limpopo River, a grueling trudge through thick bushveld and syrupy marshland. They finally pitched camp in Gubulawayo, the royal capital of the Matabele king Lobengula, on August 12, 1888, joining a scattering of missionaries and prospectors.

The Matabele had not been in the region that long. They were actually Zulus who in 1827 had fled north across the Drakensberg Mountains to escape the wrath of the Zulu king Shaka and then had fled farther north across the Limpopo in 1838 after losing several battles with the Afrikaner Boers in the Transvaal. Under King Mzilikazi, the Matabele had employed the same warlike practices as their Zulu brethren and subdued the incumbent Shona and Tswana tribes. Over the next thirty years the Matabele prospered and multiplied. And by the time the first whites—missionaries from Catholic and Protestant churches—had found their way to the area, they ruled a vast tract of land from the Limpopo up to the northeastern plateau.

Lobengula, who was Mzilikazi's son and successor, had named the royal kraal Gubulawayo, which means Place of the Killing. The name was significant, as Matabele Wilson and his fellow settlers soon discovered. Lobengula ruled with a ferocity that quite shocked the whites. They found themselves in a dark, heathen kingdom. "We were told of a rival chief and under-chief who surrendered to Lobengula without fighting," the Jesuit priest Augustus Law wrote, "and were brought to Gubulawayo and assured they would be given a place to settle in. Instead they were taken away by a party of men and one account says their fingers and toes were cut off and then they were flayed alive. Another account says that all the sinews of their body were cut and they were left there to die, being told that now they would understand Lobengula's power and their weakness." A few weeks later, as he watched one of Lobengula's *impis*, regiments, marching off to attack yet another poor tribe, Law wrote, "When, dear God, will we be able to put a stop to so much cruelty and depravity?"

Into this harsh medieval society Matabele Wilson, the missionaries, the traders, and the adventurers threw themselves, going about their business cautiously, deferentially, taking care to maintain good relations with the king and his people. Although Lobengula saw no threat from the whites, his kingdom was being eyed by the great empire builder himself, Cecil John Rhodes, the millionaire mining magnate who bestrode colonial Africa at the peak of the first scramble. Rhodes was now prime minister of the British Cape Colony, and his ambition was to paint the African continent British Empire red from the Cape to Cairo. In the land beyond the Limpopo River, South Africa's northern boundary, he saw vast potential mining wealth and another step in the empire's march north to Egypt.

Eager to head off competing mining companies already jostling for land concessions from the Matabele king, Rhodes dispatched to Lobengula's kraal two of his most trusted lieutenants, Charles Rudd and J. Rochfort Maguire, and a third man, F. R. Thompson, who was chosen because he was supposed to be empathic toward the African, a rather dubious claim given that as a boy he had witnessed his father murdered in the most hideous fashion during a revolt in South Africa.

Although Lobengula was wary of Rhodes's emissaries, he had been made aware of the value of British patronage by a rival, King Khama of the Bechuanas. In 1885, Lobengula's marauding *impis* had suffered a rare defeat at the hands of Khama's warriors in a battle at the Okavango River. Khama's forces had received rifles and horses from the British. So, on October 31, 1888, Lobengula signed what was to become known as the Rudd Concession, which granted Rhodes's company "complete and exclusive charge over all metals and minerals situated and contained in my Kingdom, principalities and dominions together with full power to do all things that they may deem necessary to win and procure the same." In exchange Lobengula was to receive one hundred pounds a month, one thousand Martini Henry rifles, one hundred thousand rounds of ammunition, and a steamboat on the Zambezi River. Based on Lobengula's claim that he ruled over all territories to the northeast, including the land of the more populous Shona, Rhodes and his British South Africa Company assumed they had rights to all the land between the Limpopo and the Zambezi and began raising the money to send pioneer columns into the uncharted territory.

The first column, led by the hunter-explorer Frederick Courteney Selous, skirted Lobengula's territory and arrived on the northeastern plateau in September 1890. By the time the second pioneer column arrived at Gubulawayo, in September 1893, Lobengula was already beginning to regret signing a deal with the British. What he had assumed would be a trickle of miners prospecting on remote, scattered sites was turning into a flood, and he wrote to Queen Victoria complaining that there were too many white men coming into his country. He repudiated the Rudd Concession, refusing to accept the monthly stipend of one hundred pounds, and ordered the execution of Lotje, the *induna,* or chief, who had most vigorously supported the signing of the agreement, and all his relatives—up to three hundred of them, according to some reports.

Although Lobengula promised not to attack the settlers in Gubulawayo, he refused to stop the cattle raids on neighboring tribes. These raids soon led to clashes with British South Africa Company police, a force of some two hundred men, and in two battles in October 1894 they routed the Matabele *impis.* The settlers, who had barely one thousand men, were far outnumbered by Lobengula's eighteen thousand warriors, and as the battles intensified, the whites began to fear that Lobengula was preparing to wipe out the settler community near the Gubulawayo kraal. At the end of October, just before the rainy season, Dr. Leander Starr Jameson led a column of two hundred volunteers into Gubulawayo to subdue Lobengula. When they arrived, they found that the king had burned his kraal to the ground, blown up the ammunition his warriors could not carry, and led his people north, away from the white man. True to his word, Lobengula had spared the lives of the whites living around the kraal.

The historian Robert Blake has cited three incidents during these crucial weeks that "had lasting consequences on Rhodesian history." It is here that one finds the roots of misunderstanding and mistrust that would end in full-scale war eighty years later.

The first incident took place in the days before Lobengula fled north. In an attempt to reconcile his differences with the settlers, Lobengula had sent a trusted white settler, James Dawson; two senior *indunas;* and his half brother to the whites' army headquarters at Tati, just outside Bulawayo. On arriving, Dawson went off for a meal and left the three Matabele envoys with a mine manager. The camp commandant, assuming that the three were merely Dawson's guides, ordered their detention lest they flee back to Lobengula with details of the camp's layout. A skirmish followed, one of the bewildered *indunas* stabbed a camp guard, and he and his fellow induna were killed. Lobengula's half brother was unharmed and returned to Gubulawayo with further evidence that the white man could not be trusted.

Lobengula's misgivings were given more substance at the end of November, when the king sent another trusted *induna* to meet with the whites. This time the *induna* carried a bag containing a thousand gold sovereigns and a message from the king that read, "White men, I am conquered. Take this and go back." The bag was handed to two ordinary troopers, who pocketed the gold and said nothing more. (A year later the men were found out, tried, and sentenced to fourteen years' imprisonment. But by then the damage was done.) Knowing nothing of Lobengula's attempt at capitulation, Dr. Jameson and the pioneer leaders decided that the only way to secure long-lasting peace for the settler community was to pursue the main Matabele army to their northern retreat and capture Lobengula. A mounted force of 160 men under Major Patrick Forbes was sent out.

The third and most significant event that would prove seminal to Rhodesian history occurred early in December, when Forbes's platoon encamped on the banks of the Shangani River. Major Allan Wilson was sent with a small group beyond the Shangani to reconnoiter Lobengula's encampment. As night began to fall, Wilson decided to disobey orders and make a strike at the king's camp at first light, probably calculating that if they ran into serious trouble, Major Forbes's main body of men would not be far behind. But this was at the height of the rainy season, and an overnight downpour made the river impassable. The next day Forbes's men came under attack from Matabele *impis,* and short of food and supplies, they were forced to retreat to Gubulawayo, where they waited with increasing pessimism for news of Allan Wilson and his thirty-six-man patrol.

The last stand of the Shangani Patrol gave the whites their first martyrs. Wilson's men had indeed been consumed by a mighty army of Lobengula's warriors and through the day of December 4, 1894, had fought with true heroism as wave upon wave fell upon them. Legend has it that when their final round of ammunition was spent, they stood shoulder to shoulder and sang "God Save the Queen." However apocryphal, it was a defining act of patriotic heroism that would help forge white Rhodesia.

Soon after, Lobengula died. Some say he drank poison; others believe he contracted smallpox. His body was never found, but as his *idunas* began to give themselves up in the early days of January 1895, it became clear that Matabele resistance had, for the time being at least, been crushed.

All this time the pioneers and prospectors and merchants who'd settled beside the Matsheumhlope River had been building a town. It was formally inaugurated on June 1, 1894, when Rhodes's friend and partner, Dr. Jameson, climbed on top of a wooden box in Market Square and announced with typical frontier brevity: "It is my job to declare this town open. I don't think we want any talk about it. There is plenty of whisky and soda inside, so come in and celebrate."

Bulawayo grew with astonishing speed. The pioneers drew up a plan for the town center—a rectangular grid, influenced by American city planners, that ran fourteen blocks north to south and seven blocks east to west—and located the industrial sites to the west. The residential suburbs were set to the east of the city grid in a greenbelt that ran alongside the Matsheumhlope River. Within four years of its founding, Bulawayo had a rail service, a civil administration, postal and telegraph services, reticulated water and electricity supplies, shops, churches, and even a public library. Lord Milner, soon to become the scourge of the Boers in South Africa, opened the library, and it received great support from the likes of Rhodes, Earl Grey, and other empire builders. Rudyard Kipling donated books and offered advice on how to protect them against the ravages of white ants and dust.

The white settlers' progress was not without setbacks, however. In 1896, the Matabeles rose up again. They were upset at the diminution of their cattle herds due both to drought and the settlers' propensity to raid, steal, and tax the symbols of Matabele wealth. The women and children among the settlers were moved into an ox-wagon laager—an encampment surrounded by two rows of wagons chained together and protected by sandbags—formed around Market Hall. Barbed-wire coils were strung along a protective perimeter, and a thirty-yard-wide no-man's-land was strewn with broken glass. A Hotchkiss machine gun was placed at each of the four corners of the compound. The rebellion was put down within sixty days.

Neither hardships nor the threat of native resistance seemed to deter the settlers, and by the turn of the century five thousand whites were living in Bulawayo. In a little more than a decade a mere handful of Europeans had cut their way through raw bushveld, subdued an entire nation of indigenous people, and established the framework of a modern, Western society in a country that had known only feudalism. In a blink of the eye, the Matabele kingdom was no more.

BY THE TIME MY FAMILY ARRIVED IN BULAWAYO HALF A CENTURY later, there was little visible evidence of the culture that had flourished at the time of the settlers. The blacks now lived in squalid, overcrowded townships beyond the city's borders. They were bused in to work at the white factories and commercial centers and carted back after dark. The only blacks who remained in the city were domestic servants—the "boys" and the "girls" who maintained the households, raised the children, and tended the glorious gardens. They were called boys and girls even though most were adults and many were grandparents. They lived in tiny, two-room concrete boxes, called *kayas,* located at the back, out of sight of their masters' houses, and although they were allowed to have their wives or husbands stay overnight on the weekends, on week nights they lived and slept alone.

For our part, we barely noticed the existence of the black community. The success of colonial occupation appeared to be measured by how close the whites could come to re-creating life in the mother country. So we named our streets after British counties, made parks and flower gardens in the image of Kew, created a gentleman's club with deep leather armchairs and dress codes appropriate to Northern Hemisphere winters, stood stiffly at attention when "God Save the Queen" was played at the end of every film screening, set up a civil service, a judicial system, and a parliament that were carbon copies of those in Great Britain—all this under the governorship of the most appropriately and resonantly named Sir Peveril William-Powlett.

THE RHODESIA BROADCASTING CORPORATION'S ANNOUNCERS had plummy BBC voices, and much of the programming was lifted straight off the venerable Beeb. At Christmas the Queen's speech crackled through the ionosphere, and we gathered round the radio as dutiful subjects should, thrilled to be in such close contact with the empire, proud to be part of this intrepid community taking British civilization to the outside world. When television arrived at the end of the '50s, it brought America into our living rooms, and programs like *The Jack Benny Show, Huckleberry Hound, Wagon Train,* and *The Loretta Young Show* provided us with an entirely new vocabulary. Primitive though communications were in those times, we found ourselves wired up to the West from whence we had come and increasingly remote from the land we were living in. We inhabited an artificial environment of imported television, jokes, mayonnaise, and HP Sauce. We had all the comforts of Africa—warm climate, servants, large houses with gardens for the price of a motorcar back home—and the culture of Europe and America piped in.

At the white schools the second languages were French and Afrikaans, but there were no courses in Ndebele, the Matabele tongue. Although we lived among Africans, we had almost no social contact with them. We were told by our parents that the Africans were very happy. They weren't ambitious and hardworking like white people, so they had easy, carefree lives with food and accommodation provided on top of the five pounds a month they received in wages. On weekends they went to places called native locations, crowded aggregations of tin shacks on dusty streets far beyond the white suburbs that we were warned never to go near, and they drank *chibuku,* African beer, until they fell down. (Until 1960, blacks were forbidden by law to drink "European" liquor.)

Rhodesians took their holidays down south, in South Africa, which was a modern, industrialized country in comparison with our cottage-industry colony. The border at Beitbridge was only a three-hour drive from Bulawayo, and the Natal coast a day's drive beyond that. During the long summers a regular flow of vehicles traversed the narrow strip of tarmac road that linked the two white tribes. A strange relationship existed between the 220,000 colonials of Rhodesia and the 3 million white South Africans. In 1923, a referendum had been held in Rhodesia to determine whether it should join up with South Africa, already the economic powerhouse of the region, and the settlers had voted overwhelmingly to retain their autonomy. Since then the two communities had moved further apart philosophically, mainly because of the militantly anti-British stance taken by the Afrikaners. This was exacerbated by the fact that during World War II a large section of the Afrikaner community had openly supported Hitler's Germany while in Rhodesia every able-bodied man had rushed to volunteer to fight the Hun. Rhodesians committed more men per capita to the war effort than any other Allied country. We were Brits, make no mistake of that, and there was something rather dubious about a country run by the grim-faced Afrikaners who'd taken the Nazis' side.

Nevertheless, we took our holidays there and enjoyed the modernity of big cities like Durban and Cape Town, in spite of the unpleasant customs of what was clearly a harsh people. I remember when I first became aware of the signs affixed to park benches in Durban that read BLANKES (whites) and NIE BLANKES (nonwhites). I was with a boy named Norman, the son of family friends, and I asked him what they meant. "It means if you catch a kaffir sitting on a bench for whites, you can kick him and chase him away," he said. "They're not allowed to sit on our benches because they've got diseases." For the remainder of that vacation, I found myself staring at passing Africans, looking for the terrible diseases I assumed must be seeping through their clothing.

We had no such benches in Rhodesia, and after taking our vacations down south, we were glad to return to the genteel surrounds of our British colony in the bushveld. Blacks lived separately there too, but the way we understood it, this was a matter of mutual agreement. Of course that was rubbish. In the 1930s, the white government had imposed a raft of legislation that would consign blacks to second-class citizenship for half a century. The key acts were the 1930 Land Apportionment Act, which stipulated that no black was entitled to hold or occupy land in white areas, and the 1934 Industrial Conciliation Act, which barred blacks from qualifying for skilled jobs or joining trade unions. The land act was particularly odious because it repudiated a commitment made under an Order in Council at the end of the nineteenth century that "a native may acquire, hold, encumber and dispose of land on the same conditions as a person who is not a native."

The prime minister in the early 1930s, Godfrey Huggins (later to become Lord Malvern), was in no doubt about the rectitude of the legislation or the duty of his government. "The Europeans in this country can be likened to an island of white in a sea of black," he said, "with the artisan and the tradesman forming the shores and the professional classes the highlands in the centre. Is the native to be allowed to erode away the shores and gradually attack the highlands? To permit this would mean that the leaven of civilisation would be removed from the country, and the black man would inevitably revert to a barbarism worse than before."

The Rhodesians felt they had to be firm with the African. The memory of the murderous black tide that overwhelmed the brave men of the Shangani Patrol remained fresh in their minds. The idea was that Africans would slowly be brought into government and some time in the next century would share power with whites.

It all sounded reasonable to us, particularly after the Belgians had come and gone. Until then there had been no evidence of racial conflict in our daily lives. All the conferences and referendums and demands about Rhodesia's future had been just newspaper headlines and cocktail party conversations. The government had revoked most of the petty discrimination—blacks were allowed into hotels and cinemas, municipal swimming pools and parks were integrated, separate lines at bus stops and elsewhere were abolished. Africans would ride by smiling and waving on their heavy black bicycles, or they would walk in loose-limbed gaggles along the dusty roads, laughing and clapping and holding hands. We would say "*sabona,*" and they would reply "*sabona,* baas." They were always so disarmingly friendly, so receptive and open, that it was difficult to connect them to the dangerous, volatile savages the government claimed to be protecting us from.

The only African I knew was a man named Barnet William, a sweet-natured Nyasa who was for twenty-five years the family's manservant, retainer, whatever—a confidant and caretaker to me and my young brother, a great comfort to my mother, and my closest friend. Barnet wasn't very tall, about five foot eight, but he was powerfully built. His muscles rippled under polished ebony skin. He liked a couple of beers on the weekend, and now and again he came home reeling all over the place, eyes blazing red. He would stand before my mother, saluting and slurring, "I can assure you, madam, that I am not quite drunk." After my father died, my mother often took Barnet to the cinema, and in those awkward, early days of integration that caused a bit of a fuss. Some said she was going too far, setting a bad example. Others said, "Well, you know what she's like. A bit odd."

Barnet would talk about everything and anything except politics. If we asked him which black leader he supported, he would laugh uncomfortably and leave the room. He wanted the vote, surely? Silence. Would Joshua Nkomo make a good leader of Rhodesia? He didn't want to know.

Around the time the Belgian refugees were in town, I decided to take Barnet fishing at the Hillside Dams, a nature reserve no more than fifteen minutes' walk through the bush from our house. I'd seldom fished before, but it seemed like a good excuse to get him away from the house and make him open up a little.

At first Barnet was evasive. Then he turned very grave and gave me a lecture I shall never forget. He said it was easy for white people to laugh about politics. For Africans it was a serious business. In the townships there was widespread intimidation and violence as the rival nationalist movements fought for power, and Barnet said he had seen people beaten to death because they supported the wrong party. He carried three different party cards when he visited the townships, and he just hoped he'd pull the right one out when the time came. "And what will Nkomo do for me if he becomes prime minister? He is a Matabele. I am a Nyasa. The Matabele hate the Nyasa."

Things were fine as they were, he said.

Of course, they were not.

THE BELGIAN REFUGEES DISAPPEARED AS SUDDENLY AS THEY HAD appeared, and by the end of July they were all back in Europe. Bulawayo, however, did not return to normal. On July 22, riots had broken out in the Highfield Township outside Salisbury, and the police reserve was called up. On the following Monday morning, three days later, rioting hit Bulawayo. Gangs roamed through the city center, stoning cars and buildings. More than five hundred policemen were called out to chase off the mob and to form a cordon between the white city center and the black townships. There were riots in the townships, and buildings were set alight. On Tuesday more troops were called in. At that point the only white casualty was a little girl who had been hit by a brick. The Model Dairy announced that there would be no milk deliveries.

Throughout the day a procession of residents not involved in the rioting and eager to leave the townships approached the military cordon, asking to be allowed through, but they were turned back. They sat huddled and frightened in little groups, hoping the mayhem would not spill over onto them. They were afraid to return to their homes, so they sat in a no-man's-land between the troops and the burning townships. In the afternoon fifty policemen in battle formation moved to break up the mob. They found themselves facing two thousand rioting Africans and withdrew with due haste, leaving a spotter plane to dive down and drop CS gas on them.

The factories in Bulawayo's industrial site had come to a standstill after workers arrived and then turned around and marched back to the townships. The police said that small gangs of intimidators had toured the factories and threatened the workers.

That Tuesday, I had my first glimpse of the struggle for the soul of emerging Africa. We were halfway through the morning's classes at the all-white Hillside School when the assembly bells went off and we were herded into the great hall. The headmaster told us that there had been more rioting in town and that the school would be closed forthwith. Parents had been telephoned and were on their way to pick us up. Soon convoys of cars were snaking their way from the school into the white suburbs under armed police escort. Once home, we were ordered to stay off the streets, which were now being patrolled by army vehicles bristling with weapons and soldiers. This was what the hard-liners had been warning us about. You give the blacks a bit of slack, and the next thing they're rampaging through the suburbs.

That afternoon I was wandering around the garden, trying to figure out why black people would want to riot, when an army vehicle pulled up alongside three young African men who were walking past. Two white soldiers leaped out of the vehicle and began questioning the men. One of the soldiers stepped forward and flattened one of the blacks with a single backhand swipe of his riot shield. As the young man lay dazed and bleeding in the road, his two companions were handcuffed and thrown into the back of the vehicle. He was then lifted to his feet, and with his head lolling onto his chest, he too was dragged off. As he was being pushed inside, he revived briefly. Staring past his tormentors, he croaked hopelessly, at no one in particular, "Help me."

I was too terrified to move. Only after the army vehicle had driven off down the road did my limbs unfreeze and was I able to take a few faltering steps toward the front gate. I stood there for ten minutes looking at the glistening pool of blood on the black tarmac. Then it began raining—the large, heavy drops that precede a torrential African storm. Within a minute the blood was flowing down the road with the rain, and a minute after that it was gone.

When I told my parents what I had seen, they said the three blacks must have been up to something. But they were just walking along the road, I said. Yes, but they must have been up to something. Otherwise the army wouldn't have arrested them. Lest I damn my parents, this was 1960, and we were all, adults and children, imbued with the belief that Her Majesty's forces of law and order were of impeccable moral fiber. It was only later that we learned they were beating the shit out of black people because they were black people.

The next day I scoured *The Chronicle* for a report on the incident, but of course there was none. This sort of thing was happening all the time, and if my parents were right, with jolly good reason.

What *The Chronicle* did tell me, however, was that white rule was under siege. The newspaper's lead story, placed beside an official portrait of the Queen Mother on her sixtieth birthday, ran under the banner headline NO SURRENDER TO THE AFRICANS HERE, SAYS GREENFIELD. Julian Greenfield was the minister of Law and Order in the Federal assembly, and he said that "we are determined that Europeans are going to play their part with Africans in the administration of the country." By this time black-nationalist aspirations had evolved from polite requests for equal representation with whites to unequivocal demands for black majority rule. White reaction had been to move further right, and while politicians like Greenfield were publicly espousing power sharing, what they really believed in was white rule in perpetuity. Now I knew what that confronation beyond the garden wall had been about.

But in our house, as in most Bulawayo homes, politics was not a popular subject. It was an unsavory business, according to my mother, practiced by ambitious and unscrupulous people who were in it for their own gain. Except for Churchill. He was the last great politician. So, we talked about books, plays, films, and anything else that steered clear of the unsettling events taking place around us. That, interspersed with hearty walks through the bushveld, endless games of cricket in the back garden, and holidays down south, was how my family kept its eyes averted as the storm clouds gathered.

There were other choices. You could go the way of the Robertsons next door and drink yourself into a coma every evening, starting with sundowners on the stoep at around five and finally collapsing wherever you were at ten o'clock. Or you could go bush, like the Tuckey family up the road, who were forever going off on mini-safaris, with Ma Tuckey leading the two boys, Ken Tuckey and Ricky Tuckey, and whoever of their friends was straggling along with them.

We would often go to the Motopos Hills, a magnificent gathering of granite hills, kopjes, some twenty miles south of Bulawayo where the splendor of the African bushveld played host to the myths of colonial white Rhodesia and the magic of ancient Africa. On top of the largest kopje are the tombs of Cecil John Rhodes and his friend Dr. Jameson, hewn into the giant rock face itself. To the west is the large stone monument dedicated to Allan Wilson and the Shangani Patrol. It bears the legend TO BRAVE MEN. Rhodes called this place World's View, but long before he had sent his pioneer columns rumbling past, long before even Mzilikazi had brought his runaway Zulus here, the occupants of this land had called it Malindidzima—the resting place of the spirits. To the west was Fumukwe, the hill that must not be pointed at, and the hills of the animal spirits—Shumbeshabe, the red lion; Ingwenya, the crocodile; and Kozi, the eagle. It was to this place that the *impis* retreated during the Matabele uprising, taking refuge in the Inungu Gorge. There were high grasses, impenetrable caves, and a small stone amphitheater near Fort Umlugulu, where Rhodes held his first meeting with the dissident Matabeles.

These trips into the Matopos gave a glimpse of an Africa very different from our Surrey-in-the-bushveld, but we were for the most part caught up in the stuff we'd brought with us from the Old World—rugby, bridge . . .

HOWEVER APOLITICAL WHITE RHODESIANS LIKE MY PARENTS professed to be, it seemed to me that in the year of my political awakening they began talking about politics all the time. That Harold Macmillan's British government was selling us down the river was taken for granted, so the debate revolved around which political leader was offering the best solution to the dilemma. Three courses were being offered. Garfield Todd, the New Zealand–born missionary who had been prime minister of Southern Rhodesia

from 1953 to 1958, insisted that the only course was enfranchisement of qualified blacks and immediate power sharing. The federal
prime minister, Sir Roy Welensky, a former railroad engineer and
boxing champion, endorsed a more gradualist approach, one that
would leave the whites in power until well into the next century and
offer equal representation to the blacks on a distant date. Ian Smith,
a cattle farmer and former Royal Air Force pilot, stood for white
rule in perpetuity.

Predictably my household plumped for the middle road, and we
had Sir Roy around for drinks when he was in town. He was a huge
man, well over six feet tall and weighing more than 250 pounds,
with great, gnarled workingman's hands. He had gained political
power through the trade union movement and was, in my parents'
view at least, a man of integrity and moderation, a rare bird indeed.
My parents' exchanges with Sir Roy did not, however, provide
comfort for the future, since he said he could see the white electorate drifting to the right, the blacks to the left into the arms of extremists, and the British just wanting to get the problem off their
hands as quickly as possible.

What we should have known was that by 1960, Sir Roy's political influence was on the wane and that the debate centered simply
on outright rule, whether white or black. Garfield Todd had been
ousted in 1958 for endorsing the latter, but he remained a significant leader in Rhodesian politics, a rallying point for integrationists,
black and white. Their numbers were comparatively few, however,
and most whites abhorred his support of black-nationalist demands
for "one man, one vote" and his calling on the British to act against
the Salisbury government if it refused to accede. After the Belgian
refugees had gone and the townships had quieted down, the white
Rhodesians stuck their heads above the parapets, took a long look
around, and decided that to follow Todd would be a calamity. It
was at this moment of uncertainty and fear that Ian Smith gained
ascendance.

The stage was set for one of the great dramas of African colonial
history, a twenty-year struggle for the soul of Rhodesia, featuring
constitutional rebellion, international intrigue, a deadly civil war,

and two principal characters straight out of Central Casting. Todd and Smith inhabited the two philosophical extremes of the white colonial mind, and their parallel journeys from 1960 through to the end of white rule in South Africa thirty-four years later serve as vivid reminders of the complexity and ambiguity of the white man's role in Africa.

THREE

Worlds Apart: The Missionary, the Farmer, and the Search for Truth

The Belgian refugees from the Congo were not the only harbingers of doom to visit Rhodesia that fateful year of 1960. The British prime minister, Harold Macmillan, came too, and the message he brought was as blunt and unequivocal as the sight of hapless Belgians fleeing the rising tide of black Africa. Britain had voted to join the European Economic Community and wanted to dismantle its African empire as quickly and as painlessly as possible. The British had watched France become embroiled in a bloody conflict in Algeria and had already had their own problems with the Mau Mau uprising in Kenya. The time had come to cut their losses. So Macmillan came to tell the white colonials to prepare to hand the occupied lands back to their original proprietors. Ghana had been the first sub-Saharan colony to go, and it was in Accra, at the start of his African tour, that Macmillan delivered the Wind of Change speech for the first time: "The wind of change is blowing through this continent, and whether we like it or not, this growth of national consciousness is a political fact, and our national policies must take account of it."

Not surprisingly, the white settlers, who previous British governments had cheered and urged on in their colonial endeavors, were none too pleased at the turnaround. Their numbers were too small in Nigeria, Kenya, Uganda, and Tanganyika to withstand the process, but when Macmillan touched down at Salisbury Airport, he knew he had arrived at the front line of white resistance. Here was a population of almost two hundred thousand whites with roots in their adopted land far deeper than those of the itinerant colonials in Kenya or Nigeria. Their children were being raised as Rhodesians, not as British expats, and they were determined opponents of the kind of political changes Britain had in mind.

On the second day of the visit, the British High Commission organized a sundowner party to introduce Macmillan to the Rhodesian government's senior ministers, all whites and all members of Sir Edgar Whitehead's United Federal Party. The idea was that they would convince Macmillan that the colony's future stability lay in the hands of a white government. If he would only hear them out, surely he would understand their position.

That afternoon Macmillan was to meet with a group of young black political activists. He also asked his staff to arrange a meeting with Garfield Todd—Whitehead's predecessor—whose liberal integrationist leanings had led to his overthrow three years earlier. Todd was loathed by most white Rhodesians and loved by the Africans, whose enfranchisement he had championed. Needless to say, Todd had not been invited to the sundowner, and Macmillan's staffers were forced to squeeze him in for half an hour between the black activists and the gin-and-tonic party.

Todd arrived promptly at five to discover that Macmillan had not returned from his meeting with the activists. When he did arrive, some twenty minutes later, he was excited and enthusiastic. He told Todd he had been enormously impressed with the young blacks and said he believed he had met the future leaders of the country. They had articulated their demands in the most reasonable manner. Todd was delighted, and the two men fell into an intense discussion. Throughout their conversation the prime minister's secretary kept interrupting, pointing out that the dignitaries were arriving and that Macmillan was late for the party. Macmillan kept putting the secretary off and finally instructed him to have Lady Macmillan meet the ministers. He would be along when he and Todd were through talking.

Eventually Macmillan stood up, put his arm around Todd's shoulders, and led him out of the office and along the corridor toward the party, all the time talking animatedly about his afternoon meeting with the black activists. As the two men walked into the sundowner, Todd looked up and saw all his political enemies gathered in the room. "This is where I stop," he said. Macmillan nodded, and they shook hands. As Todd headed for a side exit, the prime minister called after him, "Keep up the good work. You're right, you know."

A week later Macmillan stood before the South African parliament in Cape Town and delivered his famous speech to a glowering assembly of granite-faced nationalist Afrikaners. "I thought you would wish me to state plainly and with full candour the policy for which we in Britain stand," he said. "It may well be that in trying to do our duty as we see it we shall sometimes make difficulties for you. If this proves to be so, we shall regret it. But I know that even so you would not ask us to flinch from doing our duty."

When Garfield Todd read Macmillan's speech, he was convinced, he told me thirty years later, that that day in Salisbury had inspired Macmillan to take his liberation message into the heart of the Boer laager. It was more likely, actually, that the Salisbury meetings with the black activists and the liberal missionary had merely reassured Macmillan that there were at least some people prepared to support Britain's withdrawal. The deal had been done months before, thousands of miles away, in the corridors of Whitehall, and this was little more than a polite end-of-empire tour. The truth was, in fact, just as Todd's political opponents in Rhodesia and the Afrikaners in South Africa had seen it—Britain wanted out.

Todd described to me how excited and exhilarated he'd felt after his meeting with Macmillan: "I found a man who had been enlightened that afternoon, and he needed someone like me to reassure him he wasn't making a mistake." But his joy was short-lived, for as logical and inevitable as black majority rule appeared to these two men, Todd's fellow Rhodesians could not see anything beyond white government, and their myopia would commit southern Africa to decades of confrontation and civil war. This shortsightedness, Todd has always maintained, was due to their isolation from black Africa. They lived in colonial cocoons that mirrored life in Europe, and they ignored the world beyond their model gardens and picket fences.

Todd had been lucky. Fate—and his vocation—had thrown him into the heart of black Africa, and he could hear it beating when most of us didn't even know it was a living organ. He had watched at first hand as the blacks recovered slowly from the wreckage of the colonial scramble, dusted themselves off, and then began the long march toward liberation. When the harbingers arrived in 1960, Garfield Todd was ready for them.

GARFIELD AND GRACE TODD ARRIVED IN RHODESIA FROM NEW Zealand in 1934 to take charge of a small mission established by the Church of Christ. Forty years had passed since Lobengula's Matabeles had attempted and failed to resist the invasion of the white men. The towns had grown—there were ten thousand whites in Bulawayo and five thousand in Salisbury—but in the rural areas little had changed. The Todds found themselves in a tribal society that was deeply suspicious of the white intruders and far from enamored of their attempts to introduce Christianity and education to communities steeped in long-established customs. Although Todd managed to lure some of the young boys into his classrooms by lavishing gifts on their parents, he was unable to bribe the Matabele to allow their daughters to be educated. Many years later Todd's school at Dadaya would become an important education center for the first generation of African leaders, but it was no easy sell at first.

One reason the black tribesmen resisted Todd and his fellow white settlers was that they traditionally enjoyed a rather laid-back lifestyle while the women bore the brunt of the workload, tilling the fields, maintaining the homes, and caring for the children. With the introduction of a money economy, the men were goaded into going out to work, and they saw their carefree days coming to an

Garfield Todd around the time that he became prime minister
of Southern Rhodesia in 1953.

end. When a local agent for the Johannesburg mines—a little Scots-
man named Jameson—tried to recruit men from the Shabani area,
he was treated with derision. They called him Kandodo, the Mos-
quito, on account of his large proboscis and pebble spectacles, and
in the beginning only a few of the younger ones succumbed to his
promises of big money across the Limpopo. For a time Kandodo
was forced to travel far into the interior to find mine labor—into
the Congo and Portuguese East Africa and Tanganyika, where
there was no work at all—but as soon as the younger men started
coming home dressed in sharp Western suits and pushing shiny new
bicycles, others began to fall in line outside Kandodo's offices.

Gradually the Todds were able to break down the instinctive mistrust of whites. Garfield performed burials even for Catholics, was a
teacher, a builder, an arbitrator in community disputes, and—most
dramatically—a doctor. He had arrived equipped only with aspirin,
quinine, and castor oil but quickly discovered he could improvise
potent treatments. He recalls that within weeks of his arrival at Dadaya, he received a message from a local priest saying that a man
named Jonah Mantjontjo had had an accident and was lying in a
Bulawayo hospital suffering from terrible burns over most of his
body. The priest persuaded the newly arrived missionary to care for
Mantjontjo, but when he was brought in, Todd was appalled—he
was covered in filthy bandages, smelled to high heaven, and could
not move. Two of his staff members fainted at the sight of the poor
man.

Todd had heard that petrol was a good disinfectant for burn victims and sent someone off to the garage to fetch a can of engine oil.
He soaked cotton pads in the oil and placed them on the man's in-
fected flesh. The next day he lifted the pads and the infection was
gone—"and from that day," says Todd, "we always used engine oil
on burns." Some weeks later, when Mantjontjo was sufficiently recovered, Todd took him back to his village. His relatives and friends
at first recoiled in fear and shock—they had thought he was dead,
and seeing him actually standing there and talking, they concluded
that the white missionary had raised him from the dead.

By the late 1930s, there were fifty thousand whites in Rhodesia. The 1930 Land Apportionment Act had set aside fifty million acres of the country for them (the one million Africans were allocated thirty million acres), and they began to establish schools, civic associations, and recreation areas in the image of the mother country. The thirty-seat parliament in Salisbury was dominated by Sir Godfrey Huggins's United Party, and all legislation was ratified by the British government. There were only a handful of registered black voters, and neither Westminster nor Salisbury spent much time debating the "native question." The issues of the day revolved almost exclusively around white investment, development, immigration, and so on. In the early 1940s, however, things began to change. More and more blacks were moving into the cities, and with their exposure to Western ways came their desire for Western education.

It was around this time that Garfield Todd was drawn, rather by accident, into politics. He had attended a meeting in Shabani at which Sir Godfrey Huggins was the main speaker. Huggins had made derogatory remarks about New Zealand's social welfare policies, and when he finished, Todd leaped to his feet and explained why the distinguished gentleman was wrong. Huggins was so impressed that he asked Todd to stand as a member of parliament at the next election, which he did, and he was elected. The 1946 election saw Huggins's party scrape in with thirteen seats, just beating out the inappropriately named Liberal Party, which was staunchly right-wing. (Just over half of the thirty-seven thousand registered voters actually voted. Some MPs got into parliament with barely five hundred votes.)

While Todd was moving cautiously into politics, a vocal and articulate group of white Rhodesians was beginning to debate the possibilities of a multiracial future. Two Oxford graduates, Hardwicke Holderness and Pat Lewis, started up the Interracial Association, which was aimed at taking the issue of black enfranchisement into the public domain. They held a series of lectures and on one occasion invited Todd to speak. His subject was to be "The Native as a Human Being," but he canceled at the last minute, after Huggins warned him it was too contentious a subject for a member of parliament to address.

At another of the Interracial Association's lunchtime lectures, in September 1948, Gideon Mhlanga, the first Rhodesian African to receive a university degree, was invited to speak. The organizers, Holderness in particular, were so concerned about the white reaction to this that they hired two former boxers as marshals in case there was trouble. In fact, the lecture was a tremendous success. Mhlanga's story of how he had risen out of poverty was a moving celebration of the human spirit. He described a life that none of the four hundred assembled whites knew anything about. When he was a boy, his only article of clothing had been a piece of cloth wrapped around his waist. He'd walked twelve miles every day to attend a mission school. In 1922, he and a cousin decided that the only way to get a decent education was to go to a big town, so they walked 140 miles through lion country to Umtali. The journey took them five days. They worked for fifteen shillings a month and slept in the rough to save money for schoolbooks and fees. They finally ended up living in the African township outside Bulawayo, where the drunkenness, gambling, whoring, and wild ways shocked them deeply. They were, after all, rural God-fearing Christians who had never encountered this kind of thing.

Finally Mhlanga saved enough money to travel to South Africa, where he scratched out a living for nine years, eventually emerging from Lovedale College with a diploma. When he returned home, he supported his brothers and sisters by teaching in the local school. He studied at night for a university degree, which he got in 1944 at the age of forty.

Gideon Mhlanga's speech to the Interracial Association was given with the dignity, humility, and optimism that characterized black leaders of that time: "There is a growing need among Africans for more schools," he explained. "The existing ones are full to capacity. One school had over a thousand applications and only one hundred could be accepted. I am sure this need will be met. The majority of our people are illiterate, but I am not a pessimist. I believe things will right themselves. Our being here is not accidental.

It is the will of God. I would like to add that I think it is an honour as well as a great pleasure to be asked to address this gathering. Being an honour, it is also a matter of duty."

The white audience applauded enthusiastically. How could they not? And they agreed that winter afternoon that more had to be done to bring the Africans along. Holderness and his post-war idealists had won the day. It was here, they believed, at the meeting point of black and white Rhodesians, that the journey to black emancipation would begin.

Garfield Todd was to the right of liberals like Holderness at this time. He believed in the measured integration of blacks into Western society but stopped short of advocating black majority rule. He was a good constituency MP who seemed eager to dispel any thoughts that his missionary background had made him soft on native policy. Education, orderly advancement, and proper representation—that was where Garfield Todd stood.

In 1953, Southern Rhodesia joined with Nyasaland and Northern Rhodesia to form the Central African Federation, and Sir Godfrey Huggins became the first federal prime minister. To everyone's surprise the United Rhodesia Party (URP), a coalition of the old United Party and the right-wing Rhodesia Party, elected Todd as its leader. On September 7, 1953, he became prime minister of Southern Rhodesia.

Todd's party won an election held the following year by stressing the need for economic development before power sharing. As prime minister, Todd took a tough position against civil unrest. He sent troops in to quell a strike at the Wankie colliery in 1953 and a year later endorsed a piece of harsh legislation known as the Public Order Act, which gave the state free rein to quash all political opposition with force. For all that, he led a group of nine liberals inside the URP who endorsed electoral reform and black participation. Their buzzword was "partnership." For the time being, the white man would be the senior partner, and the relationship would be reviewed over time.

The real liberals—the Holderness group—supported improved housing and education, freehold tenure for blacks in urban areas, a broad electoral franchise, development of local government, and legislative reforms that would abolish the color bar. Holderness complained that the government was not even addressing these issues and pointed out that parliament was spending only 20 percent of its time debating African affairs. But he knew that he represented only a small group of educated liberals and that the main body of political thinking lay somewhere to the right.

Todd's pragmatism in his early days as prime minister was borne out of frequent encounters with the hard-line whites who ran the factories, the businesses, even the government offices. These first- and second-generation colonial scramblers subscribed to the pioneer doctrine of keeping your boot heel firmly placed on the black man's neck. They would regale you with stories that were intended to display their abiding affection for black people, but they felt they had to keep their guard up. For example, soon after Todd became prime minister, a celebration was arranged for Father Aston Chichester, who had just been appointed the first archbishop of central Africa. A state banquet was to be held at Meikles, the best hotel in town, and the archbishop went off to draw up the guest list. When he took the list to the manager of Meikles, however, there was a problem. The bishop from Basutoland was to attend. "You mean he's black?" the manager asked. "Yes, is there a problem?" said the archbishop. "Well," said the manager, "if it were the holy father himself and he were black, I wouldn't have him in my hotel." Todd and the archbishop finally decided to hold the banquet in the parliament buildings and found a restaurateur who would deliver a takeout banquet by van.

It was a parliamentary debate in April 1957 on the Immorality Act that finally drove Todd into the arms of the liberals. Two MPs moved to amend the act, which forbade sexual relations between black males and white females. The MPs complained that this was discriminatory because relations between white males and black women were not covered. Todd wanted the Immorality Act struck from the statutes altogether. This was the first of a number of run-ins he was to have with his Cabinet over the following months, and by the end of 1957 he had come to be regarded as a liability to his party. The white public, the conservative sons and daughters of the pioneers, would not have elected him again.

Garfield, Grace, and their fourteen-year-old daughter, Judith, had spent Christmas 1957 on holiday in South Africa, and when they returned on January 9 they were met at the airport by Patrick Fletcher, one of the stalwarts of the United Party and an old friend of Garfield's. He told them that the entire Cabinet had resigned. For a short time Todd resisted, even fought back. Instead of stepping down, as his party had hoped he would do, he obtained permission from the governor to form a new government. But on February 8, the party congress voted Todd out of power by 193 to 129.

AFTER HAROLD MACMILLAN RETURNED TO BRITAIN AT THE END of his Wind of Change tour in 1960, the South Africans set in motion plans to abandon the Commonwealth and go it alone. The Rhodesians briefly attempted a different tactic. Todd's successor as prime minister was the eccentric intellectual Sir Edgar Whitehead, who although not as committed to African integration as his predecessor, was convinced that Britain would grant Rhodesia independence only if the colony made significant concessions to multiracialism. In his attempts to win over the British and the African moderates, Whitehead made a number of significant changes to race legislation: municipal swimming pools and public parks were opened up to Africans, separate waiting lines at post offices and banks were abolished, Africans were allowed into previously white-only hotels and cinemas, and they were allowed to purchase European liquor. Private schools were allowed to take in African students, and jobs previously reserved for whites were opened up.

But poor old Whitehead and his middle-of-the-roaders failed to satisfy anyone with this program of cautious, orderly advance. It did not go far enough for the British government, which wanted Africans in parliament immediately, and it went much too far for the white Rhodesian electorate, who were increasingly dubious of any African representation at all. They looked to the north and saw the catastrophe in the Congo, the economic chaos in Uganda, the accession of the Marxist Julius Nyerere in Tanganyika, and then began casting around for political leaders prepared to stand up against the slide toward Africanization.

In 1961, after protracted negotiation with the British government, Sir Edgar placed before the Rhodesian parliament a constitution that he hoped would be acceptable to the British, the African nationalists, and his white electorate. The constitution proposed increased African representation in a sixty-five-seat parliament, a justiciable Declaration of Rights, and a plan under which Africans could gain an equal share of power somewhere in the distant future. Whitehead promised to repeal the 1930 Land Apportionment Act, the bedrock of white privilege, and told the United Nations that African voters would be in the majority within fifteen years. In exchange, Britain would cease to have a say in Rhodesia's constitutional affairs. The British government endorsed the plan, the white Rhodesians voted for it in a referendum by a majority of two to one, and very briefly the black-nationalist leader Joshua Nkomo agreed to it. For ten days it seemed that a negotiated independence was within the country's grasp. Then, on the eleventh day, Nkomo succumbed to pressure from the militant factions of his nationalist movement and rejected the constitution.

Whitehead's gambit had failed, and as the black nationalists became more militant, the whites began moving to the right—not just the working classes, who were most threatened by the prospect of liberalization, but also the middle-class establishment. Late in 1962, only nine months after it had been formed, the Rhodesian Front, a hastily cobbled together alliance of conservative politicians, came to power. The new prime minister was Winston Field, a conservative fiercely loyal to the British Crown. His deputy was Ian Douglas Smith, the former RAF fighter pilot and cattle farmer who viewed the mother country with far more skepticism.

In June 1963, Field and Smith reluctantly engaged in talks with Macmillan's emissary, R. A. Butler, on the breakup of the federation. They came away believing that the British had promised Southern Rhodesia independence without strings. (Both Field and Smith always claimed that Butler had made an unambiguous verbal commitment to them.) But, not for the first time, the British wriggled and obfuscated under pressure from the Organization of African Unity, and as Field haggled and negotiated to no avail, his constituents began to grow impatient. The British were selling them down the river, and they needed someone to stand up to the British. Winston Field had to go.

IN APRIL 1964, FIELD WAS DEPOSED AND IAN SMITH BECAME Rhodesia's first native-born prime minister. His predecessors—Lord Malvern, Garfield Todd, Sir Edgar Whitehead, Winston Field—had all been settlers. Smith has said to me several times that one has only to look to his boyhood, when he grew with rural Africans as his friends and companions, to find proof positive that his political beliefs could never have been grounded in racism. He was born in 1919 in the small mining town of Selukwe, the son of a Scottish immigrant who had arrived in the country in 1898. His father had stopped in Bulawayo, but when Cecil Rhodes officially opened the first mine at Selukwe, some one hundred miles to the east, he decided to take a chance in the hinterlands. By the time Ian was born, his father was a major supplier of provisions to the mining camps and owned four butcher shops, two bakery shops, and a garage.

Smith grew up on the family farm, Gwenara, and had little contact with the scattering of white settlers in the area. His father's top men were all Matabeles, as were the farmworkers, and his playmates were their sons and daughters. He says he became so integrated into the local community that his mother complained she could not understand a word he said. Oddly, the young Smith spoke neither of the prevailing indigenous languages, Shona and Sindebele. The language his mother couldn't understand was known as kitchen kaffir, a patronizing pidgin tongue that mixed English, Afrikaans, and Portuguese words in with simplifications of indigenous languages. It was a kind of bushveld Esperanto invented by the whites so their black workers could understand their orders. Smith says the language is called Fanagalo and insists that it should have become the common language of sub-Saharan Africa. "I can make myself

Ian Smith took Rhodesia to war to preserve white rule.

understood in Zululand or in the Transkei," he says. "I think it is a wonderful language."

The young Smith's studies at Rhodes University in South Africa were interrupted by the outbreak of World War II. Like many patriotic young colonials, he had joined up, flown Hurricanes in North Africa, and fought with the partisans in Italy. A horrific plane crash led to reconstructive surgery on his face and left him with his famously droopy right eye. After the war he completed his degree, married a widow with two small children, and in 1948 moved into politics, standing against Huggins and Todd's liberal UFP. His mission, he has always claimed, was to uphold "civilized standards," and these standards, broadly defined, meant the customs and lifestyle of pre-war Britain. That the British themselves were attempting to undermine this outpost of white, Christian civilization was, in Smith's mind and in the minds of the majority of white Rhodesians, the ultimate betrayal. Britain was succumbing to the forces of decadence and fashionable liberalism and in the process throwing the baby—Rhodesia—out with the bathwater.

Through the first half of 1965, Smith was locked in endless negotiations with his British opposite number, Harold Wilson, but with each diplomatic shuttle, each flurry of statements and near breakthrough, the hopes of negotiated independence grew increasingly faint. The question became whether the community of 220,000 whites was prepared to go it alone.

In May 1965, Smith called an election of the predominantly white electorate and won a resounding victory with the support of almost 80 percent of the white voters. It had been only five years since the Belgian refugees and Harold Macmillan had passed through. Not long before, the Todd-Whitehead governments had been within touching distance of a multiracial democracy. Now the talk was of rebellion and white rule in perpetuity.

SMITH'S AND TODD'S WORLDS FINALLY COLLIDED AT THE END OF October 1965. Todd had accepted an invitation to give a talk at the University of Edinburgh, and on the day he was to fly from Salisbury, he drove up from Hokonui Ranch—a five-hour journey—did some last-minute shopping in the city, and then went to the home of his friend Eileen Haddon for an early dinner before the flight. As they were finishing their meal, the phone rang, and a man asked to speak to Mr. Todd. When he picked up the phone and identified himself, the line went dead. He thought nothing of it and gathered up his suitcases and began to load them into his car. As he was saying good-bye to Mrs. Haddon, Garfield saw two cars pull into the driveway and a man emerge from each. He assumed they were journalists, and as they came up, he shook their hands and began explaining that he didn't have time to do an interview because he was late for the plane already. "We have come to arrest you, Mr. Todd," said the one. They were Special Branch. Government orders were to escort him back to Hokonui.

As the convoy pulled away, Eileen Haddon ran to the phone and called Grace. She said, "Brace yourself," and Grace thought there'd been an accident. "Garfield is on his way back to you with a police escort," said Eileen. "He's been arrested."

"Thank God! How marvelous," said Grace.

Minutes after Todd arrived at Hokonui, the phone started ringing. It was the BBC. Reporters were on their way to interview him. Then the calls came pouring in, news organizations from around the world wanting to talk to the former prime minister who was now a political prisoner. Todd told them he had no idea why he had been detained, although he presumed it was to silence his opposition to Smith's government. A banning order restricted him to the farm and forbade him to engage in any political activities.

Many years later Todd would be told by the British prime minister, Harold Wilson, that the Smith government had arrested him because it feared that if it declared unilateral independence while he was in Britain, he would set up a British-sanctioned government in exile. But the idea had not entered his mind. He didn't believe Smith would go that far.

TWO WEEKS AFTER TODD'S ARREST, ON NOVEMBER 11, 1965, IAN Smith made a Unilateral Declaration of Independence (UDI). It was an act of high treason, and we were now officially a rebel colony.

I remember that day. Hot. Dry. Early summer. My A-level English class argued listlessly about the pros and cons of rebellion before everyone subsided in laughter as the chief mimic did impressions of Ian Smith's foreign minister, the absurdly pompous P. K. van der Byl. Walking home that afternoon, I thought that I rather fancied the idea of being a rebel. Who were the British to tell us what to do, anyway? Fuck 'em. Good Old Smithy says we'll have it all sorted out and be back to normal in a couple of weeks.

Arriving home, I found a gang of friends and neighbors on the veranda. They were slinging back gin and tonics and arguing loudly about sanctions, terrorists, and civilized standards.

"The majority of the blacks don't want the vote, you know. It's just a few troublemakers who are being paid by the Russians."

"You'd think the British would realize the Reds were behind it. Some kith and kin they turned out to be."

"Sanctions will never work. South Africa will always support us."

"I hear the Robinsons have taken the chicken run. Whole family piled into the car and went south."

"Who would want to live in South Africa? If I have to leave, I'll head straight for the U.K."

"They're not moving me. This is my country. Bloody British. Bloody Wilson."

"Good Old Smithy."

They drank and argued well into the night, their voices carrying across the still Bulawayo suburb out into the African bushveld. The reason they were in a state of high agitation, I have now come to believe, is that no one really believed that Smith and his government would go through with it. Until that day it had all been politicians blowing off steam. Now it was us against the world.

Harold Wilson's response was to call for international sanctions against Rhodesia and to promise the British Parliament that the rebel colony would be brought to heel within weeks. Rhodesian monetary reserves in London were frozen, the importation of rebel tobacco and sugar into Britain was banned, and pretty soon oil imports into Rhodesia were also banned. Smith scoffed at all this and warned that Rhodesians were made of stern stuff, the same stuff that the British themselves had once been made of, before they'd capitulated to the forces of moral decay.

White Rhodesia rallied around Good Old Smithy, and at every meeting his delirious supporters sang "For He's a Jolly Good Fellow." It was some kind of weird mantra affirming his—and their own—decency and simplicity. He told them that they had struck a blow for the preservation of justice, civilization, and Christianity; it was up to the Rhodesians to defend the standards that had once been the measure of an Englishman. If Churchill were alive today, he said, he would surely immigrate to Rhodesia. Communism and corruption were rolling through Africa like a summer thunderstorm, and if our British colonial masters weren't prepared to stop it, then we would have to go it alone.

This was stirring stuff. It wasn't about suppressing the Africans at all. People who lived five thousand miles away and didn't understand Africa were telling us how to run our country. The Africans we knew seemed perfectly happy—Good Old Smithy assured every visiting politician that Rhodesia had the happiest Africans on the continent. We weren't apartheidists: there were Africans in parliament, even some at private white schools; they were allowed into our cinemas and bars and hotels. And Good Old Smithy said that when they had the appropriate qualifications, they would be rewarded with political representation. We were raising them to our standards, and that, surely, was no bad thing.

It had been only five years since the Congo had gone up in flames, and the memories of those hapless, dispossessed Belgian refugees—and their terrible tales of barbarism and anarchy—were burned into our cerebellums. There was no way Rhodesians were going to end up like the Belgians. No way. As petrol rationing was introduced and supplies of HP Sauce, Marmite, and Scotch whiskey began to dwindle, the Rhodesian resolve stiffened.

The quality of life we were defending was there for anyone to see—in the bustling, modern little cities, the factories, the impossibly neat suburbs—and we would do what was necessary to defend it. Damn it, we'd make our own tomato sauce and whiskey and wine. And if we had any doubts, all we had to do was ask anyone who'd been abroad recently. They'd return pale and wan from Northern Hemisphere winters and regale us with stories that seemed to confirm Smith's catechism on the collapse of Western society: you could buy a house in Bulawayo for the price of a steak in London; the British seldom took a bath and were dressed in rags; the Spanish had long-drop toilets just like the munts did here; you never saw the sun, and it rained everywhere, all the time.

So for a while at least, the whites would stand foursquare behind Good Old Smithy and hope that he could talk some sense into the British. A further Smith-Wilson summit, however, conducted somewhat melodramatically on board the British warship H.M.S. *Tiger,* collapsed in bitterness. Smith appointed a commission to look into a new constitution. He appointed an old friend, the prominent Salisbury lawyer Sam Whaley, to head the commission, and after a year of deliberation it proposed an electoral timetable that would ultimately produce an equal number of white and black MPs, but never a black majority.

This was going too far for the right wing of Smith's Rhodesian Front Party, and its members responded by proposing a *bantustan,* or homeland, system of tribal self-government that was ominously similar to apartheid. Smith compromised and in May 1969 announced a new constitution that introduced some element of African representation but nothing near as much as was now being demanded by African nationalists. There would be two houses: the lower house would have sixty-six members, of which fifty would be voted in by whites, Asians, and coloreds and sixteen by Africans. The upper house would comprise ten whites elected by the lower house, three whites chosen by the prime minister, and ten tribal chiefs. The whites endorsed the new constitution in a June referendum, but the black nationalists condemned it out of hand.

In 1970, the Conservative Party gained power in Britain, and the foreign secretary, Sir Alec Douglas Home, flew to Salisbury with Lord Arnold Goodman, Britain's chief negotiator on Rhodesia, and after some hard bargaining they arrived at an agreement for a constitution that lay between the previous Labour government's demands for majority rule as a condition of independence and Smith's doggedly conservative 1969 constitution. This one proposed a franchise that remained racially segregated but would eventually lead to an African majority of ten seats. "Eventually" was the operative word here, and observers calculated that the majority was unlikely to take its place until well into the twenty-first century.

The Home-Smith agreement had to be accepted by the majority of the people of Rhodesia, and another commission was appointed, this time led by the Tory peer Lord Pearce, which would travel throughout Rhodesia for two months canvassing the opinions of rural Africans. Lord Home and Smith thought the Pearce Commission would be a formality and that the response would be a resounding yes. But there was gathering opposition from the African nationalists, who used the government's relaxation of rules on political activities to campaign openly for the first time. They urged—and urging often became intimidation—the blacks to reject the agreement because it was not based on immediate majority rule. The expectation of a unanimous yes vote appeared to be evaporating in the heat of the summer.

IT WAS ON A SUMMER'S DAY, ON JANUARY 18, 1972, IN FACT, JUST AS the blistering heat of the afternoon was giving way to the liquid warmth of the early evening, that Sir Garfield was once again joined in battle with Ian Smith's government. During his years of banishment, Todd had played no role in the political comings and goings, although he continued to tell anyone who would listen—mainly itinerant journalists and the occasional visitor from Westminster—that majority rule was the only solution. His daughter, Judith, had been studying abroad and had been a constant thorn in the Smith government's side, leading demonstrations, giving speeches, and writing articles that supported her beloved father's position. Now she was back in the country, and for the past two weeks father and daughter had been traveling into the rural areas—at the request of the local communities—debating the merits of the Pearce proposals. (At the time, Sir Garfield was incorrectly quoted in *The Sunday Times* of London as having accepted the proposals. He has consistently told me that he had merely urged the rural communities not to reject them out of hand.)

That summer afternoon the Todds were driving in a convoy back toward Hokonui Ranch after attending a political meeting, and as they turned a corner on the narrow dirt road, they almost collided with an Austin Westminster speeding in the opposite direction. As the vehicles screeched to a halt, two men and a woman piled out of the Austin. They were Special Branch, and as they reached Garfield's car, they said, "Mr. Todd, we would like to speak to you and your daughter."

"Fine," said Todd affably. "We're on the way to our house. Would you care to join us?"

By now two more police vehicles had arrived, and once they had all pulled into Hokonui, the man in the gray suit introduced himself as Superintendent Tomlinson. He said he had orders to detain Garfield and Judith under the Law and Order Maintenance Act. He wanted to conduct a search of the Todds' office in nearby Bannockburn, and then he would drive them off to jail, Garfield to Gatooma Prison, two hundred miles away, and Judith to Marandellas, a further hundred miles. The police spent hours rifling through the files at Bannockburn, and by the time they returned to Hokonui so the Todds could pack their clothes, it was nine o'clock. Grace had prepared a meal for all of them, and the police sat on the stoep while the Todds had their last hours of freedom, talking and eating in the dining room.

The convoy drove through the night, and after dropping Garfield at Gatooma, they passed through Salisbury just before dawn. While they were parked at a filling station, Judith caught a glimpse of the morning newspaper. The headline read GARFIELD AND JUDY HELD. It was official.

There was an outcry in the world press and official approaches from some governments, but Smith remained firm—the Todds were a threat to the country's stability, and until his government established formal charges, they would remain out of harm's way. The

Pearce commissioners were allowed to see the Todds, and when they visited Judith, one of them, Lord Harlech, told her they had made the strongest protests about the detentions, and the only protest left would be to stop everything and return to Britain, a course they thought unwise, given what was at stake. Judith agreed.

Out in the country Lord Harlech's fellow commissioners were encountering vigorous, well-organized resistance to the terms of settlement. The Africans argued that the Smith government was committed to the perpetuation of white supremacy and that the whites had given them no indication that there would be power sharing. In other words, they were rejecting the proposals.

After two weeks of imprisonment, Judith began to despair. She had not been charged with anything, and she felt quite alone, with no access to the outside world and no way of communicating with her father. She announced that she was going on a hunger strike. Four days later she was transferred to another prison and force-fed. She abandoned her protest after two days of this, but by then her hunger strike had been so widely publicized that Ian Smith found himself fending off questions on British prime-time television. At a press conference he told journalists that criminal charges would be brought against the Todds and that they had been responsible for "burning, intimidation, violence, rioting, and looting."

At dawn on February 22, five weeks after she had been picked up by the Special Branch at Hokonui, Judith was told she was being taken back to the farm. The same car, the Austin Westminster, carrying the same Special Branch officers, came to pick her up, and they greeted her like an old friend. At Gatooma her father emerged, stooped and thin, his skin gone from burnished gold to a deathly gray and his hair hanging white and lifeless.

ON MAY 23, 1972, AT FOUR-THIRTY ON AN APPROPRIATELY OVER-cast afternoon, the findings of the Pearce Commission were announced over the Rhodesia Broadcasting Corporation. The settlement proposals were not, according to Pearce, acceptable to the majority of Rhodesians. That was it. The last chance. Ian Smith responded in typical fashion. "The report of the Pearce Commission shows that the overwhelming majority of Europeans, Asians, and Coloureds in Rhodesia supported the settlement," he said in a national broadcast. "So did a considerable number of Africans who realized the benefits which would flow from the agreement. Regrettably, however, Lord Pearce and his colleagues formed the opinion that a majority of Africans were opposed to the settlement. . . . I would not have credited that any report could contain so many misinterpretations and misconstructions of the true position."

There was no turning back now. As the black-nationalist guerrilla forces began massing on Rhodesia's borders—the Matabele Zimbabwe African People's Union (ZAPU), led by Joshua Nkomo, to the north and the Shona Zimbabwe African National Union (ZANU), led by Robert Mugabe, to the southeast—white Rhodesians started realizing they were facing a full-scale civil war.

Until then whites had experienced only minor inconveniences. Every hustler along the world's trade corridors was rerouting goods to and from Rhodesia, and the only things you couldn't get were real Scotch whiskey and decent wine. Most important, the bush war was functioning at a very low intensity. Apart from the occasional, usually failed guerrilla attack on remote farming areas in the southeast of the country, there were no signs of war.

All that changed in the early hours of the morning of December 21, 1972, when a guerrilla unit launched an attack on Altena Farm, a remote farmhouse in the country's picturesque northeast highlands. Margaret de Borchgrave and her two daughters, eight-year-old Ann and nine-year-old Jane, were lucky to survive—the guerrillas emptied two AK-47 magazines into the main bedroom and threw a grenade into the room where Margaret's parents usually slept. She and the girls lay flat under their beds, and somehow the bullets missed them. The only injury was a small gash on Jane's foot, which made her the first casualty of the Rhodesian war proper.

FOR THE NEXT FEW YEARS THE COUNTRY BOTH SMITH AND TODD wanted to save seemed to be slipping beyond salvation. Smith continued to seek a negotiated settlement and an end to the war but found himself obliged to make ridiculous statements to placate the right. "There will never be majority rule in this country, never in a thousand years," and "we will never negotiate with terrorists" consigned him to the history books as a myopic bigot. Garfield Todd, meantime, was living out his banishment in the relative calm of Hokonui farm. Every afternoon he would sit on the farmhouse veranda and count the tankers that passed by on the railway line carrying gasoline to Salisbury. These were the sanctions-busting shipments from South Africa that kept the white regime functioning, and Todd would maintain detailed notes of their movements and pass them on to MI6 contacts operating in southern Africa. And while most white farmers found themselves the target of frequent guerrilla attacks and turned their farmhouses into armed fortresses, the Todds left their doors unlocked and didn't possess so much as a handgun among them. This was because they were providing a safe haven and food and clothing for the black guerrilla soldiers passing through the area.

These activities finally brought Smith and Todd to their last confrontation. In February 1980, just a month before the election that would sweep Mugabe to power, Smith ordered Todd arrested on charges of treason. The penalty was hanging. It was, however, too late for the Rhodesian government to rid itself of this turbulent priest. Although charges were formally made and Todd was briefly held in jail, the case did not go to court before the elections, and once the new government was in place, it was struck from the books. Had the election gone the other way—an alliance between Smith's party and the moderate blacks, as the British had expected—then Todd may well have had to appear in court and face a death sentence.

"And I could not have denied the charges," he says.

FOUR

And So to War

I had tried to be a true Rhodesian, but I was never as enthusiastic about the idea as some of my friends were. First of all I didn't buy the Good Old Smithy thing. I didn't doubt his integrity, but his refrain of how the Rhodesian way of life was the most decent and civilized and perfect in the world and how we should resist the decadence and declining standards of the mother country—this bothered me. Everything that was coming out of Britain in the 1960s—the music, plays, films, journalism, fashion—seemed quite brilliant and original to me. I thought we were hicks from the bush and that the world, the rest of my generation, was leaving us behind.

Second, the cause seemed a lost one. The idea that a quarter of a million whites could deny political rights to 5 million blacks with the world on their side seemed ridiculous. I had seen the first signs myself, all those years before in the turbulent winter of 1960, when the Belgian refugees arrived and the townships turned to rioting. Even then the logic and inevitability of the black majority rising up to reclaim what had been theirs made me realize we were living the last days of empire.

In the late '60s, during the days of student protests all over the world, I spent three years studying for an economics degree at the University of Natal, and some of the edges were knocked off my

The author in Durban in the early 1970s.

rough-hewn Rhodesian ways of thinking. But it was eighteen months in London that changed me profoundly.

The day I arrived in London in 1970, I headed for Foyle's book-shop in Charing Cross Road and bought up all the agitprop litera-ture I could find—Angela Davis, Cleaver's *Soul on Ice,* Fanon's *Wretched of the Earth,* Marx, Lenin, Mao, and even Timothy Leary. Later that day I saw two movies—*WR: Mysteries of the Organism* and *Easy Rider*—and took in an anti-apartheid demonstration out-side the South African embassy in Trafalgar Square. Then, after a few pints in a pub in the King's Road, I went on to the 100 Club in Oxford Street to hear the exiled South African saxophonist Dudu Pukwane playing township jazz. This was the first time in my life I had been able to read or see or listen to anything I wanted. Before then my choices of entertainment and education had been regu-lated by groups of old white men in shiny black suits: censorship boards. Anything these reactionary Christians deemed politically unsound or morally offensive was struck off the lists. No *Playboy* or *Penthouse,* no Black Panthers, Marxist writers, or Martin Luther King speeches. No *Jesus Christ Superstar* and, for a time, no Beat-les, because John Lennon had said they were more popular than Jesus.

So it was with mixed feelings that I returned to South Africa in 1972 with a headful of new ideas about freedom and a mountain of hair that quite startled the little old ladies in downtown Durban. I also had plans to become a journalist, but before I settled into my new career, I decided to take a short holiday to Bulawayo, a some-what chancy venture given my status with the Rhodesian authori-ties. Technically I was obliged to serve a nine-month stint in the Rhodesian Army, having used up my college deferment some time back. The idea of the army filled me with horror. Much as I loved the country and felt attached to my friends, I could not bring my-self to feel patriotic enough to want to join the bush war. I thought Smith was nuts and the war was pointless.

Unfortunately my early-'70s London-look hair mountain at-tracted as much attention in downtown Bulawayo as it had in Dur-ban, and word soon got out that I was back. At the end of the first week, on a lazy summer afternoon, my back-to-my-roots reverie was interrupted by a frantic telephone call from my mother, ordering me to pack my suitcase and prepare to flee immediately. A friend working at army headquarters had tipped her off that the military police knew I was in town and were planning to pick me up.

With their increasing isolation and the gathering threat of a full-scale civil war, white Rhodesians were becoming more patriotic and less tolerant. It was backs-to-the-wall time, and they gave short shrift to whites who had taken the chicken run down south or to young longhairs like me who weren't doing their bit. Most of us had been granted army deferments to attend college, but we had been expected to return and to serve, and the MPs were always on the lookout for students, musicians, or academics who had sneaked back to visit their families. Sometimes they would get their information from customs officers, but mainly they picked it up from the grapevine. Once they knew you were in town, they swooped in. It had happened to an old friend of mine only weeks earlier. He was a drummer in a rock band that was enjoying some success in South Africa and, as was the fashion of the time, wore his jet-black hair very long. Dressed in flowing hippie raiment in a place populated by men with short hair, short trousers, and veldschoens (literally, bush shoes), he was spotted on his first trip downtown. That afternoon the MPs descended on his home and took him directly to Brady Barracks, Bulawayo's army base, where his head was shaved and his army kit issued before he had time to call his father.

Within half an hour of the phone call from my mother's friend, the family Austin Cambridge was rattling up the driveway at speed, my myopic mother set rigidly in the driving position she favored in times of emergency—arms wrapped round the steering wheel like tentacles and body leaning so far forward that her nose almost touched the windshield. After executing a violent three-point turn that dented the front fender and obliterated a rear light, she flung open the door and shouted at me, "In the boot! In the boot!"

What, me?

"No. No. The suitcase. The suitcase." Then she ordered me to lie flat on the backseat. We argued all the way to the airport, me protesting that the melodrama was unnecessary, she insisting that it was not worth taking a chance. "That Forbes boy up the road was shot in the head last month," she said. "Now he's in Ingutshene [an institution for the mentally ill], and he can't feed himself. His wife's just had their first child." Case closed.

I clambered onto the day's last flight to South Africa, knowing that I was leaving Rhodesia for the final time. It seemed an undignified and rather craven way to depart a country that had nurtured me from childhood to manhood, and as the plane banked over Bulawayo, I felt rising anger at the politicians who had forced me and so many of my generation into exile. For the past ten years most of the country's bright young whites had been leaving to attend universities in South Africa, Britain, and America, and fewer and fewer were returning.

Many, like me, drifted to South Africa, but things were hardly any more encouraging there. Under H. F. Verwoerd's hard-line successor, John Vorster, the Nationalist government had been remorselessly grinding apartheid theory into everyday reality. Millions of blacks were uprooted from their homes and dumped into remote wastelands that Pretoria's apartheid architects had designated "tribal homelands." Jailings, bannings, and assassinations were commonplace, and Special Branch heavies followed you everywhere.

Vorster's support for Rhodesia was capricious and self-serving. While recognizing Rhodesia's value as the last white buffer zone between South Africa and the rolling tide of black nationalism from the north, Vorster was also happy to use the country as a bargaining chip with the West. Take the pressure off South Africa, he told Western shuttle diplomats like Henry Kissinger and Lord Carrington, and he would force Ian Smith to go to the negotiating table. Rhodesia was entirely dependent on South Africa, its supply route linking the landlocked rebel colony with the outside world, and Vorster had no trouble keeping his side of the deal. He simply stopped the trains carrying oil and munitions north. It was, Smith would tell me years later, the greatest betrayal of all. The Afrikaners, who had promised their white neighbors unconditional support, were now prepared to sell them off like a secondhand car. In the time of the Rhodesians' greatest need, at the height of the guerrilla offensive, their last white ally turned its back on them. So much for the brotherhood of the white African.

As a Rhodesian living in South Africa—even an unpatriotic draft-dodging Rhodesian—I too was appalled at the duplicity of the Afrikaner government. They had always said, "We're in this together. Joined in the final battle of white Christian standards against the black Communist onslaught." Now they were like everyone else—putting self-interest and expediency before principles. I had come to hate this iron-fisted, iron-hearted society filled with more race hatred than Rhodesia had at the height of its civil war. The harshness and corrosiveness of apartheid had robbed South Africa of its humanity.

Given that I was armed only with a lazy man's bachelor of economics degree and a strong distaste for nine-to-five office jobs, journalism had seemed a likely career to pursue. There were two options in Durban—the reasonably conservative but lively afternoon paper, the *Daily News,* and the very conservative, old-fashioned, and very dull morning paper, the *Natal Mercury.* Both were English-language papers, and both supported the weak-kneed opposition, the United Party, which didn't in fact seem to me much different from the ruling Nationalists. The petit apartheidists of the UP simply had better manners and more refined English accents.

I started out as a beat reporter on the *Daily News,* following cops around and chasing ambulances. Many of my friends were student activists, so I had a direct line to the white left, and it was their involvement in black trade unions that drew me into black politics. The modus operandi was to find a government-instigated outrage, provide vivid details of the victims and their families, get a single-sentence standard denial from a government spokesman, and then roll the presses. The headline would read either GOVERNMENT DENIES INVOLVEMENT IN WHATEVER MASSACRE or GOVERNMENT ACCUSED OF WHATEVER MASSACRE, depending on whether the lefty night editor or the rightist day editor was on duty.

These were strange times. While I felt a certain moral rectitude about what I was doing—peripheral and insignificant though my contribution undoubtedly was—I was also aware that constant exposure to apartheid's iniquities was bad for the spirit. Student leaders, black unionists, and liberal journalists were being harassed by Vorster's government at an accelerating pace—their telephones were tapped; some were taken in for interrogation by South Africa's Special Branch; others were given five-year banning orders that abruptly cut them off from their careers. One of my close friends, the affable human rights lawyer Charles Nupen, was charged with treason, a hanging offense, for leading a campaign that called for Nelson Mandela's release from prison.

In the summer of 1974, I discovered that the net was beginning to close in around me. It was absurd that Nupen was charged with treason—but it was sheer lunacy that the secret police would waste taxpayers' money on me. I had taken my girlfriend, a high school teacher, on a driving vacation to Cape Town, and we had stayed with friends and then driven back along South Africa's marvelous coastline in convoy with Charles Nupen and his wife, Drene. At one point we had stopped off for a couple of days at Jeffrey's Bay, a remote surfing spot where we could see for miles around us and where we did not encounter another human being the entire time we were there.

Soon after we arrived back in Durban, my girlfriend was picked up by the Special Branch for questioning. It was an informal interview, the officers assured her. They simply wanted to warn her that even her closest friends might, unbeknownst to her, be Communists and that she should be careful. They told her they knew everything and proceeded to describe our day-to-day movements over the past fortnight, right down to what we were doing at Jeffrey's Bay.

I had wandered into the crosshairs of apartheid's surveillance network, and I did not feel comfortable about this.

IT WAS WITH NO GREAT SURPRISE THAT A FEW MONTHS AFTER THAT summer holiday I accepted a registered letter from the South African government that declared me an "undesirable alien" and ordered me to leave the country within a month.

Within hours of receiving the letter, I had booked passage on the final voyage from Durban to Southampton of the *Pendennis Castle,* one of the Union Castle mailboats that had through the 1950s and '60s acted as a kind of conveyor belt for white colonial families like mine, ferrying tens of thousands of immigrants from Europe to the African colonies. We had arrived on the *Windsor Castle* twenty-three years before, and now I was leaving for good.

The Rhodesia I was leaving behind was now at the peak of its civil war, and South Africa was being driven to the brink of catastrophe by a gang of white zealots. My friends were moving on, scattering to safer colonies like Australia, New Zealand, and Canada. Those who stayed behind seemed doomed, and I was sure I would next see them on BBC news bulletins manning the barricades or fleeing as refugees. The banishing order I had received deepened my sense of gloom. Would I ever set foot in Africa again?

During the coming years Africa would get along without me, although I was soon to realize that I could not get along forever without Africa. From my new home on Hampstead Heath, I watched the Rhodesian bush war unfold on television. Names from the past were constantly leaping out at me, but they evoked death and destruction rather than warm childhood remembrances. Every few weeks a new tale of horror would make its way into my living room, along with ghastly pictures of murdered children and razed villages.

One story in particular left me so enraged that I decided I would forsake my impotent exile and return to Rhodesia and take it on the chin. (This impulse passed before I got to a travel agent.) The story involved an Air Rhodesia commercial flight that had taken off from Kariba carrying fifty-two passengers, mainly vacationers who'd been fishing or sailing or viewing game at the lake. Five minutes into its climb, the Viscount had shuddered violently, and a starboard engine had burst into flame. The pilot, Captain John Hood, knew what it was immediately—they'd been hit by a heat-seeking missile.

Captain Hood managed to maintain some control over the damaged plane and aimed it at an open patch of veld. The Viscount touched down intact, but a hundred yards along it struck an irrigation ditch, cartwheeled, and broke into pieces. Eighteen survivors, all seated in the tail section, scrambled from the wreckage. After they had tended to the wounded, a group of the fittest struck out toward a village to raise the alarm. They were a few hundred yards away when they heard African voices and saw half-crouched figures running toward the Viscount. They were Zimbabwe People's Revolutionary Army (ZIPRA) guerrillas, Matabeles fighting for Joshua Nkomo's ZAPU party. Minutes later the survivors of the crash heard the crackle of automatic-rifle fire. Among those shot dead were two girls, aged eleven and four. There were ten victims in all; three others had managed to hide in the fuselage.

As I sat watching the story unfold and saw the charred bodies lined up alongside the ditch like little lumps of charcoal, the words "black savagery" and "white martyrs" crowded into my head. I heard Nkomo, the ZAPU leader, who would undoubtedly have ordered the missile attack, come on the radio and laugh about it, and I howled for the spirits of past martyrs—the soldiers of the Shangani Patrol, Piet Retief and his fellow Boers slaughtered by Dingane's warriors—to avenge this terrible act. (Nkomo later claimed that he had not been laughing about his soldiers' handiwork but about his own guarded response to the question of what weapon the ZIPRA guerrillas had used to bring down the Viscount. He couldn't admit they'd used a SAM-7 missile and had said they'd thrown rocks at the plane.)

I had hoped I would find sanctuary in Britain, far away from the blood and thunder of African life. But I was beginning to realize that Africa would not leave me alone. I began a correspondence that some years later would result in the withdrawal of my banishing order, a maneuver secured by the South African opposition MP Helen Suzman. And after six years' absence, now as a rehabilitated, no longer undesirable alien, I began to travel back to Africa.

FIVE

The Most Dangerous Man in the Country: Rick Turner and the Durban Moment

The anti-apartheid movement I had come in contact with in Durban before I was thrown out of the country was in fact one of the most significant threats to white rule in South Africa. There was a reason why even a peripheral involvement such as mine with its activists led to a banning order. During its brief and brilliant flowering, the Durban Moment redefined South African politics.

Durban was the least likely African city to nurture a revolution. It was tropical, easy-paced, a holiday resort and a harbor city bursting with extravagent flora and ringed with golden beaches. Its inhabitants were the English-speaking South Africans of Natal whose nineteenth-century pioneer forebears had hacked this pretty city out of rough bushveld and fought off bloodthirsty Zulu armies while they were hacking and building. They were proud of their British heritage and called Natal the last outpost of the British Empire. Traditional enemies of the Afrikaners, they had always opposed the National Party, voting instead for the watery opposition United Party, which was almost as conservative as the Nats, but at least its members spoke English. The sybaritic citizens of Durban, living in luxury on the shores of the Indian Ocean, went about their good lives—watching cricket and rugby, surfing, sailing, having beach parties up the Zululand coast—and accepted their reputation

Rick Turner, the political science lecturer who was banned for his
anti-apartheid activities in the 1970s.

as easygoing low achievers with a lazy grin and another bottle of ice-cold Castle lager.

The students at the University of Natal, up on the hill, were tolerated by the citizens, and little attention was paid to them. They were longhairs who drank too much and filled the movie houses at afternoon matinées instead of attending lectures; the rest of the time they seemed to be protesting or sitting in or boycotting something. If anything, the students added a little color to the landscape, mild divertissement and a couple of column inches in the morning newspaper. Every now and then one would have his or her passport withdrawn by the government "for reasons of national security" or would be picked up by the Special Branch for questioning. There would be a flurry of protest meetings and letters to the *Daily News,* but then things would die down.

It was an unlikely setting for a revolution, indeed, and yet Durban became for a time the crucible of anti-apartheid political thinking and organization. It was here that white liberalism came of age and black consciousness was born.

IT ALL BEGAN WITH THE ARRIVAL IN JANUARY 1970 OF A UNIVERsity lecturer named Richard Turner. Just turned twenty-eight, Turner was a brilliant graduate of the University of Cape Town who had studied for his doctorate at the Sorbonne. His subject was the philosophy of Jean-Paul Sartre, and the fact that he had actually met the great man added substantially to his reputation. Like most other South African students traveling abroad for the first time, he had been enamored of the academic and social freedoms that were traditional in Europe's universities but very much forbidden at home. He had been exposed to the great political debates of the 1960s and carried along by a restless Parisian student movement, and when he returned home toward the end of the decade, he was fired up with visions of a new South Africa.

For a short time he combined part-time lecturing jobs with the running of his mother's farm outside Stellenbosch. Jane Turner's only son was her raison d'être, but it wasn't long before the iron-willed matriarch and the young idealist were at each other's throats.

Rick wanted to raise the wages of the farmworkers and build them proper homes, and Jane wondered where he had picked up these mad ideas. He was also spending more and more time at the University of Cape Town, organizing teach-ins and becoming embroiled in student politics. When he was offered a part-time post at Rhodes University he leaped at it, finally cutting his ties with his mother and the farm.

By the time Turner arrived in Durban at the beginning of 1970, he carried a reputation as a fierce and articulate activist. The University of Natal was historically in the intellectual shadow of the country's two main English-language colleges, Cape Town and Witwatersrand, but it had a decent economics department, and the sciences were good. The campus was an odd mix of rugger buggers, cheerleaders and drum majorettes, dopeheads and lefties, Rhodesians and Kenyans, and although there was a small nucleus of politically active students, most were driven by either academic or hedonistic pursuits. The first thing Turner did was find his way to the small nucleus.

He soon discovered that the student movement was in the throes of serious turmoil. Up on the hill, in the leafy serenity of the white campus, student politicians were doing what they had been doing throughout the 1960s—thundering familiar condemnations of the apartheid system, attending sit-ins and protest meetings in response to the latest injustices, and generally wringing their hands in impotent despair as the Vorster government tightened its grip on the country. Meanwhile, down the hill, in the far less salubrious confines of the UNNE—the University of Natal, Non-European—students were beginning to group around a young medical student named Steve Biko. Although they had always enjoyed good relations with their white counterparts and indeed were members of NUSAS, the white-led, nonracial National Union of South African Students, the UNNE students felt the time had come to step out of the shadows.

Within weeks of his arrival on campus, Turner was invited to a discussion group of white and black student leaders. There he met Steve Biko for the first time. Biko was gregarious, charismatic, great fun—the very antithesis of the wild-eyed, scowling revolutionary the Vorster government was to conjure up in the coming years. He was also a determined and driven political activist, and Turner was impressed with his clear-headed intelligence. Biko was taken by Turner's intellect, and he asked the lecturer to give a talk on black power at UNNE the following week.

Although there was isolated heckling ("Who are you to come here and tell us about black power?"), the talk was very well received. Turner had access to foreign publications the members of his audience hadn't even heard of, and he understood the complexities of the black power movement in America. He explained how fragmented it was and described the philosophical differences between the civil rights movement and the Nation of Islam and Malcolm X and Stokely Carmichael and the Black Panthers. To his audience these were just righteous names, symbols of defiance, slogans to be chanted in the streets. But Turner could explain why the American civil rights campaigns were important to black South Africans. "Black power is not a racist doctrine," he said. "It does not mean that blacks should dominate whites. The aim is not to subjugate other ethnic groups but to develop sufficient strength to be able to participate with them in equal terms in a plural society."

A striking young student of Cape-Malay descent named Foszia Fisher was in the audience that night. She was impressed that a white man had been bold enough to come into the home of the emerging black-consciousness movement, and she was impressed with what she heard. Turner urged his audience to study the American black power movement, and he handed out reading lists at the end of the lecture. Later, at a party given by Biko, Foszia found herself locked in conversation with Turner, bewitched by his eloquence. They talked for hours, and she was flattered and delighted when he invited her out to dinner.

Within months of arriving in Durban, Rick Turner had become a focal point of liberal activism. With his fellow lecturer, the laconic opera lover Michael Nupen, a perfect foil, Turner transformed the university's moribund political science department into a hotbed of intellectual debate. He also began hosting weekly reading-and-discussion sessions among black activists like Biko and an emerging group of white students. He was constantly prompting debate, arguing with Biko that he should not allow the black-consciousness ethic to blind him to the fact that the movement's power lay in the unorganized black working classes. He cajoled whites into agreeing that it was not race but the capitalist system that explained the exploitation of South Africa's black workers.

In his writings and lectures Turner continued to amplify his vision of the future South Africa as a participatory democracy. He believed that through collective organization—trade unions—South Africa's black people could begin to exercise some control over their lives. He rejected the African National Congress's armed struggle as an unrealistic strategy for the time and regarded international sanctions against South Africa as counterproductive, reiterating that the power behind realistic, revolutionary change lay with the black workers. The creation of black trade unions would lead to a change in the balance of power without the overthrow of the white ruling class, which was the "revolutionary rupture" that the old-style Leninists had long predicted for South Africa. The ascendancy of the black working-class movement would, in Turner's view, be achieved through gradualism, flexibility, and compromise with employers and the government.

Turner was in fact quite moderate and pragmatic, which was the interesting thing about both him and Steve Biko. They were realists and even conservative, if not in their thinking then most definitely in their strategies.

Turner's place in the history of white opposition to apartheid is interesting. Ever since the inception of apartheid, in 1948, there had been white liberals prepared to take on the Nationalists. Whether they were hard-line leftists or social democrats from the Progressive Party, these anti-government whites were invariably middle-class, educated, and representative of a tiny minority of the ruling class. Mainstream white South Africans kept away from politics, feeling safe in the belief that the Nats would preserve white rule come hell or high water. Even if they didn't approve of everything the Nats did, they liked the results.

Through the 1950s and early '60s, the outlawing of the Communist Party and the main African nationalist movements, all of which had significant white membership, drove the true radicals into exile. What remained behind was a ragtag alliance that included the multiracial Liberal Party, of which Alan Paton was the most famous member; the small but valiant Progressive Party, most vocally represented in parliament by Helen Suzman; and assorted academics, trade unionists, and students. The last act of white terrorism had taken place in 1962, when John Harris, a schoolteacher and Liberal Party member, planted a bomb in the Johannesburg Railway Station. It killed an old woman and disfigured a little girl named Glynnis Burleigh and turned the nation against violent resistance. After Harris was hanged, the Liberal Party demanded the resignation of any member who had taken part in acts of sabotage.

In 1968, when the Prohibition of Political Interference Act was passed and whites and blacks could no longer legally belong to the same political party, the last legitimate enclave of radical white resistance, Alan Paton's multiracial Liberal Party, was finally overwhelmed, and its eight thousand members called it a day. All that remained of the white left in mainstream politics was the Progressive Party, with its sole member of parliament, Helen Suzman, carrying the banner of liberalism in a house filled with die-hard separatists.

By the time Turner arrived in Durban in 1970, the white liberal movement had been all but silenced, its followers reduced to occasionally sticking their heads above the parapets and complaining about censorship laws or detention without trial or bannings. The ladies of the Black Sash would hold silent vigils on the steps of City Hall, and students would periodically march down West Street waving banners, but these dignified and infrequent protests rather suited the government, since they could be used as proof that South Africa was upholding the values of Western democracy.

With the coming of the Durban Moment, however, this cozy relationship was extinguished once and for all.

STEVE BIKO MADE THE FIRST MOVE. AT THE ANNUAL STUDENT congress in Pietermartizburg in 1970, he announced that he and his exclusively black South African Students Organisation (SASO) were walking out on the multiracial National Union of South African Students. The announcement caused uproar and confusion among the white liberals. The intelligentsia of Cape Town and Witwatersrand Universities, inheritors of an English liberal ethic that had prevailed for a century, were apoplectic and accused SASO of applying the same racial policies as the Nats. Only the Durban delegation, the members of Turner's reading group, understood what was going on. (As Biko left the assembly, he handed the Durban student leader Paul Pretorius a note that read, "Thanks for all your support.")

SASO had been two years in the making and was born out of the disaffection Biko's generation of young educated blacks felt toward white liberalism. They thought that white liberals demonstrated their identification with black people only to the extent that they did not threaten their ties to their white peer group. Biko wrote in 1972 that the liberal "possesses the natural passport to the exclusive pool of white privilege from which he does not hesitate to extract whatever suits him. Yet, since he identifies with the blacks, he moves around his white circles, whites-only beaches, restaurants, and cinemas with a lighter load, feeling he is not like the rest."

While the black-consciousness movement was finding its feet, the white members of Turner's reading group were beginning to take action themselves. Charles Nupen, Karel Tip, and Halton Cheadle launched the Wages Commission at Natal University to conduct investigations into wages paid to black workers in the Durban area. The commission highlighted, through press accounts, the appalling circumstances of black unskilled workers, and it also provided statistics and information to government wage boards responsible for labor legislation. The students began publishing a workers' newspaper, called *Isisebenza*, which they distributed from the backs of their 50-cc Hondas outside factory gates, much to the disgust of the white factory bosses.

Modest though the Wages Commission's aims now appear to have been, at the time they were very important. The commission gave the student politicians a point of contact with a sector of South

The student leader Charles Nupen with Harold Nxasana, a trade union-
ist, at a rally in Durban in 1973. Nupen became the top labor arbitrator
in South Africa after Mandela's government came to power in 1994.

African society that had long been ignored and at the same time allowed them to put into practice the ideas coming out of Turner's reading groups and the university's political science department. For the first time, white students were moving beyond the confines of the politics of reactive protest, away from the marches and the endless public meetings, where denunciations of apartheid fell on the ears of the same like-minded people year after year. Now they were out there in the real South Africa, on the docks, in the abattoirs and the union halls.

Rick Turner inspired all this, although he did not specifically encourage the students to get involved in the workers' movement. What he did was provoke them to think more creatively about practical actions that would have a direct impact on the black masses. He encouraged them to apply in practical ways the methodology he described in his political science lectures, to attempt to emulate the Marxist utopia he chose to call a participatory democracy. Gravitating toward the black working class, the most exploited, the most unorganized, and the most discriminated-against sector of South African society, was logical but their own idea.

EARLY IN 1971, SOON AFTER FOSZIA FISHER MOVED INTO TURNER'S house at 32 Dalton Avenue in the Durban suburb of Bellair, they were married in a Muslim ceremony. These were the days of unyielding, relentless adherence to the laws of racial separation, and by marrying, Rick and Foszia were breaking three fundamental race laws: the Group Areas Act (Foszia, classified as a nonwhite, was living in a white area), the Immorality Act (intercourse across the color line), and the Mixed Marriages Act. But the government chose not to take any action against them, and when the local police were preparing to raid the Turner home for evidence of interracial felonies—which traditionally involved checking bedsheets for semen stains—the Special Branch ordered them to desist. The security police were apparently hoping to bring down the Turners with heavier charges than race transgressions.

The house at 32 Dalton Avenue was a modest bungalow in a white working-class neighborhood that had been established for railway workers in the 1930s and '40s. What Rick liked about it was that it was remote, set apart from the neighbors, hidden by trees, and difficult to find. It was located in the middle of an oblong piece of land at the end of a narrow stretch of dirt that passed for a road. Pretty soon the road was clogged with battered jalopies belonging to students and lecturers and transient activists, and the Turner home was the center of a throbbing little universe.

It was a year later, in the summer of 1972, that Rick Turner's battle with the South African government was formally joined. On Thursday, February 10, Prime Minister Vorster won the approval of parliament to set up a commission of inquiry into the activities of four anti-apartheid organizations: NUSAS; the South African Institute of Race Relations, a welfare and research organization; and two church groups—the Christian Institute and the University Christian Movement. Thus the Schlebusch Commission was born, a mad and tortured attempt to shut down meaningful political opposition for good. It began as high comedy, with a bunch of old duffers conducting excruciating interviews with students who had nothing to hide, and ended in tragedy, with the mass bannings of the country's brightest young men and women and the eventual deaths of their leaders, Steve Biko and Rick Turner.

The Schlebusch Commission was created at a time of bullish optimism for white South Africa. Over the previous ten years the country had achieved the second fastest economic growth rate in the world—second only to Japan's. International trade was booming, foreign earnings were up sixfold; there was even a net gain of a quarter of a million white immigrants. Nelson Mandela and the leaders of the black opposition had been safely tucked away on Robben Island for some time, and there was little sign of trouble from the masses. In spite of incessant complaints and hostile resolutions from the United Nations, student demonstrations that disrupted overseas sporting tours, and liberal lobbies' calls for disinvestment, things were going rather well. To the north the Rhodesians seemed to be holding their own in their war with black-nationalist guerrillas, while on South Africa's northeastern and northwestern flanks the Portuguese had Mozambique and Angola under tight control. After almost a quarter of a century of Afrikaner rule, it seemed that the whites might have worked out how to hang on to power.

To maintain this stability, successive Nationalist governments had wrapped the country up in a tight web of apartheid legislation. The Prohibition of Political Interference Act outlawed interracial political parties; the Suppression of Communism Act hovered over anyone to the left of Martin Luther King, Jr., who dared criticize government policy; the Terrorism Act was used to quash critics who never dreamed of taking up arms; the Immorality Act and the Mixed Marriages Act, the race legislation that Rick Turner and Foszia defied, brought heartbreak and destruction to families and communities throughout the land.

Under Vorster, these laws were enforced by a growing army of secret police and Special Branch operatives who went about their work with considerable enthusiasm. Student leaders found that they were being tailed and their phones were being tapped; trade union officials had their offices broken into and the brakes on their cars tampered with. Passports were withdrawn to prevent apartheid's opponents from carrying their messages overseas, and political activists were locked away in solitary confinement under the 90-day and 180-day detention laws that gave them no access to attorneys.

Opposition to the government implied, inter alia, association with the government's enemy. The government's enemy was communism, and so "fellow travelers," a popular catchphrase of the time, were as dangerous to the country's stability as full-blown Che Guevara–type guerrillas. If you had simply spoken to a Marxist, you were tainted, never mind whether you had actually read a Marxist book or pamphlet. The consequences of sleeping with one did not bear thinking about.

Vorster's police arrested people on the flimsiest pretexts, holding them in solitary confinement and subjecting them to techniques of torture and interrogation usually associated with Latin American juntas. The torturers became famous in their own right. There was Spyker van Wyk, who is said to have nailed a prisoner's penis to a table and who broke the ankle of an ANC politician, Stephanie Kemp. Van Wyk arrived to interrogate another ANC activist, Jeremy Cronin, wearing a bloodstained jacket and fiddling obsessively with a pair of electrodes. Then there was Theunis "Rooi Rus" Swanepoel, who also favored electric-shock treatments but whose favorite forms of torture were kicking his victims senseless and taking a pair of pliers to their genitals. (Mac Maharaj, South Africa's first nonwhite minister of Transport, was subjected to Rooi Rus's pliers treatment.)

With the appointment of the Schlebusch Commission, Vorster and his advisers saw their chance to finally smash the last enclaves of significant resistance. "The years ahead will be most important," Vorster intoned, "especially if one looks at the progress of Communism and the conflict, bloodshed and unrest which is taking place." What he meant, one assumes, is that the four organizations under investigation were hotbeds of revolution capable of, if not already up to their necks in, the kind of subversive activities that would lead to conflict, bloodshed, and unrest. It was not quite so, and a quick study of the four institutions offers some insight into the full extent of the government's paranoia at the time.

The National Union of South African Students was founded in 1924 by the educationist-author Leo Marquard "to encourage the interest and participation of students in educational welfare, cultural and community projects . . . to promote and defend democratic practices in student affairs and in South Africa."

The Institute of Race Relations was founded in 1929 by Johannesburg academics to study interracial relationships objectively. It still collects data and statistics, conducts surveys, and publishes studies that academic institutions throughout the world regard as essential reference sources. Among its four thousand members in the early 1970s were Sir de Villiers Graaff, leader of the opposition United Party, and the Progressive Party MP Helen Suzman.

The two Christian bodies, established in the 1960s, were active in community work—literacy campaigns and self-help programs. They also published studies on various aspects of apartheid.

The commission, headed by Kroonstad MP Alwyn Schlebusch and comprising seven Nationalists and three members of the opposition United Party, swung into action in the middle of the year and began summoning academics, students, and church leaders to Pretoria to give evidence. At first the students refused to testify, but Turner argued that they had nothing to hide and that their evidence would surely exonerate them. What he had not bargained for was the blinkered intransigence of the commissioners and the grueling Kafkaesque interrogation sessions that were intended to do nothing beyond confirm the commissioners' paranoid fantasies.

The commissioners arrived armed with the firm belief that the four organizations were run by cliques of revolutionaries intent on bringing down the state. Their "evidence" of subversion amounted to little more than a grab bag of newspaper clippings, public statements, published lectures, and diaries and personal correspondence pilfered by the Special Branch. The commissioners did not, however, allow the paucity of their claims to interfere with the purpose of their work. Their task was simply to prove to themselves something they already knew—that these people were dangerous subversives.

Rick Turner, as a member of the NUSAS advisory panel, was summoned to give evidence in November. The commissioners sat grim faced, convinced that this was the ringleader, the head of the beast threatening their culture. They were looking into the eyes of a revolutionary.

"Is it correct," asked one, "that in [an] address you referred to legislation such as the Terrorism Act and that you said that this legislation is being used as an instrument of intimidation?"

"Yes," said Turner.

"Not only against guerrillas but against anybody who speaks out against the government?"

"That is certainly my opinion. Yes."

There was a long and solemn pause as the weight of these words descended on the commissioners. He has already admitted to sedition, they were thinking, without even knowing it. The commis-

sioners leaned forward and proceeded with the calm assurance of
the righteous. They brought out a letter, solemnly recorded it as ex-
hibit 85, and asked Turner whether he recognized it. It was a letter
he had written to his first wife, Barbara, that had apparently been
taken from his files by the Special Branch. In it he complained that
he was beginning to find himself propelled into a leadership role on
the Durban campus that he found "both embarrassing and undesirable." Proof enough for the commissioners that he was indeed
the ringleader they'd believed him to be. They had their man.

ON THE AFTERNOON OF TUESDAY, FEBRUARY 27, 1973, RICK
Turner was working at his office on the university campus, and Foszia was grappling with trade union problems down the hill at
Bolton Hall. A number of strikes had broken out in the Durban
area, and her office was in chaos. Rick had taken a transistor radio
to work that day because the prime minister was due to make an important announcement to parliament concerning the Schlebusch
Commission.

At three o'clock the station switched to parliament, and Turner
turned up the radio to hear the slow menacing slur of John Vorster.
He was saying that an urgent interim report submitted by the commission had warned that a cabal of NUSAS leaders was threatening
the country's security and that eight of them were to be banned
immediately under the Suppression of Communism Act: "Paul
Pretorius, NUSAS president; Paula Ensor, head of NUSWEL,
NUSAS's welfare arm; Philippe le Roux; Sheila Lapinsky, . . . Chris
Wood, . . . Clive Keegan, . . . Neville Curtis, . . . and Dr. Rick
Turner, lecturer at Natal University." Vorster went on to reassure
parliament that the doughty commissioners were still pursuing
their inquiries, and he promised that the final report would make
South Africa's blood run cold. In the meantime, this interim re-
port would provide enough damning evidence to justify harsh executive action.

The most serious accusations were that the students were a
"clique" that ran the student body and lived in "communes," that
they accepted donations from foreign organizations and might have

been influenced by them, and that they had made public statements that might be construed as sympathetic to Communist doctrines. Even the overwrought language used by the commissioners and their penchant for drawing sinister conclusions from everyday events could not conceal the shallowness of their findings. The "clique" was in fact a group of intelligent, like-minded university students, and the communes were two large houses in middle-class Cape Town suburbs that some of them shared. Donations were made quite legally by two international student organizations, and their allocation within NUSAS was monitored by the donors.

Rick Turner, the commissioners found, did not live in a commune, but he exerted a great deal of influence on many of those students who did. He was described as "a revolutionary," "a radical," and "an activist."

As he listened to the broadcast, Rick phoned Foszia and told her the news. Shocked though he was, he remained calm and suggested they meet and visit some friends. He was determined not to sit quietly waiting for the police to deliver his banning order, and the couple drove around Durban, dropping in on colleagues such as the banned lawyer Ismael Meer and chewing over the repercussions of the government's actions. By nine o'clock they were at Professor Lawrence Schlemmer's apartment with a small group of close associates. An hour later there was a knock on the door. It was the security police. They asked Turner to step outside so they could read him the banning order. Instead, he stood in the doorway, briefly straddling his two lives, the old and the new, the Special Branch officers on one side, explaining how they were going to ruin his life, and his friends on the other, sitting silent and helpless as the banishment was made formal. In a suitably grave voice the senior Special Branch cop, Colonel Herman Stadler recited Turner's restrictions. He was forbidden to attend "any gathering at which the persons present also have social intercourse with one another; or any gathering at which any form of State or any principle or policy of the government is propagated, defended, attacked or discussed; or any gathering of pupils or students assembled for the purpose of being instructed, trained or addressed by you."

At the end Colonel Stadler told Turner he would have to leave Professor Schlemmer's apartment, since it now constituted an illegal gathering. Rick and Foszia drove home with the Special Branch on their tail. It would be a familiar scenario over the coming years.

A month later Steve Biko and seven other black-consciousness leaders were served the same five-year banning orders. It was, as one student remarked bitterly, a shining example of the prime minister's separate-but-equal policy. Sometime later another round of bannings struck at the white students, led by Halton Cheadle, who were working inside the black union movement from Bolton Hall.

Someone once said that being banned was rather like being on holiday and half-dead, because time was meaningless and people were always offering their condolences. The banned were permitted to speak to only one person at a time. Any more would constitute an illegal gathering. So if a banned person bumped into a group of friends walking along West Street in downtown Durban, the friends would have to line up behind one another in single file and talk to him one at a time. If more than one person visited a banned person and his or her family at home, each guest would have to sit in a separate room.

The bannings were met with a blizzard of contempt both inside the country and from abroad. The English-language press ridiculed the commission's findings as ludicrous and a joke, and an outraged Helen Suzman warned parliament that such harsh executive action would drive some of the finest young people out of the country. "This was not a proper inquiry," she said. "It was much more like an inquisition."

But even as Vorster's government was banishing and jailing its opponents by the hundreds and stalking, tailing, and eavesdropping on thousands of their followers, the tide of history was beginning to turn against apartheid. The townships had been simmering with discontent for some time, and on June 16, 1976, the schoolchildren of Soweto rose up and, armed only with rocks and dustbin lids, fought fully equipped government troops for weeks on end. More than two hundred children died in the uprising, and everybody knew that South Africa would never be the same again.

Everyone, that is, but the government. Applying the same kind of faulty, misguided logic that had fueled the Schlebusch Commission, the government chose to believe its own propaganda and ignore the real reasons for the uprising. Instead of recognizing the school kids' deeply rooted hatred of apartheid and their unequivocal rejection of Afrikaans, the language of their tormentors, as their teaching medium, the government saw only the hand of Communist agitators at work, and they responded with yet another ferocious crackdown.

The main targets were black-consciousness leaders such as Biko, Saths Cooper, and Strini Moodley, who found themselves arrested, detained, interrogated, released, rearrested, detained, and so on. Many were tortured, and all were subjected to terrible abuse at the hands of the Special Branch. I remember Saths Cooper's wife, Vino, telling me how she had been forced to stand on a brick for hours, until she collapsed. She had just been released from solitary confinement and was still shaken up and fragile.

The police had told her that her husband, who was being held in another prison in similar circumstances, had been diagnosed with advanced syphilis. Denied any contact with the outside world, she was left to stew over this terrible news in solitary confinement. I tried to persuade my newspaper, the blessed old *Natal Mercury,* to run my story on Vino's grotesque experiences in detention, but the editors ended up spiking it. The law forbade newspapers from quoting banned people, and nothing could be printed about conditions or treatment in prisons without clearance from the prime minister. So people were getting the shit beaten out of them, and nobody could say anything about it.

To further tighten the stranglehold on apartheid's enemies, Vorster's secret police were also continually extending the tentacles of their surveillance systems, now as elaborate and as expensive as any in the free world. In Durban alone the Bureau of State Security (BOSS), Special Branch, and Department of Military Intelligence were tapping more than two thousand phones, with rooms full of little old ladies transcribing the calls and sending transcripts daily to the head office in Pretoria. They called the objects of their attention "targets," and high-profile people like Rick Turner were subject to the full treatment: phone tapping, twenty-four-hour surveillance, and regular vehicle tails.

The BOSS agent assigned to monitor Rick Turner was Martin Dolincheck. He first appeared on the scene in 1973 and for a while went under the name Martin Donaldson, making himself known to local journalists as a police auxiliary who had been Bobby Kennedy's bodyguard on his 1966 visit to South Africa. Dolincheck drank in the journalists' pubs and started turning up at parties and even on press trips. He was particularly keen to befriend Dick Usher, a local journalist who lived with his girlfriend, Kathy Thompson, also a journalist, in a cottage on the Turners' property. Dolincheck took to phoning Usher at his newspaper, asking how Rick was doing. On one occasion Usher drawled, "Oh, haven't you heard? He's gone to Botswana." Dolincheck choked. Within fifteen minutes there was a police raid at 32 Dalton Avenue, and a bemused Rick Turner watched as half a dozen security policemen swarmed through the place looking for evidence of his disappearance.

Dolincheck was furious at Usher's deception, but he maintained contact with the journalist. Then sometime in December 1977 he received orders to interview Turner. His handler told him there was a feeling that the ban on Turner should be lifted. Dolincheck studied the BOSS files on Turner—he later said he was surprised that there was nothing striking or even mildly interesting in the six volumes the bureau had assembled—and phoned Dick Usher to ask him to arrange a meeting. He suggested they have dinner. Usher passed the message along, and although Turner dismissed the dinner idea "because it would break my banning order," he agreed to see Dolincheck at Dalton Avenue. Dolincheck found Turner to be reasonable and sensible and nothing like the maniacal, incandescent revolutionary he was supposed to be. Turner was also surprised by Dolincheck; he was street smart and shrewd and seemed to have a good understanding of South African politics. For almost three hours the radical and the secret agent sat and talked quietly about their differences, and when Dolincheck left, Turner felt optimistic.

Dolincheck had secretly taped the conversation, and he later sent the transcript to his masters in Pretoria with two observations of his own: that Turner was a highly intelligent man and that far from being a Communist, he appeared to be a middle-of-the-road Euro-socialist.

The Dolincheck visit apart, life was rather routine in those last weeks of 1977. In the days leading up to Christmas, however, a man with a well-bred English accent telephoned several other Turners in the Durban area, asking whether he could speak to Rick. When they said he must have the wrong number, the caller became insistent and agitated. Richard John Turner, an accountant, said the man persistently asked for an interview "even though I had assured him I wasn't Dr. Turner. He asked me if I knew Donald Woods and if I had come from Stellenbosch. Eventually I invited him to come to my flat and see for himself. He said he would, but I never heard from him again."

The caller didn't visit the Turner home on Dalton Avenue. The only foreign visitor the Turners had was a journalist named Ken Pottinger, who had once lived in Durban but had by then settled in Portugal. They were surprised when he arrived, unannounced, but they had known him years ago, and didn't think anything of it.

SIX

——

Death of a Patriot

Rick Turner was hoping for better things in 1978. His banning order was to expire at the end of March, and there were rumors that it would be lifted. The prospect of the government's renewing it was too terrible to contemplate. The isolation of the previous five years had left him depressed, so depressed that he was thinking of fleeing into political exile.

These were heavy days in South Africa. Vorster's Nationalists were engaged in one last grim attempt to force apartheid on a reluctant populace, and any resistance was met with cold malice. Academics and trade union leaders regularly received death threats. Some, like the liberal sociologist Fatima Meer, had had shots fired into their homes. The previous September, Turner's friend Steve Biko had been beaten to death in police custody.

Turner knew very well that he presented apartheid extremists with a plump target. The minister of Justice had identified him as "the most dangerous man in the country," and even in the twilight world of the banned he represented a rallying point for anti-government ideas. He was the Nationalists' worst nightmare—an idealist, a fiercely intellectual academic, and a charismatic leader of the student revolt that was beginning to seriously undermine apartheid. If the government was to stave off the rising demands of the black underclass, it had to neutralize people like Rick Turner.

It was ironic, therefore, that Turner's glimmer of hope that New Year's had appeared in the unlikely form of Martin Dolincheck, the BOSS agent. When Dolincheck came to interview him, Turner took it as a sign that moves were being made to lift the banning order. Their three-hour meeting left him with a clear impression that the government would prefer to free him. Lifting Turner's ban would go some way toward muting the howls of international rage over the murder of Steve Biko.

In those first few days of 1978, Turner tried to put all this aside. His two daughters from his first marriage had arrived from Cape Town for their annual holiday, and he was determined to relax and enjoy their company. Jann was thirteen and fully aware of what her father stood for and why he was banned; Kim was nine, and all she knew was that she seldom saw him and was told not to talk about him at school. Their mother, Barbara, had been Turner's childhood sweetheart, and although the couple had divorced in 1972, they'd remained close friends. She had been in Durban recently and during the visit had taken a long walk on the beach with Rick to talk about the future. She was worried about his state of mind and felt he was losing touch with reality. She told him she thought that he should skip the country. Rick had agreed but said he didn't know how to go about it.

This, too, he wanted to put out of his mind, while the girls were there at least. They were disappointed that they couldn't take their usual trip to the game reserves up the Natal coast. Turner had to apply for special permission to take these trips, and in previous years it had been granted. This year for some reason the local magistrate had said no. The weather had been rather dreadful—hot, clammy, and oppressive, with great torrential thunderstorms that had swept through southern Natal and left parts of Durban flooded—and the girls had spent most of the time at the Dalton Avenue house with Rick and Foszia. Jann had a new guitar that she was learning to play, and she and Kim would read aloud the books they'd taken from the library the day they'd arrived. They'd all been to a wedding of one of Foszia's cousins, but Rick's banning order forbade him to attend social functions, so he had to sit in his parked car and watch. He slipped into the gathering for a few minutes while a friend kept a lookout for the Special Branch, but it wasn't worth the risk, and he returned to his car with a glass of orange juice and sat out the rest of the party in solitude.

The two girls worshiped their father. Jann's childhood fantasies were not of romance or innocent adventure but of confrontation with her father's chief tormentor, Minister of Police Jimmy Kruger. She imagined arguing with him, demanding that he explain how he could punish a good man like her father while all the bad guys were running loose on the outside. "His banning wasn't portrayed to us as something sad or dangerous," she once told me. "It was a part of his life and of our lives that we had to get used to. In very simple terms I understood that he was on the side of the black people who were oppressed and what he was doing was right and that the government was wrong and unreasonable and that banning was just another thing they did to him."

Over the first weekend of the new year, the rain continued to pour down, and on the Monday afternoon Rick, Foszia, and the two girls drove across to the the banks of the Umfolozi River, where massive flooding had taken place and a rescue operation was in progress. They tramped through the long wet grass, past houses whose occupants were bailing out water and assembling their mud-caked furniture to dry in the afternoon sun. Although saddened by what they saw, Turner and his daughters were in a strangely exuberant mood as they wandered barefoot through the thick, sodden grass. They sang Elvis Presley songs. Rick was tone-deaf, but he liked Jann to sing, and he sort of muddled along, wavering from flat to sharp depending on how well he knew the words. They were still singing when they piled into his mustard-colored Fiat and headed home.

It was on the drive home that things changed. The Fiat was chugging toward Bellair and the girls were chatting idly about what they were going to cook for dinner when Turner hit the brakes and stopped the car dead in the middle of the road. As cars swerved around them, Jann screamed, "Daddy, what are you doing?" Her father pointed silently to a poster advertising the afternoon news-paper. It read, WOODS FLEES COUNTRY. Donald Woods was a news-paper editor who, like Turner, had been a close friend of Steve Biko's and who, like Turner, had been banned by the government. As they stared at the billboard in silence, they felt the fog once more descending on their sunny Durban day.

When they arrived home, they found Kathy Thompson, the jour-nalist who lived with Dick Usher on Turner's property, waiting with the full story. Woods, who was under twenty-four-hour Special Branch surveillance, had slipped out of his home the previous Thursday in the trunk of his wife's car. Then, disguised as a priest, he had hitchhiked five hundred miles to the Lesotho border. His wife and five children had crossed into Lesotho separately, and from there they had flown together into exile in London. Just weeks be-fore, a parcel of T-shirts addressed to Woods's children had arrived in the mail. The T-shirts turned out to have been soaked in acid, and Woods realized that his family was no longer safe.

Dinner at Dalton Avenue that evening was a somber affair. Rick seemed anxious and talked glumly about Biko's death and Woods's escape. He was also worried about a trip Foszia was planning to take to Botswana at the end of the week. Initially he had wanted Jann and Kim to travel with her, and had telephoned the girls' mother several times about mailing their passports to him. But now he was glad they were not going, and that night he tried to per-suade Foszia to cancel the trip.

Despite Rick's misgivings, Foszia and her friend Margie Victor set off early that Friday morning for Botswana. Rick spent most of the afternoon pacing around, waiting for Foszia to call to say they'd arrived safely. By dusk he was frantic and phoned Barbara in Cape Town to check whether she had heard anything. Finally the phone rang, and it was Foszia. She said she and Margie had been held at the South African border for almost three hours and had been strip-searched by the police. Then, Foszia said, something strange had occurred. One of the cops had put a call through to Special Branch in Durban and, after a brief conversation, had returned with a dramatically changed attitude. He offered to drive their car across the border and fill it with gas and inquired politely whether they would care to leave excess South African currency in his safekeeping until they returned. He wished them a pleasant holiday in "lovely Botswana." Foszia wondered what the Durban Special Branch had said to transform this cop into a PR flack for the Botswana Tourist Board.

Rick was just relieved to know she was safe and told her not to think about it. But it nagged at him too.

ON SATURDAY, JANUARY 7, RICK AND THE GIRLS WOKE EARLY AND made breakfast together. Jann thought her father seemed tired and distracted. It was a damp, warm, overcast day, and after breakfast they pottered around the garden, pulling weeds from the flower beds and feeding the rabbits, as storm clouds gathered overhead. In the bright, glowing light that precedes such African thunderstorms, Jann noticed how vivid her father's red hair was against the dark blue of his denim jacket and jeans. The casual clothes, the shock of wild hair, and the stocky build—he was about five eight and weighed 175 pounds—gave him the appearance of a slightly mad farmer. Closer inspection revealed a more refined being: the pale skin of a bookish person; a beaked, inquisitive nose; and eyes alight with intelligence behind a pair of preposterously old-fashioned black-framed glasses.

While Rick and Kim continued gardening, Jann took her new guitar across to Kathy Thompson's cottage, and for a while they practiced chords together. They tried to sing "Blowin' in the Wind," but it was so rough that Rick and Kim came running across the lawn, hands held to their ears, complaining about the noise. As the sky darkened and the first plump drops of rain began to fall, Rick shepherded his daughters into the house, and they began preparing supper.

After dinner Kathy said good-night and walked across the lawn to her cottage, leaving the two girls playing cards and Rick working at his desk. Sometime after ten o'clock the girls took baths, and Rick promised to read to them once they were in bed. He was a little worried about Kim—a few nights earlier she had woken up screaming that she could see blood everywhere and that everything was on fire. She was so shaken that he'd taken her into his bed for the rest of the night. But now they were fine, and they both fell asleep while he was reading.

An hour later Jann was tossing and turning, kicking the sheets off and trying to get back to sleep. The storm had still not broken, and the night was so hot and humid she felt she could touch it. Finally she got out of bed, wandered through the house, and found her father lying in the bath reading. She complained about her insomnia, and Rick suggested she try counting the planets. So for a while she lay counting, and as she was dozing off, she heard Rick walking through the house switching the lights off.

It was just after midnight that a loud knocking brought Turner to the front door. "Who's there?" he called. There was no reply. Jann awoke as her father entered her bedroom, drew open the curtain, and peered out the small window onto the front veranda.

Suddenly there was a deafening bang and a flash of light. Jann sat bolt upright in her bed. She thought a bomb had gone off. Her father fell to the floor, screaming, his body convulsing in pain and shock. Then she saw him pick himself up and stumble toward the kitchen, collide with the doorway, and collapse to the floor. He lay facedown, and a pool of blood quickly spread under him.

Jann ran to the kitchen door, flung it open, and shouted out, "Kathy. Come quick. There's been a bomb." When Kathy arrived, she found that Jann had turned Rick's body over, and with his blood-spattered head in her lap, she was trying to revive him with mouth-to-mouth resuscitation. Kim was sitting in a chair looking on, still and silent, her knees pulled up to her chin. All they could hear was a terrible gurgling noise, choking attempts to breathe, growing more and more faint. The little girl kept saying, "Don't worry, Daddy, I'm here," but as Kathy began dialing for help, Jann turned toward her and said, "I don't think he's going to live. He feels cold. I think he's dying." She wiped the blood off his face and noticed how pale his skin was.

The phone was disconnected. Kathy cursed; then a terrible fear began to rise up in her. They'd been cut off. Deliberately. Were the gunmen coming back? For several minutes she banged away at the phone; then suddenly it was connected. She called the police, an ambulance, and Lawrence Schlemmer. As she was talking, she saw Rick's mouth tremble briefly, and his eyes suddenly quivered. Then he was dead.

Within minutes carloads of policemen and ambulance attendants were swarming all over the place. A rude young lieutenant ushered the three trembling females into Rick's bedroom, and when Jann picked up the telephone to call her mother, he ripped it from her hand and disconnected it from the wall socket. Kathy protested, and the lieutenant wagged his forefinger at her. "We don't want any trouble from you," he said. "I'm in charge here."

For more than half an hour, the three sat hugging one another on the bed while the cops and the medics came and went around Rick's body in the next room. Then the head of the Durban Murder and Robbery Squad, Major Dan Mathee, arrived and immediately gave them permission to use the phone. They called to break the news to Barbara in Cape Town. They had no way of contacting Foszia in Botswana, since the house she was staying in did not have a telephone.

Schlemmer picked them up and took them back to his house, where shocked friends were beginning to gather. The girls were given a bath. At two o'clock someone finally managed to get through to some friends in Botswana, and they drove off to bring Foszia to the phone. They woke her from a deep sleep, telling her that there had been trouble at home and that she had to phone the Schlemmer home. She called and was given the terrible news.

THE FOLLOWING DAY RICK'S DOUGHTY SEVENTY-YEAR-OLD mother, Jane, and the girls' mother, Barbara, flew in from Cape

Town. "My blood has turned to acid," Jane said to reporters at the airport. Meantime, still in Botswana, Foszia was too afraid and too shocked to move. Friends were warning her that she would be putting her life in jeopardy if she returned to South Africa. Others assured her she would be perfectly safe. In the end it was a telephone call from her friend Fatima Meer in Durban that made up her mind. Meer said, "Only you can bury Rick. You have to come back." So she drove the 350 miles from Gaborone to Johannesburg, boarded a South African Airways flight under the name Brown, and arrived in Durban that evening. Jann was among those who met Foszia at the airport. Foszia seemed small and shrunken to her, as if her lifeblood had been drained away.

The murder had occurred too late to make the Sunday newspapers, but on the Monday morning there were banner headlines throughout the country. There were also signs that the government's disinformation machine had been working overtime on the Sabbath. Several Afrikaans newspapers claimed they had information that Turner had been working with the police on a terrorism case and that the assassination may well have been the work of the African National Congress. Even *The Times* of London picked up on this line and ran its report under the more declarative headline MURDERED SOUTH AFRICAN "HAD BEEN HELPING THE POLICE."

Not surprisingly, Durban's morning newspaper, the *Natal Mercury,* added its own interesting spin to the story. The front-page report linked Turner's murder to an attack the same night on a turned ANC "terrorist" named Stephen Mtshali. He had been shot an hour before Turner in the black township of KwaMashu, and the implication was clearly that both had been the victims of an ANC hit squad. This was not surprising, since the author of the story was one Leon Mellet, a breezy, easygoing man who was the paper's chief crime reporter and who, it was rumored, had links with the Security Police. (I needed little convincing of this. We had been colleagues on the newspaper, and I'd been told by an impeccable source that Mellet had played some part in my deportation. He subsequently left journalism and joined the police force, where he rose through the ranks and became a lieutenant colonel.)

Rick Turner's widow, Foszia, and his daughters,
Kim and Jann, at his funeral.

The following day the *Natal Mercury* carried another story under Mellet's byline, this one with the headline WE KILLED HIM, CLAIMS CALLER. An anonymous caller "with an African accent" had told the *Mercury* that the African National Congress and the black power movement had been responsible. Predictably the head of the security police, Colonel Herman Stadler, "described the call as very interesting."

Of course nobody outside the government propaganda machine bought any of it. As Turner's network of family, friends, and colleagues began gathering in Durban for the funeral, they talked only of a government-appointed assassin and of how they would have to launch their own investigation if they wanted to find the killer. At St. Anthony's Hall, a crowd of more than a thousand heard Charles Nupen say, "Five months ago Steve Biko died in detention—over forty had died before him in similar conditions. Rick Turner is now dead . . . the circumstances bring to mind the acts of Hitler's Brownshirts and the Brazilian death squads."

Among the most moving tributes was that delivered by the author Alan Paton, who had been writing an introduction to the American edition of Turner's book *The Eye of the Needle*. In a dry, cracked voice Paton described his friend's virtues:

One of the great points that Rick made was that work had ceased to be a meaningful and creative activity [in a capitalist society]. It's something that you do in order to eat and possess and to achieve a status. And there's a basic assumption that human beings fulfill themselves by owning and accumulating and consuming . . . and this means that people use people rather than love them. He went on to say: "In such a society I am not free to be open to the other as a person. I have to manipulate the other in such a way as to obtain things and to manipulate the other I have to manipulate myself. And this is my essential degradation, for if I manipulate myself, I finally lose my freedom." I don't think anyone could say it better than that.

What brought home most forcibly the cold cruelty of the assassination was the sight of the two little girls, Jann and Kim, dressed in white, walking hand in hand toward the stage. They stood side by side at the lectern and read in unison a speech by Martin Luther King, Jr., that ends: "A man dies when he refuses to stand up for that which is right, a man dies when he refuses to take a stand for that which is truth . . . so we are going to stand up right here letting the world know that we are determined to be free." As Kim faltered over the last words, Jann put her arm across her sister's shoulders and gave her a hug. It was enough to make the devil weep.

THERE WAS NEVER DOUBT AMONG TURNER'S FRIENDS THAT HIS murder was the work of a government agent. In the days following, the Durban Murder and Robbery Squad issued stock public statements that it was pursuing this as it would any other criminal investigation, but few believed it. Not one of Turner's neighbors had been interviewed by the police, standard procedure in a murder investigation. Nor had the police inspected the network of pathways that ran from the bougainvillea bush beside Turner's house through to a distant part of Dalton Avenue, although this was clearly the most convenient route for a killer on foot to take. Also, they managed to lose the most vital piece of evidence, the nine-millimeter bullet that Barbara had found in the sheets of Kim's bed on the day after the murder. Martin Dolincheck said that it was a minted slug, a police-issue bullet.

As the weeks dragged by and nothing happened, Turner's friends and colleagues became convinced there was a cover-up. In March they decided to take matters into their own hands and formed an organization they called the Sturgeon Trust. Through the trust's lawyers they hired a private detective, John R. Du Preez, to do the work the police appeared reluctant to do. He was a former BOSS agent who probably exaggerated his credentials and certainly oversold his detective skills. For a while he submitted regular reports to his Sturgeon Trust employers, but they were little more than warmed-over rewrites of press reports and diary entries from daft car journeys he insisted on taking, following one ridiculous lead after another. Then, just as the trust was about to fire this poor man's Clouseau, Du Preez announced that he had discovered the killer's identity but that he could not reveal it. All he would say was that the man was a BOSS agent, a partner of Martin Dolincheck, and that after the murder the man's hair had turned white overnight and his behavior had changed. "I saw him shortly after the shooting, and he acted most peculiarly," said Du Preez. "He kept forming a pistol with his hands clasped together and aiming at the corner of the wall. It was then that he said to me, 'Have you considered that Turner's death could have been an accident?' " Du Preez was also interviewed on several occasions by investigators from the Durban Murder and Robbery Squad, but they concluded that his "evidence" was just speculation and that the Sturgeon Trust was wasting its money.

There was also a spate of confessions by various former BOSS agents who had skipped the country and hoped to raise mortgage down payments by selling their stories to the newspapers. In 1979, one Alex Lambert fetched up in Sweden claiming that a Mr. K, also known as Cougar Kruger, had been selected by BOSS to kill Turner. He was, according to Lambert, a trained killer with a personal grudge. A year later another BOSS man who skipped the country, Arthur McGiven, said BOSS officials feared the killer had been a renegade agent acting independently. And a year after that the journalist-cum-agent Gordon Winter wrote a book entitled *Inside BOSS*, in which he raises the issue of Turner's telephone call to his former wife asking for his daughters' passports. "I know for a fact," wrote Winter, "that this call was bugged by the security police and someone in security wrongly deduced that Dr. Turner intended fleeing South Africa."

All three claims seemed to be as whimsical as Du Preez's detective work. The mysterious Cougar Kruger was never heard of again, and McGiven's theory about a renegade agent was based on nothing more than intelligent speculation. Winter was known around South African journalist circles as a man with a vivid imagination, and nothing he revealed had any originality to it. Everybody knew that Turner's telephone was tapped, and the conclusion that BOSS would assassinate him rather than just pick him up at the border was appropriately far-fetched.

Even the poet Breyten Breytenbach contributed a suspect. Breytenbach was jailed for terrorist activities in the 1970s, and while serving his sentence, he encountered a right-wing extremist named Arnold van der Westhuizen who was in prison for attempting to assassinate Colin Eglin, the leader of the Progressive Party. Van der Westhuizen told Breytenbach that his fellow right-winger David Beelders had said he had shot Turner. The poet immediately reported this to the police.

At first Beelders appeared to be a likely candidate. He had known ties to white extremist groups, and during his nineteen-day trial for the assassination attempt on Colin Eglin a letter he had written to a fellow extremist had been read to the court. In it he said, "What do you think of an elimination squad? Long overdue, I'd say. And it shall move the country. Just watch." The letter was postmarked January 10, 1978, two days after Turner's murder. But Beelders was able to provide a pretty convincing alibi for the weekend of the murder, and van der Westhuizen eventually admitted that he had made up the story to get back at his former friend.

As time passed, it became obvious to Turner's friends that there was little likelihood of the killer's being found. The only person who remained steadfast was Rick's mother, the redoubtable Jane. She kept a meticulous record of information relating to the murder, and every year she flew to Durban to meet with Robbery and Murder detectives to discuss any new leads. Curiously the lead that most intrigued Jane was Du Preez's implausible story about the BOSS agent—Dolincheck's partner—whose hair had turned white and who had gone quite mad.

In February 1982, fate, or rather a botched coup attempt in the Seychelles, played into Jane's hands. The white mercenaries involved in the attack were a motley crew of privateers recruited in South Africa by "Colonel" Mad Mike Hoare. Among those rounded up and thrown into the island's only jail was one Martin Dolincheck.

In February 1982, Jane, now seventy-three years old, flew out to the Seychelles and descended on Dolincheck like an avenging angel. For weeks she badgered authorities to grant her an interview with the jailed BOSS agent, and every day of his trial she sat opposite him in court, staring unflinchingly into his eyes, hour after hour. At the trial's end Dolincheck was found guilty of treason—a capital offense—but after an eloquent display of remorse, he was sentenced to twenty years in prison.

Finally Jane was granted her interview. She spent half an hour grilling Dolincheck. Throughout he insisted that he had not killed her son, nor did he know the identity of the assassin. He told her that the police had taken his nine-millimeter pistol for ballistics tests in the week after Rick's murder and confirmed that his was not the murder weapon.

So after months in the Seychelles, Jane returned to her home in Stellenbosch knowing what she had known all along. Some shadowy hired gun had emerged from the dark recesses of the apartheid edifice and disposed of her son.

By the end of 1982, the murder of Rick Turner had passed into South African history. The minister of Law and Order, Louis le Grange, had told parliament that the investigation was officially closed, and now, apart from reports on the odd flurry of activity from Jane, there was little media interest. There were more pressing issues.

Among the pressing issues was the implementation of proposals put forward by another government commission, this one the polar opposite of the lunatic Schlebusch Commission. The Wiehahn Commission had spent two years examining the issues of trade unions and had presented a six-part report recommending freedom of association, racially mixed trade unions, and the registration of black trade unions. Although the government demurred at racially mixed unions, the rest of the Wiehahn Commission's recommendations became law in the early 1980s, and the workers' power that

Turner and his colleagues had fought for for more than a decade became a reality.

By this time Turner's students from the Durban Moment had moved into positions of significance all over the country: Charles Nupen, Karel Tip, and Paul Pretorius were running Legal Resources, the country's first public-interest law firm, providing legal strategies to trade unions and offering legal services to the poor; Halton Cheadle and Nick Haysom were with the Centre for Legal Studies and involved in human rights issues; and Alec Erwin was general secretary of the Federation of South African Trade Unions and would eventually become deputy minister of Finance in Nelson Mandela's government.

The ideas of the people who had made up the Durban Moment and their commitment to the cause set off a chain reaction that led to the release of Mandela and, eventually, to the liberation of the country. Whether it could have happened without Rick Turner one cannot know. What is certain is that he inspired forces that had a profound impact on South African society.

As 1982 GAVE WAY TO 1983, RICK TURNER'S NAME SLIPPED FROM the headlines, and the newspapers went in search of the next hot story. They did not have to look very far. Just a few miles south of the University of Natal campus, another South African drama was unfolding. This one involved a cast of characters quite unlike Turner's students. Habitués of a darker, more dangerous world, they were the first victims of South Africa's labor liberalization, poor, working-class whites who had been promised jobs for life because of the color of their skin and suddenly found that the people who'd made those promises had changed their minds. Overnight they had become outsiders in their own land.

The homicidal journey of two characters from this white netherworld, Charmaine Phillips and Piet Grundlingh, filled the country's newspapers in the winter of 1983. Although it can be argued that they would have jumped the rails whatever political changes were taking place, it should also be said that people like Charmaine and Piet were the first whites to feel the seismic changes that were beginning to take place in South Africa. In Johannesburg's northern suburbs, political change was still a subject of dinner-party conversation, but on the bottom rungs of white society the barriers were coming down. Apartheid was collapsing all around them. Blacks were taking the jobs of white workers, moving into their buildings, and the whites didn't know what had hit them.

SEVEN

Pulp Fiction: The Uitlanders' Final Fling

The steamy, tropical port of Durban, an unlikely venue for a revolution led by middle-class whites, was a more natural home to a group on the far end of the socioeconomic spectrum—poor whites hovering at the edge of the abyss as apartheid wound down. The suburbs on the hill, with their shopping malls, art galleries, and the university campus, were citadels of affluent, mildly liberal English-speaking white South Africa, but downtown Durban, with its docks and waterfront clubs, was the brash and boisterous refuge of the white underclass.

Smugglers' Inn was Durban's most notorious nightclub. It was located at the far end of Point Road, an ill-lit strip of potholed asphalt that runs parallel to the Indian Ocean from the busy tourist center all the way to the docks. The bouncer was called Basie, and even in the shadows and the half light of the club's interior you could see the bulge of his handgun under his jacket. Many of the patrons also carried weapons, but Basie didn't bother to frisk them. If there was any trouble, he was prepared to go all the way, and everyone knew that.

On a good night Smugglers' was packed with hookers, seamen, roughnecks from the construction sites, drug dealers, and tough *okes,* guys looking for a fight. They would drink themselves into oblivion while they watched a tatty striptease show on a stage the size of a coffee table.

There were two rules at Smugglers': you had to drink, and you had to keep out of everybody else's business. When I was a student at the University of Natal, my friends and I would tiptoe into Smugglers', find a dark corner, and drink ourselves sick while praying that no one killed us. I remember one night when a big *oke* felled a hooker with an immaculate right cross to the chin. She dropped like a sack beside us, and when one of my well-bred friends, a political science undergraduate weighing no more than 130 pounds, tried to help her to her feet, she punched him in the face and screamed, "Fuck off. Leave me alone. Mind your own fucking business." Then she staggered back to the bar with the guy who'd just floored her.

Mondays and Tuesdays were usually quiet nights at Smugglers', and on Tuesday, June 14, 1983, it was so quiet that Basie unstrapped his shoulder holster and put it in the safe. There were four Filipino sailors sitting at a corner table, a couple of hookers standing around talking, and a solitary man sitting at the bar, drinking a double cane and water. His name was Gerald Meyer. A stocky, well-muscled fellow in his late thirties, Meyer was an electrician by trade and until recently had made a good living. But times were tight, and he'd been unemployed for several months. Earlier in the evening he had told his wife he was going for a quick drink with friends. A quick drink had turned into several, and by ten o'clock he was down to his last ten rand.

At around ten-thirty Piet Grundlingh and his girlfriend, Charmaine Phillips, came in and ordered two double brandy and Cokes. Piet was a Jo'burg ducktail, one of those mean guys from Johannesburg who would likely be carrying a chain and a knife and probably a gun too. Jo'burg duckies were the toughest bastards in southern Africa.

Hostile eyes stared out of Piet's thin face, and a scar ran down his right cheek. Then thirty-five, he had been in and out of prison for petty crimes since his teens. When he was on the outside, he worked on construction sites, earning fast bucks in short bursts and then drifting from town to town in a daze of marijuana and booze until the money ran out. He was a tools-in-the-boot boy, that is, he carried the tools of his trade around in his car. Like Gerald Meyer, he had trained as an electrician, but these days he took work as a boilermaker or a fitter and turner, anything that the blacks couldn't do.

Charmaine had been Piet's girlfriend since Christmas 1981. She was a welfare child from Durban who had run away from school at sixteen and then drifted into a subculture of wasted white trash. For two years she turned tricks to earn a living, but when she met Piet, she quit working in the streets and a year later had his child, a son they called Pietertjie (Little Piet). In the dark corners of Smugglers', Charmaine was a strawberry blonde with blue baby-doll eyes that made her seem much younger than her nineteen years. Under the naked bulb over the doorway of Smugglers', however, you could see the rough features, the hardness at the corners of her eyes and mouth.

Piet quickly fell into conversation with Gerald Meyer that night. He said he was heading for Richards Bay in the morning to find work on a new construction site, but for the moment he was looking "to get *lekker goofed*"—nicely plastered. He asked Meyer if he knew where he could buy some *dagga*, marijuana. Meyer laughed and said he had none to sell, although he did have some on him. He was carrying Durban Poison, the best dope there was, and he would gladly smoke some with his new friends. They finished their drinks and agreed that it would be safest to smoke the dope away from the city center.

Piet's blue Datsun Pulsar was parked outside Smugglers', and after Meyer had retrieved a bottle of brandy from his car, he hid the keys under the driver's seat and climbed into the Pulsar. He was surprised to discover that there was a baby lying unattended in the back, but it wasn't his business, and he said nothing.

Piet drove along Point Road and then turned onto the Marine Parade, the main strip along the beachfront, where a mile-long row of skyscraper hotels looms over a clanking amusement park. A thin and fast-disappearing strip of sand separates the hotels from the advancing waters of the Indian Ocean. Beyond the Golden Mile, as it is called, the road widens and then sweeps away from the movement and the lights, up past Fitzsimmons Snake Park toward the mouth of the Umgeni River. Piet accelerated into the dark night and told Meyer he knew of a place out in the cane fields where they could drink brandy and smoke *dagga* in peace.

At Umdloti Beach, some ten miles from the Durban beachfront, Piet turned the Pulsar off the highway and headed away from the sea into the sugarcane fields. Half a mile along a rutted dirt road he found a clearing and pulled the car over. The two men climbed out and for a moment stood still, taking in the silence and the startling canopy of stars. It was a crystal-clear winter's night, and in the sheer darkness of the Natal countryside, away from the city lights, it was as if they could see to the end of the universe.

"Come on, let's make a pipe," said Piet, gathering up an empty Coke bottle that had been kept for the purpose and leading Gerald toward a tree. Charmaine remained on the backseat, feeding her son the last of some milk. She shouted after Piet, telling him to smoke his *dagga* quickly because she needed to get back to Durban to buy more milk and diapers for the baby.

Piet found a small rock and smashed the Coke bottle against it, leaving the jagged neck in his hand. After tapping off the roughest edges with a stone, he stuffed a *girrick,* a ball of silver paper, down the bottle neck as a stopper and began mulling the sticks of *dagga* in the palm of his hand. When he had filled the bottle neck with the crushed weed, he beckoned Gerald over to light it. Even as he was firing up the makeshift pipe, taking the first sharp puffs, Piet started to laugh—hey, it was *lekker* being goofed on good Durban Poison, he thought. Gerry took a couple of hits, and he too began laughing. For a while they passed the brandy bottle between them and talked about the hard times.

Across the clearing Charmaine was sitting in the car, trying to calm Pietertjie, who was now wailing loudly. There was an angry glint in her eyes. The baby needed milk, and these two *okes* were smoking and drinking and laughing, and they didn't give a shit.

Piet and Gerry were still giggling stupidly, like kids, at nothing in particular, when Charmaine appeared at Piet's shoulder. She was pointing a Ceska Zbrojovka 7.65-millimeter revolver at Gerry's head. For a moment both men froze. Then, just as Piet found his voice and shouted, "Charmaine!" she pulled the trigger. The first bullet smashed into Gerry's brain, and as he threw his hands up in a reflex action, Charmaine pulled the trigger again. Gerald Meyer was dead before his body hit the ground.

"Jesus Christ, Charmaine, what have you done now?" yelled Piet. He grabbed her and stumbled toward the Datsun. His stoned brain hadn't quite come to grips with what had just happened, but instinct told him to get the hell out of there immediately. Piet gunned the engine and navigated the Datsun through the cane fields, headlights bouncing up and down along the rutted road like a strobe until they hit the freeway. The North Coast Road is a stretch of smooth asphalt that makes its way along the rugged Zululand coastline for 150 miles, until it reaches the Mozambique border, where it stops. Piet headed north, to Richards Bay, three hours away.

At the turnoff to Umhlali, the pretty little village that provides the surrounding sugar farmers with their supplies, Charmaine told Piet to pull the car over. "That *oke* left his car outside Smugglers'," she reminded him. "We have to move it, or the cops might connect him to us." This made sense to Piet, but he was so full of *dagga* and brandy that he didn't think he could make the drive back. So Charmaine got behind the wheel, and an hour later they pulled up behind Gerald Meyer's Ford Granada outside Smugglers' Inn.

It was by now the early hours of the morning, and Point Road was silent and empty. Piet retrieved Meyer's keys from under the driver's seat and drove the Ford off, with Charmaine following in their car. Meyer had told him he liked to drink at the Normandie Bar at the end of Bell Street, and Piet thought it was a wise move to take the car there and then set it alight. Which is what he did. He gathered up a pile of paper on the driver's seat, lit it, and left the car to burn.

Soon afterward they stumbled into a cheap boardinghouse on Gillespie Street and took a room. Piet fell into a deep sleep.

• • •

THE WORLD OF PIET AND CHARMAINE, A ROUGH-AND-TUMBLE milieu at the fringes of white South Africa, had presented a problem to apartheid's social engineers early on. The problem surfaced after the Boer War, at the turn of the century, when Afrikaner farmers, dispossessed and poor, had become *bywoners,* workers on others' lands, then drifted toward the urban centers, some getting piecemeal work, others living on handouts. In the late 1920s, a Carnegie Commission study found that one fifth of the Afrikaner population could be classified as very poor, or "unfit to find proper means of livelihood." To protect their less fortunate brothers and sisters, Afrikaner policy makers—the Nederduitse Gereformeerde Kerk (Dutch Reformed Church) and the Broederbond (Brotherhood)— began to fashion a social infrastructure that provided a cushion of financial aid to poor whites.

Poor whites, unlike poor blacks, were considered capable of being lifted out of their benighted state. Black poverty was taken for granted, and the question of whether or not it should be treated as seriously as white poverty was answered by the eugenicists. Through the 1920s and 1930s, fledgling apartheidists found support in academic circles. In one study Marthinus Laurentis Fick, a minister and educator who served as secretary for Poor Relief and was later a member of parliament, claimed that intelligence tests he had conducted proved that the average intelligence of a black man was the same as that of a white mental defective. He was supported by I. D. MacCrone, who found blacks "stupid, criminal, childish, with low standards of living." In fact, the "presence of the inferior Bantu" was given as one of the major causes of the poor white condition.

After World War II, eugenics was denounced as bad science, and the poor-white problem was passed on to social scientists. Biological racism was replaced by "cultural racism based on theology." With the accession of the Afrikaners to power in 1948, the divine right of the white man, the Boer in particular, was engraved in the constitution. Legislation such as the Mines and Works Act and the Industrial Conciliation Act threw a protective cordon around the marginal

whites, and soft jobs on the railways and in other businesses provided a comfortable lifestyle that required minimal effort.

Bloated government institutions backed by the policies of
apartheid provided sheltered employment for whites at the bottom
of the economic ladder. A generation of indolent, indifferent white
workers was spawned, many of whom worked for not much more
than an hour a day. The indolence of the South African civil service
was matched only by the inefficient bureaucracy of the Afrikaners'
mortal enemy, the Soviet Communists. By the mid-1970s, however, the government's protective legislation was beginning to take
too big a toll. Job reservation, which had prevented blacks from
taking work as artisans, had created a critical shortage of skilled
labor in a fast-expanding economy, and as an informal "skilled"
(that is, black) workforce emerged to fill the void, whites found
their protected status threatened.

Industry's dependence on black labor made the refusal of blacks'
demands increasingly difficult, and as Rick Turner and the students
up on the hill began organizing blacks into powerful, structured
trade unions, businesses moved away from the policy of protecting
white workers at all costs. In 1979, black trade unions were legal-
ized, and working-class whites on the margins suddenly found
themselves out on a limb. They had been pampered and propped
up for as long as they could remember, and now their support
structures were being dismantled. But nobody had warned them.
In fact, their political leaders were still standing up in parliament
and denying that this was taking place. Just as Ian Smith was
promising his people that there would not be majority rule in
Rhodesia "in a thousand years," so South Africa's Nationalists were
reassuring their constituents that white privilege was here forever.
But the whites on the margins already knew otherwise.

Piet and Charmaine had emerged from quite different back-
grounds—he from working-class, God-fearing Afrikaner stock and
she from a family of wild English-speaking losers—but by the time
their paths crossed, they were both bona fide members of a violent,
self-destructive subculture of outsiders that the eugenicists of the

1920s and the theologians of the '40s had promised to eliminate through their programs of social support.

Piet was born in 1948 in Potchefstroom, one of the white working-class towns that had sprung up around Johannesburg in the '30s and '40s. He was the youngest and favorite of Piet "Bliksem" Grundlingh's three sons. Piet Bliksem was an electrician with the railways, one of the new Nationalist government's most protected industries, and the family lived in modest comfort in a house provided by his employer and maintained by the family's matriarch, the kindly Christina. When the railways decided to transfer Piet Bliksem to Johannesburg, it was Christina who packed the house up and moved the furniture and the boys to Johannesburg's southern suburbs. In a small tin-roofed government-subsidized house, she meticulously reestablished their tidy, God-fearing, law-abiding family life.

But for all the security his family life offered, Piet Bliksem was a troubled man, prone to long periods of introspective gloom and wild outbursts of violent behavior. Every Saturday he would sit alone in his garden, drinking a potent brew of Paarl Perlé wine and homemade *wit blitz,* cursing passersby and threatening to beat up anyone who paused to look at him. He would drink until a combination of high-octane alcohol and righteous anger drove him out into the night, to a bar or a nightclub, where he could find a fight or a place to break up. Every Sunday morning a contrite Piet Bliksem would gather up Christina and the three boys—Piet, Adam, and Tiens—and march them off to church so they could all pray for him. It was traditional Afrikaner behavior, this wild explosion of incandescent fury followed by a somber confrontation with one's Maker.

In 1967, ravaged by the Paarl Perlé and *wit pooitjie,* Piet Bliksem died of a heart attack at the age of fifty-two. Despite the widow Christina's attempts to keep the family on the rails, her three boys began following in their father's footsteps. Piet was nineteen, and although he had qualified as an electrician and could get work, he began hanging out with a bad crowd, petty criminals who taught him how to hot-wire cars and pull checkbook scams. He had a few jobs, but he was soon banging up against the law and was jailed on and off for assault, car theft, and robbery.

Piet was hanging out in Durban when he met Charmaine. It was four days before Christmas 1981, and he'd arrived that morning from Richards Bay, where he had been working as a boilermaker. The plant had closed down for the holidays, and he planned to spend some time with his friends in Durban and then drive up to Johannesburg and spend Christmas Day with his mother. He had spent the previous Christmas in jail, and he wanted to make it up to her this year.

After a long day of jolling with his friends—drinking and smoking *dagga* in a crowded little flat on Gillespie Street—he'd decided to take a walk and get some fresh air. As he stepped out into that midsummer evening, Piet felt good about life. Things were going well at the moment. He'd been earning good money at his new job and had just bought a red Alfa Romeo—and paid cash for it.

Piet's friends had asked him to fetch his guitar, and after he'd wandered around for a while, he took the guitar out of the Alfa and headed toward the flat. As he was about to go in, a little urchin boy of ten or eleven stepped out of the shadows. "Hey, mister, can I play a tune on your guitar?" he said winningly. Standing beside him was a pretty blond girl in her late teens. "Sure," said Piet. "Come on up to the party. What's your name?" "I'm Dean," said the boy. "And this is Charmaine." The girl was his sister.

Piet was the life of the party, playing guitar, telling jokes, dancing, rolling joints, and making pipes of Durban Poison. The beer and the brandy flowed, the air thickened with the sweet, cloying smell of the *dagga,* and Piet noticed that his new friend, Charmaine, was matching him pipe for pipe, drink for drink. By eight-thirty they were the only two left standing. Everyone else lay sprawled unconscious among the empty brandy bottles and full ashtrays. "It's early," said Piet. "Let's crack one more pipe and then go for a drink at the beachfront."

Charmaine was quite taken by this genial Jo'burg ducktail, even though he wasn't particularly good looking and seemed rather thick. His slow drawl of broken English—a kind of monosyllabic

Charmaine Phillips during her trial for murder.

pidgin language known as *skates' taal* (roughneck speech)—accentuated his dimness. But he seemed kind and friendly. And Charmaine was in need of kind and friendly right then. The previous three years had been increasingly grim. After running away from school, she'd fallen in with a bad crowd and had married a Greek sailor named Gabriel Skubridis. Soon after her seventeenth birthday she'd had a son by him; but the Greek disappeared, the child was taken into the welfare system, and Charmaine was back on the streets, turning tricks with men she hated and simmering with self-loathing.

Lately things had been getting out of hand. She'd been drinking, getting into fights, ricocheting around. She had been out of jail only a week and was lucky to be out at all. During one of her drinking binges at the Belgica Hotel, she'd persuaded a man named Coenraad Els to take her for a ride on his motorbike. As they were speeding along Smith Street, Charmaine pulled out a penknife, held it to Els's throat, and demanded all his money. The police had picked her up pretty quickly, and she'd been given a two-year suspended sentence for armed robbery.

Charmaine's slide from the fringes of white society into the badlands was, in many ways, similar to Piet's. Her parents had seven children, four sons and three daughters, and for a time they maintained a decent family home. But in 1969, her father was diagnosed as having bone cancer. He couldn't work, and her mother began to drink, take drugs, and have wild, public affairs with other men. She showed no interest in the children. In 1972, when Charmaine was eight, the Durban Child Welfare Department moved in and farmed the children out to foster homes and orphanages. Their parents were committed to a psychiatric hospital. The children took this badly: Charmaine's older sister, Bernadette, was also admitted to the hospital for treatment; the two older boys, Wayne and Mark, were arrested for armed robbery—Wayne ended up in Durban Central Prison and Mark in a reform school in the Cape; the twins, Dean and Johanna, were kept in protective care.

Charmaine pretty much stayed on the rails until she was thirteen. She attended classes at Durban Girls' High School, a good school whose top pupils regularly ascended to the University of Natal up on the hill. Then one day she was called out of class by a social worker, who told her in a matter-of-fact manner that her mother's body had been found stuffed in the closet of a Russell Street flat. She had been beaten to death by a drunken boyfriend. Charmaine fainted.

As Charmaine sat drinking with Piet on the Durban beachfront the night they met, she thought she had finally found a man who would treat her well and who really seemed to like her. For his part Piet was very pleased with himself, having snagged this pretty young girl. He was even more pleased when he asked her whether she wanted to come to Johannesburg with him that night and she said yes. At that moment Piet and Charmaine both thought exactly the same thing: they thought their luck had changed.

For the next twelve months Piet and Charmaine moved around the country together, living in a succession of mobile homes, borrowed houses, and motel rooms. They traveled from Sishen in the Northern Cape to Richards Bay in Natal to Secunda in the Transvaal—the booming, belching industrial centerpieces of the South African economy. Piet was a good mechanic and electrician. He would work for six weeks at a time, putting in long hours of overtime, and then they would take off, hit the road for a few months until the money ran out.

Charmaine appeared quite content with this peripatetic lifestyle. She liked it that her man provided for her, and she even played at being a homemaker, bravely attempting to make their dismal trailer-park dwellings habitable. But every now and then the ugliness of their surroundings and depressing monotony of their lives would overcome her, and she would revert to the rages and violent outbursts that had been commonplace before she met Piet. One night in a bar in Richards Bay, two affable drunks made a pass at her, and she demanded that Piet fuck them up. He slouched across to the men and warned them to lay off his goose. They apologized, but that was not enough for Charmaine. She ordered Piet to beat the men up. Eventually, with a sigh of resignation, he crossed the bar and, in a chilling display of controlled violence, battered them both to the floor. As he was finishing, the plant foreman pulled Piet away from his victims and ordered him to stop fighting. In a flash Charmaine had leaped onto the foreman's back and, with her hands clasped firmly around his throat, began screaming that she would kill him. When everyone was pulled apart and the dust settled, the foreman ordered Piet and Charmaine off the site. "We don't mind you, Piet," he said. "But we can't deal with Charmaine."

Her rages were tempered briefly by the birth of their son, on Christmas Eve 1982, a year after they had met. But by the time they returned to the road in early 1983, with Pietertjie bundled up on the backseat, Charmaine was once again plunged into long bouts of brooding anger, punctuated by increasingly frequent explosions of rage. Piet couldn't talk to her when she was in these states. Once he had tried, but she stabbed him in the shoulder with a kitchen knife, and he decided then and there never to get in her way.

Sometime in March they arrived in Vryheid looking for Charmaine's brother Robert. It turned out that he was away on holiday, and they spent the night at a boardinghouse, where they met Danie Johannes Strydom, another hard drinker who worked the construction sites. The following morning they offered him a lift to Johannesburg, and as they were setting off, Piet noticed that among Danie's papers was a gun license. "So you carry a gat," said Piet. "Let's see it." Danie obligingly pulled out his weapon, a Czech-made 7.65-millimeter Ceska Zbrojovka revolver, but Charmaine began freaking out about having a loaded gun so near her baby and ordered Danie to put the revolver in the glove compartment.

As was Piet and Charmaine's custom, there were several stop and dops along the route, roadside pauses for a quick puff of *dagga* and a couple of hits of brandy. Danie battled to keep up with the couple's intake of drugs and booze, but by the time they reached the outskirts of Johannesburg, he had become so ill he vomited onto the baby's blanket. Charmaine smoldered about this, and when they pulled into a Kentucky Fried Chicken place, she whispered to Piet that they should dump their passenger. They woke Danie and asked him to buy some food. As he disappeared into the restaurant, Piet gunned the engine and wheeled out of the parking lot.

Piet Grundlingh in the courtroom.

Charmaine opened the glove compartment, reached in, and ran her hand over the Ceska Zbrojovka. "Now we've got a gun," she said quietly.

PIET WOKE UP ON WEDNESDAY, JUNE 15, 1983, WITH A HEAVY HEAD. He'd been so disoriented from the *dagga* and brandy the previous night that he was sure he'd hallucinated the whole thing. Gerald Meyer, the clearing at Umdloti, Charmaine's pulling the trigger—it was surely a bad dream. Even when Charmaine told him it wasn't a dream, that it had all happened, he still wasn't so sure. She said she would take him to the spots—to Bell Street to see Meyer's Ford Granada, then to the Umdloti cane fields to see his body. "OK. And then we head for Richards Bay," said Piet.

Charmaine was right. There on Bell Street was the car, the interior blackened from the fire but far from destroyed. And there, in the clearing in the cane fields, lay Gerald Meyer's body, now beginning to swell in the sun.

It wasn't long after Piet pulled the Datsun onto the North Coast Road and struck out for Richards Bay that four Indian fishermen stumbled across Meyer's body and raised the alarm. But by the time the police arrived, Piet and Charmaine were one hundred miles away, in a motel in Mtunzini, and Piet told her not to worry. "The cops can never stick it on us."

The senior policeman at the site was Captain Ivor Human, a smart up-and-coming officer who thought he recognized the dead man. Scattered around the body was the debris of the previous night's party—cigarette ends, an empty brandy bottle, the Coke bottle neck full of *dagga*. With the help of sniffer dogs, he found two cartridges in the long kikuyu grass and, after fingerprinting the victim, returned to Durban to find out who he was. He put the prints on a plane to Pretoria and sat waiting through the day and into the night for the results. At midnight the call came through, confirming it was Gerald Meyer. Human had arrested him ten years before for smoking *dagga*, a minor offense. The records showed Meyer had had no further brushes with the law.

Human managed to track down the dead man's relatives, and sometime after two in the morning he arrived at a block of flats on the Esplanade to break the news to Meyer's widow.

SATURDAY WAS WET AND OVERCAST. PIET, CHARMAINE, AND Pietertjie had spent a comfortable night at the home of a friend, Rosemary Usher. In the morning Piet had driven out to the coal terminal and successfully interviewed for a welding job. On his way home he picked up a soaking hitchhiker, a young man in his mid-twenties named Vernon Swart. Swart persuaded Piet to make a detour to a shopping center in exchange for some beers, and the two men fell into easy conversation. He told Piet that he had a job with the Oceanographic Research Institute and that he was saving money so that he could return to the Cape and start his own fishing business. Piet liked young Swart and invited him back to Rosemary Usher's for a few drinks. "What else can you do on a rainy day but drink and smoke *dagga*?" Piet said.

As they sat around the Usher house getting wasted once more, Charmaine became bored and fidgety. She told Piet she wanted to visit her recently divorced sister in Vryheid and suggested that Vernon come along. It was midafternoon, and Piet figured they could be in Vryheid by dusk. They bade a fast farewell to their hosts, piled into the Datsun, and headed off into the afternoon sun as it finally broke through the rain clouds. Rosemary Usher was relieved to see the back of them. She had quite liked Charmaine and had been touched by her concern and care for the baby, but Piet had been something else. She thought he was trouble.

Piet drove the Datsun inland through northern Natal's principal town, Empangeni, through Nkwalani, near the site of the original Bulawayo, the royal kraal of the great Zulu king Shaka, and deep into the land of Shaka's descendants. It was here more than a century earlier that the Zulus and the British and the Boers had fought epic battles for the right to rule over these rolling hills and fertile valleys. Here Shaka had created the mightiest army in Africa; his successor, Dingane, had lured the Boer leader Piet Retief and seventy-nine of the Afrikaners' finest young men to their deaths, thus instilling in these two peoples a lasting antipathy. It is a sacred part of South Africa, and one can easily imagine what it was like when the first white man arrived.

Piet and Charmaine had no interest in the history of the countryside they were speeding through. All they knew about the kaffirs was that they didn't like them and they couldn't trust them. When a friend had warned him not to drive too fast in this part of the country because if he knocked a black man over he would be in big trouble, he just laughed, pulled the CZ revolver from his waistband, and said, "This is what I'll use if any kaffir comes near me."

At Melmoth, Piet pulled into a garage for gas and some food. Charmaine suggested that since they were paying for the gas, Vernon should buy the food and some milk for the baby. But when he emerged from the café carrying a plate of grits and vegetables, Charmaine complained bitterly about the rubbish food and their passenger's cheapness. Piet told her to shut up and offered to pull off the road outside Melmoth so that she could smoke a joint, "a *dagga skyf* to make you feel better." They stopped under a tree some thirty yards off the road and for a few minutes passed around the joint in silence. "Come, Vernon, let's catch a leak here," said Piet, and the two men walked a couple of paces from the car and began urinating.

As they finished, they turned around and found themselves facing a trembling, white-faced Charmaine. She had the CZ revolver raised and pointed at Vernon's head. "Rob the *oke*," she shouted at Piet, throwing a coil of rope at him. "Tie the *oke* to this tree and rob him." He recognized the edge in her voice, the clipped insistence in her words, and knew it was pointless to resist her.

"Don't worry, my *maat*," he said to Vernon. "Just put your hands behind the tree. We'll take your wallet and go." When he'd finished binding Vernon's hands, he pulled the wallet from his pant pocket, turned, and walked toward the car. As he passed Charmaine, who was still pointing the CZ at Vernon's head, Piet saw a look of cold malice in her eyes. "Charmaine, don't shoot this *oke*," he said. "We've got the wallet. Now let's go." He got behind the steering wheel and heard Charmaine laugh. There was a single shot, and she stopped laughing. "Jesus Christ," said Piet.

He decided there was no point in going on to Vryheid and turned the car around. As the sun was setting, they headed back to Richards Bay. "Now we've got serious problems," Piet said. "What did you kill the *oke* for?"

Charmaine said she hated Vernon because of his cheapness and that it had enraged her that he'd urinated in front of her. "Don't worry, Piet, they won't know it was us," she said. Besides, they'd taken enough out of Vernon's wallet to keep them going.

After a few days drifting around Richards Bay, they decided to head for Durban. They arrived there on the day of Gerald Meyer's funeral. The morning paper—the *Natal Mercury*—carried a small story on the murder under the headline MYSTERY OVER KILLING OF KIND-HEARTED MAN.

In Durban they bumped into their old friends Tjaart and Maria van Heerdon, who were finishing up a vacation and invited them to come and stay at their home in Secunda. Tjaart said he was sure Piet would find work there, at the SASOL refinery.

At dawn on Saturday, June 25, Piet and Charmaine left Durban for the Transvaal, arriving at the town of Ermelo at around eleven. Piet said he felt like a couple of beers, and while Charmaine looked after Pietertjie in the backseat of the car, he went into the Marino Hotel in search of a cold Castle lager.

Two men were playing snooker in the hotel bar, and as Piet sipped at his beer, he struck up a conversation and issued a challenge to the winner, who turned out to be Barend Greyvenstein, a miner from Witbank who was visiting his parents in Ermelo for a few days. He bought Piet a beer and then beat him at snooker. They talked about the usual things: graft (work), drink, and rugby, and when Piet said he was driving to Johannesburg later that day, Greyvenstein asked for a lift. "That's fine," said Piet. "Only we're stopping at my *maat*'s place in Secunda for a *braai* [barbeque] and some dops on the way. So come."

When they reached Tjaart and Maria van Heerden's, the *braai* was already in full swing. Some people were standing around in the garden, drinking beers and brandies over the cooking meat, and others were inside watching the day's major rugby match, between Transvaal and the Orange Free State, on television. Someone passed around a white pipe, a nerve-deadening mix of Durban Poison and crushed Mandrax tablets, that had them staggering around helplessly, and as the rugby match began heating up, the men started laying bets. Barend was a Free State man, and he wanted to put one hundred rand on his team. "You haven't got that kind of money," said Piet. Barend pulled his Help-U cash card from his wallet and said he could draw four hundred rand from his account immediately. "So put your money where your mouth is," said Piet and took the bet.

As it happened, the match ended in a draw. Greyvenstein, however, was in an expansive mood and offered to buy everyone a drink at the Holiday Inn before they left for Johannesburg. All but leveled by an afternoon of drinking and taking drugs, the ragged band barely managed to stagger along to the Holiday Inn, but by the time they got there, they had lost their enthusiasm for Greyvenstein's drink. The van Heerdens said farewell and returned home, and Piet, Charmaine, and Greyvenstein set off for Johannesburg in the Datsun.

This time Charmaine had to drive, since Piet was slumped comatose on the backseat, next to the sleeping Pietertjie. Greyvenstein, voluble and wide awake, sat in the passenger seat chatting away and occasionally dropping his hand onto Charmaine's thigh and telling her what a nice girl, *lekker* chick, she was. She kept her hands on the wheel and stared ahead at the road, gritting her teeth as the emboldened Greyvenstein began running his hands over her body. She hissed "fuck off" at him and then shouted for Piet to "stop this *oke* trying to grip me." But Piet did not stir.

Charmaine turned the Datsun off the R29 onto the Kinross Dam road and a little more than a mile along turned again, now onto a bare patch of bushveld. Before Greyvenstein knew what was happening, she had pulled the CZ from the glove compartment and was ordering him out of the car. "This is a robbery," she said. She made him hand over his wallet and give her the numbers for his bank card. Greyvenstein did as he was told, repeating the four numbers slowly in the hope of placating the glowering woman in front of him. Charmaine told him to sit down in the dirt, and he refused, still not quite comprehending how serious she was. She shouted again, "Sit down on the ground, Greyvenstein." He hesitated, and as he looked down, she pulled the trigger, shooting him in the face at point-blank range.

After emptying Greyvenstein's pockets, Charmaine made sure she'd driven the Datsun some way from the scene before she shook Piet awake. She told him she had robbed the *oke* and dropped him off down a side road. Piet knew the truth; he could see it in her face and hear it in her voice. But he didn't say anything. There was no longer any point. They were now so far down this road that all they could do was keep moving. He decided to lie low that night and found an empty house that was located no more than a mile from where Greyvenstein's body lay. The following morning, as they drove past, the spot was swarming with people.

On Tuesday, June 28, the television program *Police File* reported the murder of Barend Greyvenstein and showed a photograph of the dead man, asking viewers to phone in if they had any information on him. Tjaart van Heerden was watching *Police File* that night and was startled to see the face of the man he'd been entertaining only days before. He called the police immediately.

CAPTAIN IVOR HUMAN WAS ALSO WATCHING *POLICE FILE*, IN HIS Durban North home. He liked the program and had found it helpful in the past. He was in need of help—his investigations into the Gerald Meyer murder were going nowhere. There was no motive, no witnesses, nobody who had seen him in the hours before his death. He wasn't robbed, and it seemed certain he was with people he knew. But that was as far as Ivor Human had gone.

Like Tjaart van Heerdon, he watched the photograph of Barend Greyvenstein as it flashed on the screen, but to Human the picture meant nothing. Then he heard something that got his attention—

Greyvenstein had been shot at close quarters with a 7.65-millimeter bullet. Just like Gerald Meyer. Captain Human went straight for the phone.

His hunch was confirmed when Tjaart van Heerdon remembered that he and his wife had bumped into Piet and Charmaine in Durban in mid-June—around the time Gerald Meyer was murdered. He also remembered that Piet had been waving a gun around, bragging how he would take out anyone who got in his way.

The following morning the police issued a warning on national radio to all motorists. They should be on the lookout for a blue Datsun Pulsar driven by a dark-haired man accompanied by a young blond woman. The couple was believed to be armed and dangerous and should not be approached.

Piet and Charmaine were by this time slipping in and out of Bloemfontein, checking into boardinghouses under the name Gerber and keeping off the streets during daylight. They knew that Tjaart had talked to the police and that the net was closing in, so they decided to dump the blue Pulsar and maybe head for Namibia. First they needed money. On Thursday evening they drove into Bloemfontein and stopped at an ATM machine on Maitland Street, hoping that their last victim's cash card would work. Charmaine, though she had a photographic memory, must have misremembered Greyvenstein's PIN, and they couldn't get into his bank account. Beside them a young black man named Martin Mofosi was also having trouble withdrawing money. It was his own account, but he didn't know how to work the cash machine. Piet and Charmaine descended on the hapless man like vultures.

OVER THE NEXT FEW DAYS THE POLICE UPPED THE TEMPO OF THEIR manhunt, circulating descriptions of the couple and their vehicle. In the meantime the fugitives had dumped the Pulsar and were heading toward Johannesburg in a hot-wired Ford Granada. So caught up was everybody in their various whirls of activity that it was not surprising a small story in the weekend newspaper passed unnoticed. It was nothing more than a couple of paragraphs reporting the discovery of an unidentified young black man's body at a motorists' rest stop outside Bloemfontein. This was the sort of thing that seldom rated many column inches in the white press. What was unusual was that the man had been shot in the face with a 7.65-millimeter revolver.

Piet decided he had to get rid of the gun, and soon after arriving in Johannesburg, he took Charmaine to visit his *sangoma* on Jeppe Street. *Sangomas* are witch doctors, possessed healers and casters of spells. Piet and his *sangoma* went back a long way. The *sangoma* was not only a provider of powerful *muti,* medicine, but also a black marketeer who was willing to move anything. He gave Piet two hundred rand cash for the 7.65-millimeter CZ. He also gave him a vial of *muti* that he said Piet should dab on his face to ward off bullets. It will make you invincible, the *sangoma* said.

Over the following days Ivor Human and his detectives made several crucial breakthroughs. The blue Pulsar had been seen at a Durban orphanage around June 14, and the visitor's register confirmed that Charmaine Phillips had visited her brother Dean on that date; when police found the Pulsar abandoned on a Bloemfontein backstreet, they dusted it down and came up with Charmaine and Piet's prints everywhere. Then Vernon Swart's decomposing body was found tied to a tree on the wattle plantation near Melmoth, and ballistics tests showed that he'd been shot with a 7.65-millimeter bullet. South Africa had a pair of serial killers on the loose, and the country began to fixate on Piet and Charmaine.

A rumor spread that Charmaine was a young Durban beauty who had abandoned her marriage to a wealthy industrialist for love of an outlaw. There were stories that the couple had murdered their victims while they were having sex, Charmaine pulling the trigger at the moment of orgasm. It was *lekker* and lurid, a distraction from the gravitas of the political issues of the day. They were dubbed South Africa's Bonnie and Clyde, but the press quickly turned the story from outlaw bio-pic to soap opera as Piet's mother made a heartrending appeal through the newspapers for her son to surrender.

At nine-thirty on the morning of July 14, there was a knock at the door of Adam Grundlingh's Johannesburg flat. Adam's wife, Isabella, answered. There stood Charmaine, thin and pale and holding a bundle that contained her infant son. Without a word Charmaine thrust Pietertjie into Isabella's arms, kicked her high heel shoes off, and sprinted away down the corridor. There were two notes attached to the baby: one had instructions to pick up his clothes from a locker at the Johannesburg Railway Station, and the other said that Charmaine and Piet were headed for Swaziland. Within minutes the police were swarming around the flat.

Now free of the responsibility of the baby, Piet told Charmaine they needed a motorbike. It would be less easily identified than a car, and the crash helmets would hide their faces, which were plastered across every newspaper. He found a 1,000-cc Kawasaki advertised in *The Star,* and that evening he and Charmaine arrived at the owner's home in Ferndale to inspect the machine. The owner and his friends were playing cards and drinking, and when Piet asked to take the bike for a test ride, leaving their car as collateral, the man cheerfully agreed. The couple disappeared into the night.

The fugitives rode southwest for an hour and pulled into Louw's Caravan Park in De Deur. With their last few rand they rented a room and huddled together on the bed. Piet said they should head for Namibia. The cops would be looking for them at the Swaziland border, and maybe they could make it. He also said that if they were caught, he would take the rap. "You're young, Charmaine, you've got your whole life ahead of you," he said. "Someone's got to look after Pietertjie when all this is over." Charmaine reluctantly agreed, and they rehearsed the confessions they would make.

The clear winter mornings on the high veld can be bitterly cold; the sun rises glowing red against a deep-blue sky, promising warmth but providing none. Chill winds blow across the flatlands, penetrating blasts of Arctic air that find their way into your bones and make your body ache. That morning Piet and Charmaine pulled out of the caravan park dressed only in cotton shirts and jeans. They rode ten miles to Vereeniging. Frozen and hungry— they had barely eaten in days—they pulled up to a Salvation Army hostel and asked Lieutenant Freddie Essenhigh for food and clothing. Meanwhile, in Ferndale, the owner of the motorbike had woken up with a hangover and a vague memory of a couple riding off on his Kawasaki and not coming back. When he saw the unfamiliar Ford Granada standing in his driveway, his memory returned, and he phoned the police.

At the Salvation Army hostel, Lieutenant Essenhigh found some clothes for Piet, and as they were leaving the storeroom, he noticed the young woman sitting on the motorbike. He recognized her immediately. Piet asked for some money, and the lieutenant, trying to conceal his fear, said he had none but he could give them some tinned food. Piet accepted and shook the lieutenant's hand. When Piet looked into the man's eyes, he knew that he and Charmaine had been recognized. No matter.

Just as Piet was kick-starting the Kawasaki, two police cars careered into view and screamed to a halt feet from the bike. Sergeant Nico Oosthuizen leaped out of one with his revolver drawn. The couple raised their hands, and Oosthuizen switched the bike's engine off and pocketed the keys. "I am de Jager," Piet said. Charmaine didn't say a word.

As word of their arrest got out, a gaggle of journalists soon descended on the home of Piet's long-suffering mother. She was telling the reporters how relieved she was that Piet and Charmaine had surrendered peacefully, and then the phone rang. One of the reporters answered.

"Could I speak to Mrs. Grundlingh, please?" said a voice.

"Who is it?"

"It's her son."

Christina took the phone and smiled. "It's my boy," she said.

PIET CONFESSED TO THE MURDERS—THE THREE THE POLICE KNEW about as well as a fourth—that of Martin Mofosi, the black man they'd met at the cash machine in Bloemfontein. Charmaine corroborated his confession, telling detectives that he had beaten her regularly and had threatened to kill her if she tried to escape or tell anyone. Although it appeared pretty straightforward, Captain Human and his colleague, Captain Johann Pretorius, needed more evidence from the murder scenes and the murder weapon if they were to make their case watertight in court. They decided to retrace the couple's murderous journey, and Piet and Charmaine agreed cheerfully to be their guides.

For four days a small convoy of detectives and their charges wove their way from Umdloti to Melmoth to Kinross and finally to Bloemfontein, camping out under the stars, sitting around *braais,* and talking about rugby and cars and the way the country was going. Although Charmaine remained brooding and withdrawn, Piet was his gregarious self. He and Ivor Human, particularly, talked as if they were old friends, and Charmaine began to suspect that they were conspiring against her. Piet called Human "Cappie" and said he was grateful that the policeman treated him with courtesy and respect.

As the journey progressed, Captain Human began to question the veracity of Piet's confession. Charmaine seemed able to describe events in far more vivid detail than Piet. At Kinross in particular, where Greyvenstein had been shot, the detectives found Piet's woolly explanations impossible to reconcile with actual events; Human wondered whether Piet had been there at all. Nor did he believe Piet's story about the gun. He told Human he had thrown it into the sea, but they had been miles from the coast when they committed the last murder with it.

Human's suspicions were all but confirmed by a deadly little exchange at a campsite outside the Orange Free State town of Bethlehem. The convoy had stopped for a midday *braai,* and while the meat was cooking, Piet and Human stood beside the picnic table talking. Suddenly, out of the corner of his eye, Piet noticed a blur of movement as Charmaine lunged for one of the kitchen knives lying on the table, raised it above her head, and steadied herself to plunge it into Human's back. "Watch it, Cappie," Piet shouted as he knocked Human to the ground and Charmaine's blade arced through empty space. As Piet and the other detectives overpowered her and took the knife away, Human looked up at Charmaine and saw the intense stare, the burning malevolence that Piet had seen when she'd come out of the darkness and shot Gerald Meyer.

Having finished the investigations at the murder sites, Captain Human was driving Piet and Charmaine back to their prison cells when a message came over the car radio. It was one of Human's ballistics experts telling him that they had identified the 7.65-millimeter weapon they were looking for—it was a Ceska Zbrojovka revolver. Human looked across to his passenger and said, "Now will you tell me where it is?"

Piet grinned and said, "OK, Cappie. On one condition. That we go visit my ma first."

Tears rolled down Christina's cheeks as she held her son. He told her not to worry, that things would work out. While they sat talking, Captain Human made a call to his office. "We've connected the CZ revolver to all four crime scenes," he said. "So if we get the firearm, we convict them."

Piet's *sangoma* was not happy to see them. He didn't like being this close to a white policeman. They sat around in the dark Jeppe Street room for a while, talking about nothing, engaging in enigmatic exchanges that ended with everyone nodding their heads and saying, "Hauw, hauw." When Human finally asked him about the gun, the *sangoma* said he did not know what he was talking about. There was no gun. Piet was making this up. Then Piet tried to persuade him, telling the *sangoma* it was the right thing to do, and Human promised he would not be prosecuted for illegal possession of the weapon. Muttering to himself and shaking his head, the *sangoma* went off, poked around in the dark, and returned with the weapon.

In July, Piet and Charmaine were formally charged with four counts of murder in the first degree and a month later, after an appearance in Durban Magistrate's Court, were ordered to undergo psychiatric examinations. Their trial was set to start on October 17.

Ivor Human's work was all but done. There was, however, one further twist. On September 27, Piet and Charmaine sent Captain Human a message requesting an urgent meeting. They said they wanted to come clean.

At three o'clock that afternoon at the police station in Lyden-berg, the three sat down at a bare wooden table.

In his slow, flat, *skates' taal* Piet began by telling Human that they had given false confessions. "Now I want to set the record straight," he said. Then he turned to Charmaine and said, "If there is any-thing you don't agree with, I want you to stop me." She nodded.

PIETERMARITZBURG IS A LITTLE COLONIAL CITY FORTY MILES IN-land from Durban and three thousand feet up from sea level. It is called Sleepy Hollow by the more sophisticated citizens of Durban, but it is the provincial capital and is decorated with exquisite Victo-rian brick-and-wrought-iron buildings and blessed with a far more pleasant climate than that of Durban. Although it started out as a Boer town in the mid-eighteenth century—it was named after two Boer heroes, Piet Retief and Gerrit Maritz—a succession of treks, internecine wars, and immigration drives have left it an enclave of British colonial society. If anywhere is the Last Outpost of the British Empire, then it is Pietermaritzburg.

It was here, at the Natal Supreme Court, on October 17, 1983, that the trial of Piet Grundlingh and Charmaine Phillips opened to a packed house. Lines had formed before dawn, and when the court-house's doors opened at nine o'clock, there was a scramble for the two hundred seats in the public gallery. Families and friends of the defendants sat shoulder to shoulder with journalists, the victims' relatives, and the blue-rinse ladies from Maritzburg who would not miss a day of the trial.

In her opening statement Charmaine said, "I shot four men, but I plead not guilty to murder and guilty of culpable homicide." Piet denied shooting the men and said he had not conspired with Miss Phillips to kill or rob them.

When Charmaine took the witness stand, the prosecution pro-duced the sworn statement she had made on her arrest in June. She had said then that Piet had done the shooting and that he had threatened to kill her if she told anyone. She'd said there were "many times when I wanted to run away, but I was scared because I knew he would kill me."

That confession was a hoax, she told the court and went on with enthusiasm to describe how she had committed the crimes: "I started laughing at him [Vernon Swart], pointed the gun at him and shot him. I can't tell you how many shots I fired."

In the days that followed, Charmaine put on a wild and explosive performance on the witness stand. She began by screaming at the prosecuting counsel that he was "fucking stupid" and inviting him to stick his theories "up your arse." On day two she threw a shoe at some newspaper photographers and directed a torrent of four-letter invectives at the judge before breaking down and sobbing as she described how Barend Greyvenstein had made her feel like a whore. On day three she refused to testify any further and wrote a note to the court saying she was stoned on *dagga* the police had been giving her. On day five she said that Captain Human had been supplying her with *dagga,* and she invited the judge down to her cell to see for himself. When a government psychiatrist described her as a psychopath whose only hope lay in becoming a nicer psychopath, she laughed hard and loud. But it was Charmaine's descriptions of her life on the fringes of white society that provided truly poignant moments amid the gore and the madness and brought on a wave of sympathy from the public.

A wealthy Durban couple, prominent in horse-racing circles, was reported to be providing Charmaine with the dresses she wore in court. On the final day of her testimony, she received a bouquet of pink and white flowers from an anonymous sympathizer. There was also a noticeably warm relationship between the fugitives and their jailers. Every morning in the holding cells while they were waiting for the day's proceedings to begin, a woman police officer would brush Charmaine's hair and adjust her makeup. Whenever officers had finished giving their damning testimonies to the court, they would smile and wave at Piet and Charmaine, often stopping by and asking whether they wanted any messages passed on to their families.

But if Charmaine was enjoying her moment in the public spotlight, Piet became more and more withdrawn as the trial proceeded. His mother sat in the front row day after day, her sad, crumpled face a continual reminder of the pain he had inflicted on her.

The court adjourned for the Christmas recess, and Charmaine was allowed a half hour with her son, Pietertjie, before he was handed over to the Child Welfare Department. When the court reconvened, on February 17, 1984, it was to hear the judge's verdict. He found Piet and Charmaine guilty of four counts of murder and said that Piet "probably shot three of the victims." Charmaine fidgeted, laughed, and scribbled notes during the reading of the verdict. Piet sat silent, staring down at his feet.

A week later Piet was sentenced to be hanged, and Charmaine was given four life sentences.

The prisoners were taken to holding cells, where they would wait for Charmaine to be transferred to Kroonstad Prison and Piet to Pretoria Central. That evening Piet had a surprise visitor. It was Captain Ivor Human, come to transfer him personally. As they climbed into Human's car, the captain turned to the prisoner and asked him whether he'd like to join the Human family for dinner. "So we'll be an hour late at Pretoria Central. They won't miss us." Piet had his last moment of freedom at the dinner table of his captor's family.

SEVEN PRISONERS WERE TO BE HANGED AT PRETORIA CENTRAL Prison on July 30, 1985. There were six black men—four Zulus, a Xhosa, and a Shangaan—and one white man—Pieter Grundlingh. Each was allowed visits from three people on the day before the executions. Piet asked to see his mother, his brother Adam, and Captain Ivor Human.

Human arrived at Pretoria Central at five in the morning on the twenty-ninth and was escorted to a small office just off death row. As he waited, he could hear the dirgelike songs the prisoners sing for the ones who are going to hang that day. When the singing stopped, there was a terrible silence. Then Piet burst into the office grinning wildly, pumping Human's hand, and moving from side to side like a boxer going through his moves. "Howzit, Cappie?" he said. "Howz your wife and daughters? Tell me about them." Usu-

ally a warder is required to be with the prisoner, but on this occasion the men were left alone. Piet asked Human whether he minded
him smoking.

Piet said he had found God and was ready to meet his Maker. He
handed Human a gift, a newspaper photograph taken during the
trial that showed the captain, Charmaine, and Piet smiling at the
camera. It was in a matchstick frame that Piet had painstakingly
constructed during his final hours on death row. Piet thanked him
for everything he had done.

"For what I have done?" gasped Human. "I've put you in the
gallows."

Piet shook his head and smiled: "You treated me like a human
being."

Piet handed Human a scrap of paper and said this was his final
confession, that he was finally admitting that he did all the killings.
"Why are you doing this?" asked Human.

"Because I want Charmaine released and for her to look after my
son," he replied.

Human heard himself saying, "Go well, Piet."

"I'm better off than you, Cappie," Piet said. "I'm prepared, and
I've fixed up my business with God. You may walk out of here and
get run over, and you won't have fixed up your business. Then
what?"

They shook hands, and Piet ambled off down the corridor with
his arms hanging loose and low, his head set slightly forward, like
that of a vulture, and his gait a model pimp roll from way back. He
paused at the door and called out, "Cheers, Cappie."

Then he was gone.

Charmaine remains in Kroonstad Prison, and it is unlikely that
she will ever get out.

EIGHT

Another Place, Another Time

In March 1990, I returned to my old hometown, Bulawayo, for the first time in almost twenty years. On the flight up from Johannesburg, a family friend I bumped into told me that nothing had changed while I had been away. It was, she said, as if the clocks had been stopped in the early '60s and the rest of the world had forgotten about Bulawayo and left it behind. Haddon and Sly, the genteel department store that supplied my parents with Daks jackets and rough-cut Oxford marmalade; Ramjis, the hip shop that brought in the first Beatles boots and tab-collar shirts and clothed a generation of young whites in neo–Carnaby Street fashion; the Eskimo Hut, purveyors of the finest ice-cream cones this side of the equator—it was, she said, all still there, just as I had left it.

This seemed too fanciful to be true. I had spent the previous six weeks in South Africa watching the impossible happen, slack-jawed in amazement as an Afrikaner president announced the release of Nelson Mandela, the lifting of the ban on the ANC and the South African Communist Party, the end of apartheid. South Africa had changed—was changing—so profoundly that I barely recognized it as the place I had left behind when I sailed off to exile in Europe. More to the point, it had changed so profoundly that I no longer felt connected to it. Although I had shared in the euphoria of those first days of emancipation, it had seemed like *their* party. I had become a foreign guest, and welcome though I was, I found myself lurking self-consciously on the fringes of a society that had once been my own.

Thus it was with some trepidation that I flew into Bulawayo on that perfect, clear summer afternoon. As I prepared to confront my past, the South African Airways 727 banked sharply over the Motopos Hills, and I swear I saw the monument to the Shangani Patrol glint defiantly in the sunlight.

Our final approach to Bulawayo Airport took us over the neat, orderly city center and the impossibly green suburbs surrounding it, then across the brown, drought-stricken Matabeleland bushveld and down onto the single strip of tarmac. As I descended the stairway, I could sense, almost touch, the African landscape of my childhood. Out there, beyond the tiny whitewashed two-story terminal and the row of msasa trees running alongside the main road to town, was the vast brown-green bushveld that had been our back garden in the colonial heyday. Untroubled, uncomplicated . . . unknowing—I cannot imagine a more perfect childhood or a more perfect setting. Then I caught my first smell of the bushveld, an intoxicating aroma of dust and wildflowers and cow dung carried on the warm afternoon breeze, and for a brief moment it was as I had always hoped it would be.

Of course it could never be the same. Too much had happened in between. When I left, rather ignominiously crouched on the backseat of my mother's Austin Cambridge back in 1972, my fellow white Rhodesians were still living out the colonial dream in relative peace and tranquillity. The guerrilla war, such as it was, seemed to be well under control, a complete mismatch between a Rhodesian Army that liked to regard itself as the best counterinsurgency force in the world and a cobbled-together band of farmworkers and garden boys armed with antiquated Soviet weapons they didn't know how to operate.

The Rhodesian forces were indeed impressive, the second largest army in sub-Saharan Africa, after that of South Africa: almost five thousand regulars in the army and air force, ten thousand territorials, eight thousand members of the British South Africa Police, and thirty-five thousand police reservists. The air force even had reasonably modern jets—Canberras, Hawker Hunters, and Vampires. By contrast, the black insurgents, trained in Russia and China and in camps in neighboring African countries like Tanzania and Zambia, were ill-equipped and disorganized, and their incursions across the Zambezi River from Zambia were infrequent and invariably doomed. (Between 1966 and 1968, for example, the Rhodesian forces lost only 13 men while killing 150 guerrillas and capturing almost 300.)

To most Rhodesians it was a small and distant war that they read about in the newspapers, and so it remained until 1972. Then things changed. A new front was opened on the country's eastern border by Robert Mugabe's Zimbabwe African National Liberation Army (ZANLA), the military arm of ZANU. They poured into the Rhodesian countryside with a new battle plan. They conducted a hearts-and-minds campaign among the rural communities, building up support networks throughout the country, and instead of taking on the Rhodesian security forces, as they had to their cost in the past, they began operating hit-and-run attacks on soft targets, like white farmsteads. At the end of 1973, the country's farmers were living behind electric security fences, their windows covered in steel gauze to stop grenades and their grounds patrolled by armed guards.

By the mid-1970s, it was no longer a small and distant war. Despite the positive gloss put on things by the government's propagandists and the tight control imposed by the censors, the white Rhodesians were becoming aware that they were getting into something serious. Firefights with guerrilla gangs were more frequent, friends were being killed in action, whole families of farmers were being wiped out. Although it was still winning the war, the much-vaunted counterinsurgency force was fast losing its aura of invincibility, and by 1976 its kill ratio had fallen from ten to one to six to one.

As the war intensified, terrible atrocities were committed by both sides. White civilians, black villagers, missionaries and the little children in their care, school kids, schoolteachers, were shot, beaten, and bayoneted to death by one army or the other. It seemed that our side was committing atrocities in the name of Western civilization and theirs in the name of black liberation, and between them they were leaving a trail of misery through the entire country. The effect on white Rhodesia was profound. Even as I strode across the tarmac toward the terminal that afternoon in 1990, after that first exotic whiff of the African bushveld, I knew I had arrived at another place, another time. My friends had been to war.

NINE

We're All Matabeles Now

Despite the flower gardens and the serene homes in leafy suburbs and the languid movements of people operating on African time, Bulawayo is in truth rather loutish. As gracious and decorous as it may first appear, it is a down-to-earth, rawboned, fighting town. In the heyday of the whites, Salisbury was the cultural and political center, but Bulawayo was the muscle and blood of colonial Rhodesia. The whites were good rugby players and hard men in the Rhodesian bush war, and the blacks were Matabeles, warriors from the same gene pool as the Zulus. You can still feel the edge—feel the hairs on the back of your neck stand up when some mean-looking bastard at the other end of the bar checks you out. Probably the same guy who was doing it to you thirty years ago, only now he's more bitter and more dangerous.

I felt I knew this place. Even though I had relinquished full-time membership, I was still an insider, still Boynton from Bulawayo. I could understand the nuances, knew the slang, recognized the abrasive exterior as a front that concealed kindness and goodwill toward most men. However much some of them disliked me for skipping the country, they seemed to accept me back into the fold with good grace. That first weekend on my return visit in March 1990, I discovered what had happened to the whites I had grown

White citizens of Zimbabwe, watching a soccer match on TV.

up with and what surely would have happened to me had I been a true Rhodesian and not fled. Most worrying was that I found myself falling right into it.

It all began around midday on Saturday at the Old Miltonians Club, an eighty-year-old sports and social club that had once been a bastion of white athletic endeavor but now fielded multiracial teams. The bar, however, the nerve center of the club, remained white by vocation. The vocation was drinking and bullshitting. Leathery old Rhodesians were perched along the bar on high stools, a row of them, like vultures at a water hole, moaning about everything from the string of failures suffered lately by the ladies' bowls team to the dismal state of the Zimbabwean economy. They'd been sitting on the same barstools since before Ian Smith had taken over the country, since before television. And they were as bad tempered and argumentative now as they had been then.

That Saturday a group of white men, the sons and nephews of the leathery old vultures, wandered in one by one, out of the bright sunlight and into the cool interior of the Old Miltonians' bar. They wore colorful, loose-fitting clothes that provided a rather garish contrast to the khaki or mottled-green safari suits of their elders. These were big fellows, with burgeoning paunches and bulging thighs and forearms. After a few breezy exchanges with the old chaps—"Howzit, Lofty, I didn't know you were still alive. How do you do it? You must be a hundred"—they settled at a table at the far end of the bar—Barry, Stretch, Dave, Bloat, and Fivey—and ordered a round of Castle lagers. Soon the beer was flowing, and they were playing roll dice for the privilege of buying the next round of drinks. Outside, the cricket team was making short work of weak opponents while a group of long-distance runners was limbering up for an afternoon outing.

"Hell, these zots are slow," said Fivey. "Come on, Gabriel, bring us six more Castles. Don't get me wrong, I like the zots, but they're very slow."

"Dave, roll the dice. Let's get another round in."

The old men at the bar were nice and mellow by now, having been here since opening time, and were settling into familiar territory, conversations they'd engaged in for decades: "Look, I don't mind doing business with Afs, but I don't want to live with them. If they leave me alone, I'll leave them alone. You know what I mean?"

They all nodded, and then another picked up the theme: "Hell, man, when we got here, they hadn't even invented the wheel. The ordinary Afs aren't interested in all this stuff. All this comrade business. Isn't that right, Gabriel?"

"What's that, baas Lofty?" said Gabriel. "You want another drink?"

"No, man. This comrade stuff. You're not interested, are you?"

"No, baas," said the bartender vaguely.

"Most of them admit they were better off under Old Smithy. Ask Gabriel. Gabriel, is that right?"

"Yes, baas Lofty," said Gabriel without listening to the question. "So where's that drink?"

Meanwhile, over in the corner, Fivey was telling his friends about events the previous evening. He'd been to the movies with a neighbor, and when they returned home, the neighbor found his house had been broken into. They phoned the police and were told that if they wanted an officer to investigate the crime, they would have to come down to the station and pick one up—there was a shortage of cars. So they drove off to pick up a policeman. When they arrived, the officer in charge apologized and said there were no policemen at the station, could they come back the following morning? "Why didn't you tell us that when we phoned," exploded Fivey.

"Because you did not ask me," replied the officer.

When he finished the story, Fivey turned to me and explained: "You see, when the blacks took over the country, we were narrow-minded, and we thought they'd fuck it up. Now we are much more broad-minded, and we know they're fucking it up."

They all laughed.

"It's your round, Bloat."

They were in their late thirties and early forties, mostly quite successful traders, skilled artisans, and entrepreneurs, all with families and homes in the better suburbs. They had fought in the bush war against the "terrs"—the terrorists—but when Smith's government had finally conceded to black majority rule in 1980, these white Rhodies had accepted defeat with a degree of relief. They'd been worn down by the war, and they'd lost too many good friends to relish its dragging on any longer. Some eighty thousand Rhodesians remained after their country became the independent nation of Zimbabwe, and encouraged by Robert Mugabe's calls for reconciliation, they decided to make a go of it. This meant that they would continue to live an easygoing, blessed existence, replete with phalanxes of servants, undemanding office hours, and as much leisure time to sit around drinking and partying as they saw appropriate.

As the shadows began to lengthen, the conversation turned to the evening's entertainment. There was to be a party at Barry's. Bring your own bottle.

"So let's have another two for the road," said Stretch, and Gabriel shuffled off to fetch a tray of Castle lagers.

THE EVENING'S FESTIVITIES CONSISTED OF LOUD MUSIC, DANCing, and drinking. It was like Saturday night 1964—the same warm, liquid evening, the same clear, star-lit skies. Even the music—the Hollies, old Rolling Stones, Beatles, Swingin' Blue Jeans—was the same. Old Peugeot 304s and Morris Minors and those mid-'60s Ford Anglias with passenger cabs the shape of parallelograms pulled into the driveway and disgorged whole families of partygoers. It was perfectly clear that these middle-class Rhodesians who had grown up in the heyday of the white empire were carrying on as if the empire had never ended. The war had been an unpleasant interruption, but they were now back to their old ways.

The women chatted and drank large gin and tonics and chainsmoked Madison Lights while the men gathered in bunches swigging Castle lager or whiskey on the rocks. Bloat and Fivey hammed it up to "Twist and Shout," turned up brutally and distortingly loud, and their wives tried to hold conversations over the din. At the bar some of the men began telling war stories. A few had served with the Selous Scouts, the elite commando brigade said to have been responsible for three quarters of the enemy deaths in the bush war. Barry had always voted against the Smith government, but when he was called up for the army, he decided to volunteer for the Scouts because they were the best soldiers and the best chance he had of coming through the war alive. As it happened, he got badly shot up in an ambush toward the end of the war and was lucky to survive. He still carries an ugly scar on his right leg.

The Selous Scouts were named after Frederick Courteney Selous, the hunter and adventurer on whom Rider Haggard based his character Allan Quatermain, and although conceived as a specialist tracker unit, it soon metamorphosed into the deadly commando batallion of popular mythology. The commandos were trained to survive in the bush without water or rations, to eat maggot-infested meat they found by the wayside, and snakes and baboons' brains. To quench their thirst, they would slit open an antelope's stomach and drink the fluid from the half-digested grasses inside.

For a while it had been a Boys' Own adventure with live ammunition, but toward the end of the war, the boys around the bar conceded, the wheels had come off. Foreign mercenaries and all-purpose opportunists had been recruited by the Scouts, and when it became evident that the country would, after all, be handed over to the blacks, some turned to profiteering. They moved into national wildlife parks, especially Gonarezhou, on the country's southeastern border with Mozambique, declared them frozen zones—off limits to people—and cut down elephants and rhino with automatic weapons. They poached ivory, and horn was moved across the border into South Africa and fed into the smuggling routes that took it eventually to the Far East. This was the first time I had heard about the frozen zones and the ivory poachers, but when I pressed the boys around the bar for more details, they retreated rapidly. They knew very well which of their former comrades-in-arms had been involved, but they were dangerous characters who would take out their best friends if necessary. Besides, all that was long past—another time, another place.

So they changed the subject. To their other war, the so-called Dissident War. For a short time, the laughter subsided around the bar, and the din of the dancers and the music in the next room seemed to recede into the background. The Dissident War, which had flared up only months after independence in 1980, had been fought in Matabeleland, at the mission stations, on the farms, and in the black townships, and had seriously shaken the whites' hopes for a peaceful life under black rule and a secure future for their children. It had been another of those senseless African civil wars, ignited by tribal rivalries and then exploited by all manner of opportunists, and had threatened to bring Matabeleland and its people down.

It began just as the world was turning its attention away from Zimbabwe, just as the armies of diplomats, negotiators, peacekeepers, and journalists were packing up and moving on, content that they had witnessed history being made and justice being done. It had its roots in ancient rivalries between the majority Shona people, who now dominated the new Zimbabwe government, and the Matabeles, who secured only 15 percent of the votes in the election. They had fought the Rhodesian bush war as two separate armies—the Matabele ZIPRA guerrillas under Joshua Nkomo's command out of Zambia and the Shona ZANLA forces under Robert Mugabe out of Mozambique—and during the elections they were assembled and housed at camps throughout the country, pending their integration into the new national army. Skirmishes broke out in some of the camps first, then pitched battles with heavily armed platoons going at each other, and by the year's end hundreds of armed ZIPRA guerrillas had returned to the bush and declared they were at war with the Shona government.

The government's response was immediate and unequivocal. The Matabele leader Joshua Nkomo was sacked from his Cabinet post after a cache of arms and explosives was found on a farm owned by his party; under the Law and Order Maintenance legislation inherited from Smith's government, Mugabe rounded up leading Matabele politicians and subjected them to detention, interrogation, and torture; army task forces, most notoriously the North Korean–trained Fifth Brigade, were deployed to Matabeleland to sort out the ZIPRA problem.

As had been the case in the bush war, the victims were the peasant villagers and the white farmers living in the outlying areas. Attacks were frequent, random, and invariably brutal, the black villagers slaughtered because they supposedly supported the wrong political party and the white farmers ambushed because their deaths brought international publicity. By the middle of 1983, it was no longer clear who was killing whom and for what reason. The army had adopted the "pseudo-operations" tactics perfected by the Selous Scouts in the bush war and were roaming Matabeleland disguised as dissidents. They were responsible for many of the atrocities the government claimed were the work of ZIPRA rebels.

According to survivors, pseudo-gangs would descend on a village, demanding food, clothing, and money in the name of ZIPRA, then return the following day in conventional uniforms to persecute the villagers for helping dissidents. So nobody was sure who had been responsible for the massacre at Beitbridge or the unspeakable cruelty of Mafunga Ndebele's execution at his kraal outside Kwekwe. At the Beitbridge cattle farm twelve armed men had arrived and herded some thirty-five men, women, and children into a single thatched hut. After berating them for being "sellouts"— deadly shorthand for "supporters of the opposition party," the identity of which depended entirely on who was asking the question—the bandits set the hut on fire, then gunned the people down as they tried to flee the flames. Among the dead were nine children, including two two-year-olds. At Masolo Village outside Kwekwe, four men armed with AK-47s demanded to see Mafunga Ndebele, and when he arrived with his wife and eldest son, they shot him dead. Then at gunpoint his wife was ordered to chop off his head, hands, and legs, and his son instructed to take the body parts to the local police station. Soon after, Mrs. Ndebele committed suicide.

The Zimbabwe government cited the Ndebele atrocity as another example of dissident barbarism and the reason it was having to pursue this unpleasant campaign, although witnesses identified the four men who killed Mafunga Ndebele as government soldiers. Only when the Catholic Commission for Justice and Peace announced to the press that it had evidence of almost five hundred civilian deaths at the hands of the Fifth Brigade did Mugabe take some action, withdrawing the brigade and promising a government inquiry. If the inquiry ever took place, its findings were never made public, and what followed was a concerted campaign of intimidation and repression of Matabele leaders and the continued harassment of the rural population.

Through the middle 1980s, Matabeleland was a very dangerous place to be. The dissident gangs were joined by common criminals and a hard core of disillusioned guerrillas. They were called Super ZAPU and were armed and abetted by agents from South Africa, where the apartheid government saw that it was to its advantage to destabilize the new black governments of the subcontinent. The army's pseudo-gangs were also running amok, answerable to no one. The white farmers had never seen anything like it, not even at the peak of the bush war. Over a period of three years, more than forty farmers and their families were killed in attacks, and by 1984 half a million acres of commercial farmland in Matabeleland had been abandoned as their owners fled to the safety of Bulawayo. Those who remained were always heavily armed, always connected to their neighbors by Argric-Alert, always watching, listening, anticipating.

"Then it just stopped," Bloat was saying from across the bar. "Over a single weekend. On the Friday we were going out to the rural areas with G-3s on the dashboard and sidearms at the ready, and by Monday the weapons were in the gun cupboard." What had happened was that in December 1987 the two arch rivals, Robert Mugabe and Joshua Nkomo, had signed a Unity Accord, and Nkomo became Zimbabwe's vice president. Just like that.

"But it's not over," I heard the Bulawayans around the bar saying. "Zimbabwe is nothing to do with black and white anymore. It's the ruling Shona against us, the Matabele. They're getting rich, and we're getting screwed." They said the white Shonas, their former Rhodesian comrades-in-arms, were just as bad as the black government officials. Shifty Shonas, they called them and started laughing. "That's the difference between the Matabeles and the

Shifties," said Bloat as he crossed the room to turn up the music, "We don't talk bullshit."

BY MIDNIGHT, THE WEIGHTY ISSUES LONG BEHIND US, BLOAT and a few others were twitching sporadically to the now deafening and distorted music, their gyrations clear evidence that there was no longer conscious connection between the rhythms of the music and their body movements. The songs were being changed every thirty seconds; one minute it was Led Zeppelin, the next Neil Diamond or Ella Fitzgerald. Bloat's body lost interest around the time they put Nat King Cole on, and his gimlet eyes flicked around the room looking for alternative amusement. He slumped down at the dinner table and threw a bread roll at the man sitting opposite him, one Andrew Hastings MacGregor, a giant former prop forward and Bloat's longtime business partner. It struck him on the temple.

"If you do that again, I'll flatten you," Andrew snarled.

Direct incitement for an encore. Bloat's second roll struck Andrew's glasses and broke the frame. Within seconds the two were face-to-face—pointing, grunting, pawing at the ground. As they went for each other's throats, the party stopped dead in its tracks, and the other men piled on the two adversaries, attempting to prize them apart. Two very strong men these, Bloat and Andrew lurched and ricocheted from the dining room through the bar into the living room. Furniture clattered, glasses were smashed, and women screamed above the unholy din of the hi-fi—and still the two bulls and their clinging friends banged from wall to wall.

Finally there was a moment of calm, as if the entire scrum of heaving men had paused for breath at the same time, and the two bulls were separated. As Bloat and Andrew stood trembling, eyeball to eyeball, nostril to nostril, the group decided that one of them would have to leave the party. So Bloat gathered up his wife and his two sleeping children and walked off into the night. Then the others put the Rolling Stones on the turntable and danced and drank the night away.

It was a scene straight out of the Bulawayo handbook, a reprise of the belligerence that carried these frontier communities through the hard times. It had been like that when the pioneers were hacking a town out of the dry, dusty bushveld and, decades later, when the whites were fighting a no-win war against the rest of the world. For those growing up here, there were only three things that really counted: one was to play rugby, the second was to get overwhelmingly pissed on Saturday nights, and the third was to get into fights regularly and fearlessly.

I had managed a passable game of rugby, and getting pissed was easy. But I really hated fighting. My stomach would knot up; I'd freeze, get smacked around, then offer a few token counterpunches before being humiliatingly overwhelmed. There always seemed to be hard men after me, engaged in vendettas turned manhunts that were conceived on the flimsiest of pretexts—you went to the wrong school, you dressed a bit fancy, they just didn't like your face. I once heard that a real puncher named Billy had been looking to knock me about for six months, but every time he'd seen me in public, I had been with a girlfriend, and it simply wasn't on to smear your victim against the pavement in full view of a woman. It was quite common, this Victorian sense of decorum mixed with pointless violence, and I knew full well that to avoid a battering, I had to remain in female company. Which I did.

In spite of my own congenital cowardice, I had always been proud of Bulawayo's hard-boiled reputation and disappointed that it hadn't rubbed off on me. Years later, as I watched the Rhodesian bush war unfold from the safety of a historic Hampstead building, I noticed that this rawboned physical exuberance had come to serve white Rhodesians well. They were transformed from good fist-fighters into formidable soldiers, outstanding marksmen, and fearless bush warriors. I tried to picture myself in the heat of battle and concluded once more that I was a pale imitation of a true Rhodesian and certainly far too craven to call myself a Matabele.

BLOAT, BARRY, AND THE REST OF THE BULAWAYO PARTYGOERS woke up on Sunday morning with heavy hangovers. The wives were soon working the phones, comparing hangover cures, gossiping about who'd dragged whose spouse behind the hydrangeas for a bit of this and that and what they thought about Annette's whipping her bra off and twirling it above her head in the middle of "Satisfaction" and how Terri was so pissed she had passed out with her head down the toilet. They were also worried about what their foreign visitors, a barrister and his wife out from England, would make of the fight. Shirley said, "They asked me whether this was a regular occurrence. I said it had only happened once before. Then I remembered Bill and Larry two weeks ago and Bloat and Fivey a week before that and Ham and Dave. And I realized it's happening all the time."

They decided that the only way to sort it all out was to reassemble at Barry's around lunchtime and talk about it over a relaxing drink or two. By the time they started rolling back up the drive in their parallelogram Anglias and their half-timbered Morris station wagons, the television had been switched on and was broadcasting live coverage of the presidential rally in Harare. Pretty soon the postmortem prattle subsided, giving way to groans of despair over the events unfolding in the capital. It was a big day for Zimbabwe—March 4, 1990—the day that Nelson Mandela made his first official visit. He arrived early in the morning to a rapturous welcome and was due to speak at the rally in his honor at midday. When he finally turned up, at four-thirty, the well-oiled group gathered around the television was gleeful. This was typical of black politicians, they said; they leave their own people sitting around in the sun all day, and turn up four hours late.

Before Mandela was allowed to speak, the crowd at the National Sports Stadium and the nation at large were treated to a long address by President Mugabe. He used his forty minutes to berate the old enemy, Ian Smith, whose Conservative Alliance of Zimbabwe (CAZ) Party was opposing him in the forthcoming elections, and the recently acquired enemy, Edgar Tekere, a former ZANU leader, whose Zimbabwe Unity Movement (ZUM) was doing likewise. Before lavishing praise on Comrade Mandela ("If you thought ten and a half years' imprisonment was a long time, this man has been in jail for twenty-seven years"), he told the audience that his was the only party for patriotic Zimbabweans to vote for.

How things had changed. How Mugabe had changed. When I interviewed him in 1980, on the eve of his election victory, he had spoken eloquently of reconciliation and rebuilding, of accommodating former enemies, black and white, in a democratic political process. I was a young reporter, and Mugabe seemed to be on the verge of becoming a major African statesman, the first of a new breed who would eschew the venal ways of their predecessors and work for the good of their people. How things had changed.

Mandela's own speech—it was his first public appearance since being elected vice president of the ANC—was as conciliatory and gracious as Mugabe's was self-serving and hectoring. He even said that white South Africans could have their own schools in the new South Africa if they felt the need. He spoke with the quiet, dignified assurance of a great leader and appeared decidedly calm beside the sweating, twitching Mugabe.

But a Zezuru does not like to upstaged by a Xhosa, and at the end of Mandela's address Mugabe stood up again and, to everyone's surprise, announced that the following day would be a public holiday in honor of Comrade Mandela. The small crowd cheered rather listlessly, and when the news filtered out over radio and television that night, the people who were running the country's industries (largely the same whites who were the enemy a decade ago) went apoplectic. Factory furnaces had been fired up, cattle were being driven to slaughterhouses, production lines were running—it was going to be chaos.

Their worst fears were realized. The following morning a large section of the workforce set off for work, some because they had not heard the president's pronouncement and others because they could not afford a day without wages. Most had to walk—the nationalized bus company had closed down for this holiday—and when they arrived at their factories, they were told to turn around and walk back home. There were frantic phone calls to schools, restaurants, and department stores. Should they open? Should they send people home? Finally an agreement was reached: everything would indeed be closed on Mandela Day. Businessmen estimated that the country would lose four million Zimbabwe dollars.

But not every government department was inactive. In the early hours of that Monday morning, under cover of dawn's half-light, workers from the Roads and Works Department of Matabeleland were out changing Bulawayo's street names. Suddenly, silently, without forewarning, names that had survived two world wars, the Unilateral Declaration of Independence, the Rhodesian bush war, and ten years of independence just disappeared. Grey Street became Robert Mugabe Way; Borrow Street became Samuel Parirenyatwa Street; Rhodes became George Silundika—and so on.

This time it was not only the business community that was appalled. (The cost in postage mix-ups, new stationery, telephone directories, and the like would be enormous.) Members of the predominantly Matabele Bulawayo City Council were very unhappy. They had been informed of the intended move the previous Wednesday and had tried to block it, complaining that all the heroes the streets were to be named after were Shonas. They took their objections and the names of several Matabele war heroes to the Zimbabwe Central Committee but were told the whole business had been agreed on by parliament months before and they were to do as they were told.

This was the kind of high-handed behavior the citizens of Bulawayo, black and white, had come to expect from Mugabe's government. They were, after all, Shifty Shonas.

IF YOU WERE TO ASK A MATABELE, PARTICULARLY A WHITE MATA-bele, for examples of shiftiness among the ruling elite, you would be deluged with stories of corruption on such a grand scale that the famous looters of post-colonial Africa, like Mobuto in Zaire and Bokassa in the Central African Republic would appear as petty pilferers by comparison. Some said the president's late wife, Sally, was so wealthy she had made a bid for London's Dorchester Hotel. Others said that Mugabe himself had so much money stashed in Swiss banks that he was the sixth richest man in the world, coincidentally the exact ranking accorded Daniel arap Moi by Kenyans, Julius Nyerere by Tanzanians, and even the aescetic Kenneth Kaunda by Zambians. (Why they were all sixth I could never understand.) What was true, however, was that through the 1980s, Zimbabwe had become steeped in a culture of small-time corruption that found its way into every nook and cranny of business life. Import and export licenses, manufacturing contracts, land allocations, foreign currency allowances—you simply couldn't trade unless you knew whom to bribe.

The scandal cited most frequently as the defining example of this culture of corruption is an affair that came to be known as Willowgate. Unlike its American near-namesake, it did not lead to the downfall of a head of state; rather, it displayed the extraordinary contortions African politicians are prepared to go through to protect the status quo, and their instinctive distaste for the notion of a free press.

It began rather innocently in 1988, when a Bulawayo businessman and member of parliament, Obert Mpofu, unexpectedly received a check for four thousand Zimbabwe dollars from the Willowvale Company. (In the late 1980s, a Zimbabwe dollar was worth about twenty-five U.S. cents.) Willowvale was an automobile-assembly plant owned by the government and the major provider of the country's vehicles, from family sedans to trucks. Zimbabwe's chronic shortage of foreign exchange during the 1980s had placed serious strictures on the number of vehicles assembled, and the plant was now turning out only fifteen hundred vehicles a year, compared with seventy-five hundred in 1982. The country's requirements were for between twenty thousand and twenty-five thousand new vehicles a year, so there was a four-year waiting list for Toyotas, Mazdas, and Datsuns that were put together by Willowvale. Traditionally Willowvale sold its vehicles to car dealers, and they passed them on to the public at regulated prices. The only exception was a so-called strategic pool of vehicles reserved for MPs, civil servants, and essential services.

Obert Mpofu's windfall check turned out to be a case of mistaken identity—it was meant for one Alvord Mpofu, an employee of Manilal Naran, a well-known Indian businessman, as a refund for a vehicle purchased in Naran's name from Willowvale. When Obert Mpofu told the story to Geoff Nyarota, the editor of *The Chronicle,* Nyarota smelled a rat. The only way the other Mpofu or his employer could have bought a vehicle directly from Willowvale was through an approved government minister. Nyarota told his deputy, Davison Maruziva, that it looked like a case of small-time ministerial patronage, and he put an investigative reporter on the case.

With the help of some insiders at the Willowvale plant, *The Chronicle* team put together a list of cars that had been provided to ministers and through the serial numbers traced them to their present owners. The Mazda pickup truck that Alvord Mpofu had bought for his employer, Manilal Naran, had been ordered by Zimbabwe's minister of Industry and Technology, Senator Callistus Ndlovu. Naran had paid Willowvale Z$24,382, which was Z$5,000 below the dealer's price, and within three months had sold the truck to Rio Tinto, the mining company, for Z$65,000.

Nyarota and Maruziva kept following the registration numbers. They found another Mazda pickup that Naran had bought on Senator Ndlovu's instructions for the same price and this time had sold to Mac's Main Street Garage in Bulawayo for Z$75,000. Then two Toyota Cressidas were bought and sold through the same system, with equally large profit margins. They discovered that the ubiquitous Mr. Naran was doing the same deal with another big fish, the minister of Defence, Enos Nkala. And as they were coming to terms with the scale of Nyarota's case of "small-time ministerial patronage," they found another network, one that revolved around Maurice Nyagumbo, former minister of State and one of the founding fathers of black nationalist politics.

By early October 1988, Geoff Nyarota was sitting on the most explosive story in his young country's history. The question was, Could he publish it? Three years earlier the government, to the consternation of its opponents, black and white, had taken a majority share in Zimbabwe National Newspapers, known as Zimpapers, the holding company for the country's major paper. *The Chronicle,* like *The Herald* and the *Sunday Mail,* was thus government owned, and although Mugabe and his senior ministers paid lip service to freedom of the press, they were quick to come down on any editor who dared to practice it. They had already fired the editor of the

Sunday Mail, the much revered Willie Musarurwa, a brave journalist who had spent twelve years in jail for his opposition to the Smith government. Then Musarurwa's successor, Henry Muradzikwa, was "promoted" into a dead-end public relations post after running a story about a Zimbabwean student being expelled from Cuba because he was found to have AIDS. A Cuban delegation that was visiting Harare when the story broke had objected to it.

Geoff Nyarota was no dissident—he had for a time been President Mugabe's publicist—but he was too good a journalist to let the Willowvale story go. On October 21, 1988, *The Chronicle* splashed the first installment of Willowgate across its front page. There were lines at the newsstands not only in Bulawayo but also in Harare, and for the first time in ten years *The Chronicle* sold out.

Enos Nkala, the minister of Defence, telephoned Nyarota and threatened to have him arrested immediately. He demanded that Nyarota travel to Harare the following day to meet with him. "If you do not travel here, I will teach you a lesson," Nkala yelled. "I will use the army to pick you up." The chairman of Zimpapers confirmed the government's hostility and told Nyarota that he was going to be dismissed from his post and arrested. One of the prime movers against Nyarota was Senator Callistus Ndlovu.

Meanwhile *The Chronicle* kept publishing new Willowgate revelations, doubling its print run and selling out every issue. The minister of State, Frederick Shava, was involved, as were Senator Jacob Mudenda, provincial governor of Matabeleland North, and Dzingai Mutumbuka, minister of Higher Education. The scams were all the same: a minister ordered the vehicle from Willowvale's special pool; a middleman paid the manufacturer's price and sold it to a vehicle-starved public for as much as three times what he'd paid. A nice source of revenue for very little effort.

Finally President Mugabe was forced to take action, and on January 3, 1989, he reluctantly announced the appointment of a commission of inquiry into Willowgate under the chairmanship of Justice Wilson Sandura. Far from being the expected whitewash, the hearings, which began a month later, proved to be a harrowing inquisition into a parade of the president's senior ministers and the country's senators and provided the packed High Court of Zimbabwe with daily doses of grand African theater. Some officials were outraged at having to endure public humiliation. Senator Ndlovu came close to being jailed for riotous behavior. The commissioners said he was arrogant and aggressive and that he had lied to them. The minister of State, Frederick Shava, was called "an unreliable witness whose evidence cannot be believed." He at one point changed his testimony—"when he realized that he could not go far with his lies because his answers were becoming more and more ridiculous." The commissioners said Shava was behaving like a car dealer, "and in one year he made a profit of Z$140,000."

Most of the officials seemed unrepentant and came up with implausible, long-winded explanations of why they had sold the vehicles at massive profits. The commission recommended that five of them—including Frederick Shava—be charged with perjury. For one or two, however, it was a crushing blow. Maurice Nyagumbo, the old nationalist, close friend of the president's, and national hero, shuffled into the Sandura hearing a broken man. Everything he represented—the noble defiance and the moral rectitude of the African liberation movement, the glory of leading his people from subjugation to independence—stood to be wiped out as his shabby little wheeling and dealing was exposed. He was accused of profiteering on eight vehicles, and although he lied halfheartedly, he knew the game was up. Some weeks after appearing before the commission, Nyagumbo committed suicide by drinking a bottle of rat poison. He was accorded a state funeral, and at his graveside his old comrade and friend Robert Mugabe said bitterly, "Maurice is dead. He has taken his life and left us confused and bewildered, . . . guessing."

The commissioners weren't left guessing at all. They investigated Nyagumbo's bank accounts and announced that far from being an ascetic pauper, as was popularly believed, he was rather well off. "At the time of his death," they reported, "[one] account had a balance of Z$23,000, although a sum of Z$5,000 appears to have been withdrawn on the day when Nyagumbo was in the intensive care unit of Samuel Parirenyata Hospital."

The sheer scale of corruption exposed by the Sandura hearings should have justified Geoff Nyarota's decision to publish the Willowgate story. Indeed, he was formally thanked by the commission for *The Chronicle*'s exposés. But even as the commission was sitting, Nyarota and Davison Maruziva were being removed from their jobs, "promoted" to public relations positions in the head office in Harare. President Mugabe said he thought Nyarota had been "overzealous" and the promotion was appropriate to his skills. He was replaced by a more compliant editor, and *The Chronicle*'s circulation slipped back to fifty thousand.

As Nyarota languished in the head office, the subjects of his investigations were being submitted to further humiliations. Five ministers resigned, and Shava was sentenced to nine months' imprisonment for perjury. Then in March, President Mugabe convened a meeting of ZANU's high command, and the matter of a presidential pardon of all the Willowgate officials was discussed. The following day Mugabe told a press conference of the party's decision and said, "Who among us has not lied? Yesterday you were with your girlfriend and you told your wife you were with the president. Should you get nine months' jail for that?" Lying under oath, it seemed, now had the president's seal of approval.

Whereas the ministers picked up their lives pretty much where they had left off, Geoff Nyarota's fortunes continued to slide. In 1991, he spent six months as editor of Zimbabwe's independent and highly respected *Financial Gazette*. But he was soon hounded out of that job, and when I saw him in Harare, the following year, he was close to penniless and struggling to support his wife and two children on meager savings and some itinerant vegetable selling. Friends were also helping him out.

It was miserable to see Nyarota in this position. He should have been the hero of the day. But he wasn't. He was a temporary irritant that had been successfully swatted out of the way by an unrepentant government. And in 1993, further misfortune befell him when one of the ministers involved in Willowgate, Nathan Shamuyarira, filed a defamation suit demanding fifty thousand Zimbabwe dollars' restitution for claims Nyarota had made in *The Chronicle*.

Shamuyarira was, in fact, virtually the only Willowgate witness the Sandura commission exonerated. Although he had been involved in two vehicle deals, the commissioners found that he had given his evidence well and were "satisfied that there was nothing unlawful or improper in what he did." (In May 1994, the High Court ruled in Shamuyarira's favor and ordered Nyarota and his co-defendant, Zimpapers, to pay fifteen thousand Zimbabwe dollars and costs.)

THIS, THEN, WAS THE NEW ZIMBABWE. IT WAS NOT, AFTER ALL, AS I had imagined when I'd landed at Bulawayo Airport that March afternoon in 1990. I had allowed sentimentality to gull me into believing I still knew this place. I did not. As it became increasingly apparent during the visits I made over the next few years, I was as disconnected here, in my hometown, as I was amid the tumult that had followed Mandela's release in South Africa. I now realized that I was a transient voyeur watching the whites fighting among themselves on Saturday nights, the blacks dipping their fingers into the tills, and the whole damn country slipping from the Third World into the nth World while nobody was looking.

Late at night, as I lay in bed, the voices of the empire's ghosts ebbed and flowed through my head: Selous the pioneer, Rhodes the empire builder, Todd the missionary prime minister, Smith the rebel farmer. I imagined them arguing about the fate of their beloved Rhodesia, blaming one another for events now engraved in history, mourning the state of the nation as it is today. I could hear Selous lamenting the collapse of the wildlife habitats and Rhodes complaining about the suppression of the Matabeles while Smith and Todd bickered about the Unilateral Declaration of Independence and the war that accompanied it.

Todd, one of the two surviving ghosts of the empire, had been knighted at Buckingham Palace in 1986 and was one of Zimbabwe's most distinguished elder statesmen. After independence he had served for five years as a senator under Robert Mugabe and had then retired to his Bulawayo home. He dabbled in public affairs and became involved in a series of controversies surrounding Zimpapers, of which he was a prominent shareholder.

I phoned Garfield on one of my trips in 1993, and we agreed to meet for lunch at the Bulawayo Club. I found him sitting on a bench in the garden, contentedly watching a pair of hammerkops battering away at the silver oak above him. As he rose to greet me, his tanned face creasing into a warm, familiar smile, I was struck by how healthy he looked, fitter and younger than when I'd last seen him. He had just celebrated his eighty-fifth birthday, and he stood straight as a ramrod, to his full six feet two inches. He didn't wear glasses—he has twenty-twenty vision—and his thick mop of white hair was unruly, like a schoolboy's. His skin was a leathery brown hide, cured for over half a century under the African sun.

I had arrived with a headful of baggage from the old Rhodesia and the new Zimbabwe—the incorrigible whites, the corrupted ministers, the ever-present threat of tribal conflict, the seeping corruption, and the economic stagnation. My hope was that this gentle Christian liberal would help me reconcile the optimism and righteousness of the liberation movement of the 1960s and '70s with the despair at government incompetence and corruption in the 1980s and '90s. Was Ian Smith right about the blacks not being ready to govern? Did Todd regret supporting the liberation movements?

Over lunch we talked a great deal about Geoff Nyarota and the erosion of press freedom under Mugabe. Sir Garfield had bought shares in Zimpapers soon after independence and ever since had been fighting a rear-guard action against government interference. He objected to the manner in which Zimpapers had been taken over in 1985 and was now in the process of rallying shareholders for a special meeting in Harare, where he hoped to oust the government-appointed chairman, Dr. Davidson Sadza. The company's finances were in a mess, and several senior executives were about to be charged with embezzling company funds. Dr. Sadza had allowed the once thriving newspaper group to teeter on the brink of bankruptcy, and Sir Garfield wanted him out.

This confrontation with the new order described in microcosm the post-colonial liberal dilemma. There was no question that the ordinary black Zimbabwean was economically worse off now than he had been under white rule. Equally, there was no doubt that the current government was as uninterested in individuals' constitutional rights as was its predecessor. (Geoff Nyarota had told me he had had more freedom as a journalist under Smith's government than under Mugabe's.) But was all this part of the inevitable growing pains of a new order after a century of colonial rule, or was there a malaise so deep-seated in the African psyche that blacks could not successfully govern themselves in a modern democracy?

Todd's predecessors, the Victorian missionaries, had been unequivocal in their opinions. In 1873, on his deathbed at Chitambo's village in what is now Zambia, David Livingstone had written, "All I can add in my solitude is . . . may heaven's rich blessing come down on everyone, American, English, or Turk, who will help heal this open sore of the world."

TEN

Empire's Ghosts: Last Words from
the Missionary and the Farmer

"He was a nice chap, really," said Sir Garfield. "But then everybody's nice."

He was talking about a man named Ken Flower, who had been the head of Rhodesia's Secret Service during the war years and had been partly responsible for Todd's jailing in the early 1970s. He may also have been responsible for having Todd charged with treason—a hanging offense—eight years later, in the last days of white rule. So listening to Todd now was a bit like hearing Jesse Jackson call David Duke a brother. And yet he said things like this with neither the smooth insincerity of a politician nor the unctuousness of a clergyman. True to his calling, he was a man who bore no malice toward his enemies and seemed righteous in thought and deed.

Sir Garfield was now living in a Bulawayo suburb with his wife, Grace. They spent little time at the family farm near Shabani. Three blocks away, their daughter, Judith, was living in similarly leafy surroundings. These days Bulawayo seemed fond of the Todds, and they in turn seemed fond of Bulawayo. It wasn't always so. For many years they were the enemies not only of the people of Bulawayo but also of most of the whites in the country. I remembered how vehemently Todd's liberalism had been objected to. A man once threw thirty silver coins at him in Salisbury Airport and yelled

Sir Garfield Todd, with his wife, Grace, and their daughter, Judith,
at home in the suburbs of Bulawayo in the late 1980s.

"Judas," this only weeks after a baboon with the words GARFIELD TODD painted on its back had been let loose in the city center. There seemed little room for debate in those days: one was either a Smith man or a *kaffirboetie,* a brother of the kaffirs.

So despised was Todd that there were serious attempts to assassinate him. Everyone knew that a team of Selous Scouts had been dispatched to Shabani to eliminate him, but they'd never reached their target, a mystery that was resolved only years later. Two young black men confessed to one of Todd's workers that they'd been sent "by the Smith régime" to eliminate a Dr. Zhou at Mnene Hospital and Mr. Todd at Dadaya. They'd gunned down Dr. Zhou on his doorstep and for several days waited beside the dirt road to Todd's farm. He passed by two or three times, but the young men said they could not bring themselves to shoot him. They returned to face the wrath of their masters and soon after resigned from the Scouts.

Todd was also nearly gunned down in 1977; he was followed around Lusaka for two days by Rhodesian undercover agents poised to assassinate him when the order came through from Salisbury. But the order never came. However much they hated him and the ideas he stood for, it seems that the Rhodesians could not bring themselves to execute a white missionary.

Now Todd's treasonous notions of a democratic multiracial society had become the laws of the new Zimbabwe, and the citizens of Bulawayo could no longer remember what all the fuss had been about. Just as it has become increasingly difficult to find anyone in South Africa today who ever supported apartheid, so it was impossible to find anyone in Zimbabwe who'd been behind the Smith government or UDI. Of course it was ridiculous locking Todd up, the good citizens of Bulawayo clucked. We didn't go along with it, but what could we do? The country was at war. Even Ian Smith, the man ultimately responsible for Sir Garfield's many incarcerations, told me he felt unhappy about it, "but we had no choice because he was conniving with terrorists against the constitution of the country."

"We missed a golden opportunity," I heard Sir Garfield saying. "Imagine what we could have achieved in this country." He was describing the time in the late '50s when Rhodesia seemed a short step away from multiracial government. Then he admitted reluctantly that it had been an impossible dream, an outbreak of political idealism that was totally out of keeping with the mood of the time. Remember, he said, that whites simply didn't accept blacks as equals. It's the way things were in those days. He reckoned he'd had the support of 18 to 20 percent of the white population—the educated urban liberals. "The rest were not very sophisticated politically," he said. "They were ripe for the calls to patriotism of Ian Smith and the Rhodesian Front."

These days, the Good Family Todd was concerned about the country's future, more particularly about the paths—social, political, and economic—that the government was taking the country down. But the Todds were philosophical and were not alarmed because they believed in the intrinsic goodness of the black African. They were, and always had been, much more than white Christian liberals. They were Africanists.

Why weren't more of us like Todd? If we had supported him in the late '50s, we would most likely have averted a civil war and would certainly have elected a more moderate black government than that of Robert Mugabe. But we did not, and the only logical explanation is fear of the unknown. Had we followed the Todds into the heart of Africa, then we may have overcome that fear. But we got tangled up in white-man's politics and followed the wrong leaders and stayed firmly rooted on the manicured side of the picket fence.

And yet. And yet. There are many who believe that the calamities attending the first fifteen years of black rule in Zimbabwe are proof enough that Todd and his ilk were leading us down the road to ruin. They cite the corruption scandals, the government's incompetence, the economic mismanagement, and so on, and they want to know what the liberals say about black government now.

By chance, Garfield Todd had the opportunity to confront the question himself in the winter of 1993.

MORE THAN TWENTY YEARS AFTER GARFIELD TODD AND HIS daughter were thrown into jail by the Smith régime, Africa turned against them again.

As fiercely and as single-mindedly as they had opposed the Smith government through the '60s and '70s, so in the years since independence the Todds found themselves increasingly in conflict with the Mugabe government. Sir Garfield had spoken out frequently against the president's threats to turn Zimbabwe into a one-party state, and relations between the two men soured considerably after he challenged Mugabe to do something about the corruption that was seeping down from the government through the civil service and into every nook and cranny of business life.

During this time Judith Todd was becoming embroiled in a rearguard struggle to protect the freedom of the country's press. Her vocal support for her friend the sidelined *Chronicle* editor Geoff Nyarota and her investigation into the questionable goings-on at Zimpapers were being viewed with some anger at the statehouse.

One morning in July 1993, I met the Todds outside Herald House, the headquarters of Zimpapers. Sir Garfield smiled his Christian smile and promised that a mighty battle was about to commence. Persistent rumors of executive corruption at Zimpapers had been further fueled a few weeks earlier, when the managing director, Davis Midzi, and two other employees appeared in court on charges of defrauding the company. It was another motor-vehicle scam, and according to Todd it was the tip of the iceberg.

Sir Garfield's rebellion was driven by his daughter's long-running investigation into irregularities at the company under Dr. Sadza. Sir Garfield helped Judith get elected to the board of directors in 1991, and from the inside she had been able to uncover some cavalier business methods. She'd found, for example, that unconstituted "board resolutions" had been slipped into the minutes of board meetings and that Davis Midzi had been given the green light to take four million Zimbabwe dollars from the pension fund without authorization by the directors.

Judith Todd was not altogether surprised. Dr. Sadza and Midzi had only recently been forced to resign from another company in dire financial straits, Hunyani Holdings, Limited, after it had recorded a loss of Z$21.9 million. The government had rescued the debt-ridden company by injecting Z$37 million into it. So bad was

Hunyani's financial position that at one point it was unable to pay staff salaries, and another Z$2-million loan was granted by the government. At the same time it was noted that there had been a dramatic hike in the directors' fees during the same year, from Z$82,000 to Z$1.9 million. It was then that Sadza and Midzi had resigned.

When they arrived at the meeting, Sir Garfield and Judith had expected the first item on the agenda to be Dr. Sadza announcing his resignation from Zimpapers. (Midzi had been suspended when criminal proceedings were announced.) But they watched Sadza walk into the room with a little swagger and a fuck-you look in his eyes and realized something was up. Sadza sat down, gazed out at the twenty or so shareholders, black and white, in attendance, and declared the meeting open. One white shareholder rose immediately and said, "I don't know how we can expect foreign investment in this country if our companies are being run like Zimpapers." Dr. Sadza looked directly at the man with seeming incomprehension. "That's fine," he said. "Now we would like to ask you to approve directors' fees that have already been paid." Ripples of weary laughter washed over him.

He told the meeting that he had been instructed by the majority shareholder, Mugabe's government, to stay on as chairman and, since there was no point in discussing the matter further, asked that the meeting proceed to the second item on the agenda, which was the nomination of board members. Todd immediately rose to his feet and spoke: "Mr. Chairman, two years ago I found some of the board of directors were illegally in their places, and I managed to get Judith on the board so we could get some news about what was going on in the company. This has now turned into news of a flood of disasters. We need a new chairman, a new legal adviser, a new board . . . and we're not going to get this unless we get a new president of Zimbabwe, which is very sad because I have always been a supporter of the president. But if he is going to interfere in companies in this way, then it is a poor show for anyone who is interested in his company, in his land, in his economic security, in his country."

Dr. Sadza paused for a second, then said evenly, "Are there any further nominations for the board?"

Since Sadza controlled the majority vote, Judith was removed from the board, and Geoff Nyarota's nomination was quashed. Sadza told the journalist, "There are areas where your talents are far better used." It was a remark that dripped with insincerity, given that Sadza's newspapers refused to employ him.

We left the meeting and walked past the flower sellers lining African Unity Square Park and on to the Harare Club. Sir Garfield chuckled about Judith shaking hands with Sadza at the end of the meeting, wishing him all the best. "She's a real Christian, you know," he said with some irony.

Over lunch he raged on. "There is no question that Judith's removal from the board was a decision made by the government. . . . I think Dr. Sadza has been taking his directions from the president himself. It is a warning not only to all businesses but to every person who has land—communal or private—or interests in any commercial or industrial area. If a blight like this can be inflicted on a company like Zimpapers by the country's president—well, where will it end?"

Judith was no less despondent. "I'm tired of being a dissident," she said. "It was easier with Smith because it seemed so morally right, so straightforward. I was also an outsider—I was young, and I didn't know them personally. The people I'm up against now are people I've known all my life. And it's the mirror image of my struggle against Smith and UDI."

The Todds' discouragement did not mean that they had lost their faith in the essential goodness of mankind or their belief that things would improve. "It's a period of transition," Sir Garfield said as we were parting. "Post-colonial power at its worst. But things will change."

I wasn't so sure. I needed to talk to someone a little more skeptical. I dialed Ian Smith's number.

He answered right away. "Are you here now?" he asked. The familiar, clipped accent took me back thirty years. It was another voice from my youth, a voice I have carried with me ever since, that slightly nasal Rhodesian-farmer accent saying things like "All we ask is that Rhodesia be allowed to maintain civilized standards" and "Our Africans are the happiest Africans on the continent." Now he was telling me that he was inundated with journalists and film crews wanting to talk to him, but he had some time later in the week.

"Phone me tomorrow, and we'll make a plan."

IAN SMITH'S HOUSE IS NEXT DOOR TO THE CUBAN EMBASSY. FOR forty years he had been one of white Africa's most defiant opponents of the Communist menace, constantly warning his constituents that social contact with the Reds could ruin their lives. Now here he was sharing a garden fence with them, even using the same water supply and sewage system.

When I asked him whether he felt threatened by the proximity of the Commies, Smith rolled his eyes toward heaven and dismissed his reclusive, secretive neighbors with a flick of his hand. They lived behind high walls topped with coils of razor wire, and their buildings bristled with communications antennae. Armed guards patrolled the property round the clock. Smith's gate was left open and his front door unlocked. His house was modest, set amid a shaded, well-manicured half-acre garden. When I walked up to the front door and knocked, he answered. There were no guards, no rottweilers, not even a burglar alarm.

He still had that wiry, tough-as-biltong appearance, and he still fixed you with a waxlike, off-kilter stare, a legacy of plastic surgery after an injury in World War II. But the years had taken their toll. There was weariness in his eyes and a stiffness in his body that suggested a man at the end of the road. His beloved Rhodesia was long gone, and the society that had replaced it was not to his liking at all. He remained active in opposition politics but spent most of his time tending to his cattle farm in Selukwe. My visit took place before the Mandela government had come to power in South Africa, and he was still traveling there occasionally, talking to right-wingers like General Constand Viljoen, no doubt warning them of the perils of black government.

He led me into his living room, and I was once more catapulted back to my Rhodesian childhood. All our homes were furnished like this: sort of 1950s middle-class British suburban, with chairs and couches covered in chintz, and fussy little Wedgwood and Royal Doulton objects on various mahogany side tables. Heavy fringed curtains were half-drawn to cut out the afternoon sunlight. The only clue to Smith's political past was a massive painting of the Cape by Gabriel de Jongh above the fireplace, a specially commissioned work that was presented to him in 1974 by Rhodesian Front backbenchers to commemorate his ten years as prime minister. And the only concession to Africa was a semicircle of eight ceramic figurines on a marble table—all African women in traditional dress. Except for this little display, we could have been in a semidetached house in Hounslow.

It was ironic that I should visit Ian Smith in the same week that his old nemesis, the liberal Todd, had had his depressing confrontation with the African way of government. Ironic because Smith had said all along that this would happen. When he led the country into UDI in 1965, he warned his supporters that anything less than continued white rule would lead to a lowering of standards and the kind of corruption and mismanagement that was already evident to the north. The cornerstone of his political philosophy was simply that blacks were not ready to rule. He once told an election rally, "Sixty years ago Africans here were uncivilised savages, walking around in skins. They have made tremendous progress but they have an awfully long way to go." And even when he conceded defeat and accepted the inevitability of majority rule in the late 1970s, he refused to believe that a black government would benefit Rhodesians, black or white.

He still refused to believe. He said the Mugabe government was "a bunch of gangsters" and cited one corruption rumor after another as evidence of its venal nature. He had been following the Zimpapers saga and said it was yet another sign of Mugabe's determination to turn Zimbabwe into a one-party state. "You see," he explained patiently, "the Russians got into Africa after World War II, and the philosophy they preached was that once you become the government, you remain the government forever. And the African leaders took that up—just look at Tanzania, Uganda, Zaire, Nigeria. It is easy to brainwash the African people. Most of the rural people are illiterate and susceptible. A bunch of poor, innocent old chaps, dear old chaps in the bush. What decent chaps, how easy it is to pull the wool over their eyes."

Smith still talked with the patronizing confidence of someone who had God and the truth on his side. He was an awkward, prickly man, typical of the white Rhodesians who formed his core constituency. He described himself as the equivalent of a British Tory and a champion of traditional Western values, but there was more to it than that. What Rhodesians like Smith inherited from their forefathers was a frontier conservatism that was defined by the need to prevail in a harsh and hostile landscape. It was founded on the whites' conceit that most Africans preferred to be ruled with firmness, and anything less would be perceived as a sign of weakness that would result in their going straight for the white man's throat. Rhodesia's short history was strewn with white casualties: the martyrs of the Shangani Patrol, the women and children speared to death in the Matabele uprising, the passengers on the Air Rhodesia Viscount, farmers and their families during the Dissident War—the list was endless.

The iron-fisted conservatism of Smith's Rhodesians manifested itself in an unwavering loyalty to their own kind and in a lifelong suspicion of any idea that might threaten their value system. Academics and politicians of the left were branded "pseudo-intellectuals," artists were "poofters," and Africans with opinions were "cheeky kaffirs." There was never a glimmer of self-doubt, only bitterness at the way the world had abandoned the white man in Rhodesia. One word constantly resonated through Smith's conversation. The word was "betrayal." The British government had betrayed Smith by attempting to abandon the Rhodesians to black majority rule, and throughout the years of negotiations during the civil war, "Britishers," as Smith called them, of every political hue— Harold Wilson, Sir Alec Douglas Home, Lord Goodman, Lord Pearce, David Owen, Lord Carrington—betrayed him with monotonous regularity, breaking agreements, reneging on promises, kow-towing to the Organization of African Unity and the UN. And finally the cruelest betrayal of all, when John Vorster's South Africa turned its back on Rhodesia and set in motion Smith's final capitulation to majority rule.

As we sat talking, I noticed that Smith was eyeing me with some suspicion. He had already said that most journalists he'd encountered were left-wing, "and I have no doubt the press has treated me unfairly over the years." I could see he was thinking that here was another lefty come to ridicule him, so I told him that I'd grown up in Bulawayo, and he seemed to relax a little. "One of us," he laughed self-consciously. And then he drifted into a reverie about that other time. "Ah, Rhodesians," he said dreamily, as if he were recalling some mystic, long-forgotten race. "Most Rhodesians were not racists; they were not extremists. I found them to be normal, balanced people. We established a wonderful nation here—we expanded the economy at an incredible rate, and we held back the advance of communism."

As he was speaking, I couldn't help but think about our old family radio. That impressive piece of furniture, a combination radio–record player designed and built by my father, had provided the sound track of my youth, and in between Ella, Satchmo, and Ellington we had listened attentively to this same flat-voweled voice of reason defining the Rhodesian way of life. While the rest of the world was spiraling downward, free-falling into Communist-inspired satanism and liberalism, the voice told us that we were the last defenders of truth and justice and "civilized standards." We were the descendants of pioneers, making a stand, preparing ourselves to give our lives to uphold the virtues of the Old World.

Now the voice was telling me a favorite story. The day after Robert Mugabe took office in April 1980, he had sent for Smith. Now Mugabe had once promised that come liberation, Smith would be hanged in the center of Harare, but now he could not have been more generous. He shook Smith's hand and said how lucky his fellow Africans were to have inherited this jewel of a country, with its superb infrastructure and its efficient, modern economy. "He promised me he would keep it that way," said Smith. "I went home to my wife, and I was rather excited. I said maybe I had been wrong about black government. Here's this chap, and he was speaking like a sophisticated, balanced, sensible man. If he practices what he preaches, then it will be fine.

"For six or seven months it was fine. Then he reverted to form and started talking about bringing in a Marxist one-party state."

By the time I got up to leave, I found myself feeling some sympathy for the crusty old conservative. He was much maligned these days, not least by whites who once supported him but now regarded him as an embarrassing anachronism, an uncomfortable reminder of their own past. The black government no longer took any notice of his hectoring, and white liberals like Todd laughed out loud at the things he said. I felt like patting him on the shoulder and saying "Good Old Smithy" for the first time in my life. We shook hands, and he said, reluctantly and almost inaudibly, that he had enjoyed our talk. It was probably as close as he gets to friendly.

I drove out the gate and past the Cuban embassy, which suddenly seemed ridiculous, as if the Disney people had created a cartoon monument to the Cold War and dumped it in the Harare suburbs. This city was full of the humbug and pretension of Third World capitals on the diplomatic and foreign-agency circuit. There were more Mercedes-Benzes per licensed driver in Harare than in any other city in the world. The place was awash with foreigners on expense accounts. And here, in the middle of all the extravagance, all the foolish trappings of post-colonial Africa, stood the melancholy figure of the most vilified person in the country's history.

I caught a glimpse of him in the rearview mirror, and I saw the shadow of a man who once took a country to war to protect a nineteenth-century lifestyle.

ELEVEN

Playing God in Eden

I was fourteen years old when I shot my last wild animal. It was a small bushbuck on a friend's farm northwest of Bulawayo. I'd shot wildly, hitting it in the hindquarters and had had to chase after it through thick bushveld for almost a mile. When I arrived before the fallen creature, I could not finish it off. I stood frozen over its quivering body and stared into its desperate eyes. My companion slit its throat, and its thrashing stopped.

I was disgusted with myself. "Ineptitude" and "cowardice" were two words that sprang to mind. We had never questioned the morality of hunting; it was simply something everyone did from a very young age, starting out shooting birds with a .22, then dassies and dik-diks with a .410, and on to kudu with .310s and twelve-bores. But the suffering I had inflicted on that poor creature was enough to convince me that this was a sport for which I was unsuited. It wasn't that I opposed hunting—I continued going into the bush with friends who hunted—but I knew I could never kill again.

I doubt I realized it at the time, but that encounter with the bushbuck changed my perceptions about the relationship between us and them—the white settlers with guns and the wild animals. Until then I had accepted that we had some divine right to shoot the place up because we were the ones who were preserving it. The Afs, we were told, had no interest in wildlife, and if we left it to them, it would all be gone in a decade. I was to learn in the coming years that like so much of the history handed down from one settler generation to the next, this was a flawed and self-serving analysis.

In fact, before the white colonials arrived in Africa, mankind and wild animal had cohabited most successfully. Hunting was conducted on a need-to-eat basis and usually on the instruction of the tribal chief. The indigenous people recognized the relationship between a healthy, abundant habitat and prosperous fauna, and they fitted in accordingly, killing animals only for food and self-protection. Then, in the middle of the last century, in the wake of the empire builders came the white hunters, who, like an advancing army, cut down the wild animals in their path by the millions.

At the turn of the century, many of the hunters, now sated and weary of these one-sided contests, chose to channel their love of the bushveld into animal conservation. They campaigned for controlled hunting and for the establishment of game reserves, within which the animals would be the property of the state—that is, the white colonial governments. It was already too late for some species: the blaubok (bluebuck) and the quagga, an animal similar in appearance to a zebra, had been shot to extinction in the Cape, and in Natal there were no more elephants where there had once been large herds. The southern white rhinoceros was down to no more than fifty.

Game reserves were set up all over colonial Africa, invariably named after European kings and queens and inevitably conceived as playgrounds for the white elite. Tribes living in the designated areas were forcibly removed and dumped somewhere outside the fences, cut off from their ancestral lands and forbidden to hunt for food. But the whites had the power, and so for the first half of the twentieth century the game reserves prospered and were regarded as models of conservation. Among other things they provided Western academics with vast natural laboratories in which to study animal behavior and wealthy vacationers with holiday resorts where they could impersonate Victorian explorers in safety and comfort.

In the second half of the twentieth century, two other forces came into play that would transform Africa's game reserves into blood-soaked battlegrounds. The arrival of Western medicines cut infant mortality dramatically among African tribespeople. Previously a woman would have eight children and expect only four to survive. Now all eight survived, as did all their children and their children's children. At the turn of the century, Africa supported ninety-three million people, and as the millennium approaches, there are almost more than eight hundred million. This population explosion led to a demand for more land, and the resentment of the white man's reserves and the white man's animals grew stronger. The second event that threatened the game reserves was the growing demand in the Far East for ivory and rhino horn, which the Chinese believe to be a miracle analgesic. Thus the value of rhinoceroses and elephants skyrocketed just as the locals' resentment for them was building to a crescendo.

As Africa entered the final decade of the century, the last oases of wilderness and their dwindling animal populations were threatened with obliteration. Although Western conservation organizations like the World Wildlife Fund and the African Wildlife Foundation had pumped millions of donated dollars into wildlife projects and had successfully engineered international bans on the trade of rhino horn and ivory, the slide toward oblivion continued. It was clear that unless dramatic action was taken to stop the human encroachment on wildlife habitats and the poaching of key species, all would be lost.

TWELVE

Diary of a Dark Safari

One hot, dry Transvaal summer's day, I was sitting in a Wimpy hamburger bar in a one-street town called Magaliesburg with two undercover cops named Riaan and Ben. Riaan was a handsome young man with dark, curly hair. He had been a Special Branch policeman in apartheid days. Ben was blond, discomfortingly silent, and had only one leg, having lost the other to a rocket grenade in the Angolan civil war. They were detectives in South Africa's Endangered Species Protection Unit, and we were into the third day of an undercover sting operation that was intended to crack open a rhino-horn smuggling network.

The three black waitresses gathered near the till were staring at us and whispering to one another. They could tell that Riaan and Ben were cops even though they were wearing jeans and casual shirts. Maybe it was the bulge of Riaan's nine-millimeter pistol under his leather jacket or Ben's walkie-talkie lying on the Formica table beside his cheeseburger and fries. Or maybe it was because all three of us were staring out the plate-glass window at the red Ford parked across the street in front of the antiques shop. "Christ," I heard myself saying aloud, "they probably think *I'm* a cop." Riaan and Ben laughed, and I resisted an impulse to stand up and explain why I was sitting there with foot soldiers of the old apartheid establishment.

The driver of the red Ford across the street was another undercover cop. He was posing as a prospective buyer, and his passenger was Vince, a career criminal who had turned police informer and was setting up a bust. Two more cars containing ESPU detectives were cruising the dirt roads outside town, all connected by cell phones. Vince was waiting for his contact to telephone the antiques shop and set a meeting place.

For the past two days we had been playing cell-phone tag with the woman Vince had chosen to betray, a farmer's wife he'd known for some years and with whom he'd regularly done illegal gemstone deals. This time she wanted to move rhino horns and, unaware that Vince had new employers, had asked him to find a buyer. On the first day we had waited from dawn to dusk in another God-forsaken Transvaal town, Boksburg—four carloads of ESPU cops, Vince, and me hanging about hopelessly while she kept changing plans, switching times and locations with the practiced caution of an experienced criminal.

She said she was waiting for her contacts to bring the horns from Katlehong, one of the lawless black townships to the south of Johannesburg. At one point she'd told Vince she might be receiving forty horns, and this news had put the cops on red alert. They already knew there were two heavily armed ex-soldiers guarding the farm and reckoned that a major delivery like this would mean the big syndicates were involved, which in turn would mean many more men armed with automatic weapons. So they'd requested that some of the heavies from Murder and Robbery and even more serious heavies from the Internal Stability Unit be placed on standby. But nothing happened.

The same four cars and fifteen cops had returned to Boksburg on the second day while another vanload of ESPU operatives bristling with weapons had been deployed to stake out the woman's farm. The idea was that the Boksburg team would arrest the woman when she'd made her sale to Vince's "buyer," and then everyone would descend on the farm and clean the syndicate out. Although

Vince had promised me "a great show today," the woman kept up the bait-and-switch strategy until well into the afternoon, dragging us from one phony meeting place to the next. Finally the cops had decided it would be too dangerous to raid the farm after dusk, and they called the meeting off.

Now it was the third day, and the woman had lured us fifty-five miles across the northern Transvaal, to within a few miles of her farm. She had only one horn to sell, a small one weighing three and a half pounds and worth eight thousand rand, about two thousand dollars, but she promised that the rest would be delivered in the next few weeks.

At twelve-fifteen the phone in the antiques shop rang, and Vince was told that the woman's son was waiting on a dirt road some three miles away. We watched the red Ford pull out and head back along the road toward Pretoria, and we evacuated the Wimpy bar with haste, Ben leading the way with great swings of his body between aluminum crutches. As we accelerated out of Magaliesburg, the car radio crackled with instructions to take the turnoff to the Bekker School.

When we hit the dirt road, we could see in the distance the red Ford pulled alongside a gray Opel, and as we approached, the Opel took off in a cloud of dust. Another cop car flew past us, and a hundred yards farther along it eased the Opel to a halt on the side of the road. Warrant Officer Gert van der Merwe, the head of the operation, leaped from his vehicle and stood at the window of the car, pointing an R-3 automatic rifle at the head of the driver, who was just a kid, maybe eighteen years old. Van der Merwe ordered him out of the vehicle, then body-searched and handcuffed him. Riaan handed me a camera and asked me to be the police photographer. So I made the kid stand next to the trunk of the car and placed the rhino horn beside him.

It was while I was point-and-shooting away at this unfortunate khaki-clad bat-eared farm boy that the towering absurdity of all this hit me. The small horn on the trunk, wrapped in a supermarket shopping bag and looking like a piece of rotten wood, was nothing more than a clump of matted rhinoceros hair. For entirely spurious reasons it had achieved an outrageous monetary value, and so for three days some fifteen policemen had been traipsing across the Transvaal trying to stop its illicit transfer from one dubious character to another. But even as the cops were shaking down the boy smuggler, more rhinos were being killed. However many busts these cops made, there would always be more horn coming onto the market. Until, that is, there was no more left to poach.

The bat-eared boy led the convoy of cops to the family farmhouse a few miles away, and as we pulled in, we were greeted by his sobbing sister. She said her brother was innocent and that Vince was to blame; then, when the cops told her they were going to search the house, she started yelling.

It was a typically spartan Transvaal farmhouse furnished with cheap chairs, tables, and sofas and decorated with posters of sunsets, dogs, and Jesus. The search of the boy's bedroom revealed nothing more than the usual accessories of a young Hun lifestyle—nine-millimeter pistol, rifle, razor-sharp switchblades, kung fu fighting sticks, cartridges for automatic weapons. The boy's demeanor was cool until the cops began describing prison life in the new South Africa. Black felons outnumbered whites a hundred to one, and the whites were getting the shit beaten out of them, they told him. "How would you like a big black cock up your arse every night?" Gert asked. The bat-eared boy turned pale. He was looking at three years inside with good behavior, and he didn't need a mathematics degree to work out that that was a lot of black cocks. So he told the cops he was ready to cooperate if they'd do a deal. Any kind of deal. He said he could lead them to a network of Mozambicans who were bringing in a lot of horn.

The cops conferred briefly, and then Gert stepped forward and unlocked the boy's handcuffs. He instructed him to report to the Rustenburg police station the following day. The farm boy nodded and then asked to speak to Gert privately. We were filing out of the room when Gert exploded in laughter. "Listen to this," he roared. "This guy has just applied for a job as a game ranger with Natal Parks. He wants to know if the arrest will screw up his application."

We left the forlorn wanna-be conservationist and repaired to a bush bar, a ramshackle white shebeen located on a farm at the end of a dirt road in the middle of nowhere. In recent years bush bars had been springing up all over the northern Transvaal. This was the heartland of the Afrikaner right, the die-hard apartheidists, and the bars served as retreats where they mourned the passing of the old order over beers and brandy and Cokes.

Gert bought the first round, Riaan broke out smokes, and everyone agreed it had been a good day's work. There was a major from the Rustenburg drug squad with us—the bat-eared boy was also trying to move a pack of one thousand Mandrax tablets—and the major bought a round and started telling drug-bust stories, of how the rock stars pouring into the country were arriving with bags of cocaine and how the Nigerian syndicates were moving in to supply the growing local demand. A couple of rounds later the cops were telling each other dirty jokes in Afrikaans, and Vince the Informer was explaining to me in minute detail how to commit check fraud. Vince, it turned out, was a very bright customer indeed, a career criminal who seemed to have gotten away with most of it most of the time. He said he'd turned informer because he hit hard times and needed quick cash—the ESPU's informers usually received 10 percent of the value of the horn or tusk confiscated plus expenses. Vince had probably made fifteen hundred rand ($450) that day.

The ESPU was formed early in 1989 by a personable captain from the stock-theft unit named Piet Lategan. It was the brainchild of South Africa's then minister of Law and Order, Adriaan Vlok, and was intended as an antidote to the wave of allegations by Western wildlife activists that South African officials, army officers, and government ministers were aiding and abetting the illicit wildlife trade. Clearly eager to wipe out traces of the bad old days, Vlok moved Lategan's unit onto a farm outside Pretoria called Vlakplaas (Flat Place). Vlakplaas is a name that will live forever in infamy in South African history, for it had been the headquarters of C10, apartheid's notorious hit squad; Lategan's predecessor there was Colonel Eugene de Kock, a man popularly known as Prime Evil.

Lategan's unit had grown to twenty-two men and women, many of them culled from the old Special Branch, and had developed a network of informers throughout southern Africa. They'd been involved in operations as far north as Zambia and had been consulted, and had run joint operations, in several neighboring African countries. Their success at penetrating and prosecuting the smuggling syndicates was illustrated by the stockpiles of confiscated rhino horn and ivory sealed up in the storeroom at Vlakplaas. The current stocks were held as evidence in upcoming criminal cases, and I counted more than 30 rhino horns and around 120 tusks. There were boxes containing thousands of carved ivory seals. The total value was anything between one and five million dollars.

Some of Lategan's methods—and drinking companions—had attracted criticism in conservation circles, and there was a time when he and his men were thought to be on the take. Although these allegations were generated and circulated by a dubious informant, they were taken so seriously that a secret meeting was convened by a number of conservationists at a Holiday Inn to address "the Lategan problem."

Lategan angrily denied any impropriety and said his drinking relationships with known ringleaders of the smuggling networks—like the former Selous Scout Ant White and the South African superspy Craig Williamson—were all part of the information-gathering process. In the murky world of undercover policing, Lategan said, unconventional methods and unconventional alliances were the only avenues to success.

As the celebrations at the bush bar wound down, we climbed into our cars and headed back to Vlakplaas. The drinking had gone on too long, and by the time we had swerved and skidded through the ninety-mile drive, it was nine o'clock. To nobody's surprise we walked straight into a huge party taking place at HQ. A training course for regional conservationists had just broken up, and the bar was wall-to-wall bearded men in shorts, all drinking and shouting. Colonel Lategan was in an expansive mood behind the bar. "It was a small bust," he said, "but I think it will lead us to a bigger network."

Colonel Piet Lategan, head of South Africa's wildlife protection police.

The bust of the boy had taken three days and at one stage, backup paramilitary troops were on standby. All for a piddling little horn and a bag of Mandrax. As I slipped out of the ESPU bar—with great haste so as to avoid Vince, who was now insisting on taking me to Johannesburg so he could introduce me to the best whores and the best-quality coke in Africa—I couldn't help feeling that the solution to Africa's poaching plague lay somewhere else.

IN THE WEEKS FOLLOWING THE MAGALIESBURG BUST, I TRAVELED four thousand miles through southern Africa, investigating African wildlife conservation. I wondered whether the world's outrage about elephant poaching and the ivory trade and the subsequent international trade bans and fund-raising and hand-wringing had had any effect. Or whether wild Africa's demise still seemed inevitable.

In Kenya the controversial but effective head of the National Wildlife Department, Richard Leakey, had been ousted by his enemies in Daniel arap Moi's government. From Zimbabwe, which once boasted the finest national parks on the continent, reports described a park system in disarray: its rhino population had been reduced from two thousand animals roaming wild and free to a scattering of two hundred living mainly on heavily guarded private reserves. In Mozambique the cessation of the fifteen-year civil war had allowed international conservators to examine and evaluate firsthand the damage done to the animals and ecosystems during the conflict. What they saw left some in tears. In South Africa, while the political landscape was changing dramatically the organized-crime networks had been conducting business as usual, flourishing and feeding off the burgeoning democracy just as they had fed off the apartheid state. South Africa was still Africa's clearinghouse for the traffic of rhino horns and elephant tusks to the Far East.

In Europe and America increasingly grim newspaper and magazine reports of the carnage had galvanized public awareness and had fattened the coffers of wildlife-preservation organizations. In the late 1980s, a group within the World Wildlife Fund International, whose patrons included the Duke of Edinburgh and Prince Bernhard of the Netherlands, began discussing a radical plan to rid

Africa of its poaching epidemic. The plan was to mount a covert semimilitary operation against the poaching organizations, and Sir David Stirling, founder of the SAS, the elite commando Special Air Service unit, was brought in to run it. Knowing that the idea of the WWF hiring a private army in its name and with its money would not go down well with the membership, Prince Philip, Prince Bernhard, Stirling, the president of WWF, Robert SanGeorge, and its director general, Charles de Haes, cloaked the operation in secrecy. They code-named it Operation Lock.

To fund it and to conceal the WWF's involvement, the principals played a neat shell game with two works of art owned by Prince Bernhard. In December 1988, the prince instructed Sotheby's to auction the *Holy Family* by Bartolomé Murillo and *The Rape of Europa* by Elisabetta Sirani. The proceeds were to be donated to the WWF. The paintings fetched just under a million dollars, and the money was duly deposited in the WWF's account. Two weeks later Prince Bernhard called the account's administrator and asked that most of it be transferred to the account of his wife, Juliana. It was to be used to bankroll Operation Lock.

On January 18, 1989, two employees of Stirling's, Ray Harris and Jim Hughes, both ex-commandos, arrived in Johannesburg and set up base in the Mariston Hotel. Within weeks five more operatives had arrived and two safe houses—one in Pretoria and the other in Johannesburg—had been established. Stirling's commando unit was led by Lieutenant Colonel Ian Crooke, a decorated SAS officer, and his instructions were to penetrate the poaching and smuggling networks and then devise a way to bring them down.

Crooke immediately established a working relationship with Lategan's ESPU, which seconded one of its men to the Pretoria safe house. Surveillance operations were set up to monitor known smugglers like some members of the Pretoria-based Pong family and the German Hans Beck in Botswana, and Crooke's men began to infiltrate the underworld, posing as buyers and sellers of rhino horn and ivory. Crooke also sent undercover operatives into Zambia to investigate that end of the network, and into Zimbabwe, where they carried out a joint sting operation with Zimbabwe's

Central Intelligence Office to trap North Korean embassy staff who had been trading in rhino horn. They also investigated a Bulawayo businessman named Basil Steyn, who they believed was moving illegal ivory to Hans Beck in Botswana. In Swaziland they uncovered a rhino-horn smuggling network inside the Taiwanese embassy that had been established by the previous ambassador and was now flourishing in the hands of the staff he'd left behind.

Within six months Crooke and his men had identified the major operators moving ivory and horn down through Kenya, Zambia, Zimbabwe, and Botswana and out through South African seaports to the Far East. This did not mean, however, that the operators would be arrested or the trade would be stopped. Penalties at the time were insignificant, mainly small fines, and the big operators seemed to enjoy some protection from above. For all the stings and busts the big players remained in the game.

Sometime in the middle of 1989, Crooke's team decided that the most effective way of breaking up the pipeline was to remove some big players and that the cleanest method was assassination. The idea was to lure Hans Beck to a farm in the northwestern Transvaal on the pretext of an ivory deal. Once there Beck was to have been killed and his body driven three hundred miles into Swaziland and dumped. Crooke's men did a dry run of the operation, and Hans Beck agreed to meet them at the Rustenburg farm. But at the last moment a call came through to cancel everything. The operation was off. Crooke's European backers had said no.

HAREBRAINED ASSASSINATION PLOTS ASIDE, OPERATION LOCK appeared on the surface to have achieved a great deal in a very short time. But right from the outset there was disquiet among conservationists who were let in on the secret. They feared a hidden agenda. Clearly permission for Crooke's men to conduct such covert operations would have come from the top of the South African government and equally clearly the intelligence they would pick up on their operations through the subcontinent would be most useful to that high authority. There was no question that Crooke held briefings with the Department of Military Intelligence and had ongoing dealings with Craig Williamson, the South African superspy, but whether or not Operation Lock functioned actively for the South African government during its brief campaign will probably never be known.

Then, on July 5, 1989, all hell broke loose. Robert Powell, a Reuters journalist based in Nairobi, broke the story of Operation Lock and said there were suspicions that Crooke's team had been a South African–backed destabilization unit. Crooke was furious and blamed the Kenyan naturalist Ian Parker for leaking the story. But it mattered not, for the cover was blown, and the conservation world—the rich, conservative donors, the animal rights groups, everyone who held an instinctive dislike for private, clandestine armies—all came down on the WWF, which scrambled desperately to distance itself from the operations. Robert SanGeorge told the British journalist Stephen Ellis that Operation Lock had been initiated without the knowledge or authority of the director general and that "no funds for the operation were channeled through WWF International's books."

At the insistence of his boss, David Stirling, Crooke agreed to meet with the press and explain his work. He described in detail the training of anti-poaching units in Mozambique, Namibia, and Swaziland and information gathering in South Africa, but naturally he didn't mention Hans Beck. The press was duly satisfied, and the London *Evening Standard* published an apology to Stirling and Crooke: "Their objective is solely as stated by them, the legal one of keeping down animal poaching . . . and there is no question of attempting to destablize the area."

But the damage was done. Crooke had no alternative but to wind down the covert operations. While Lategan did not approve of some of Operation Lock's methods, he was disappointed that it had all come apart. "Ian Crooke's people provided us with more useful information about the trade in that short time," he told me, "than all the Western organizations like the EIA [Environmental Investigation Agency] have in the years since."

Everybody now knew who the bad guys were. At the bottom of the chain were the barefoot poachers, the African tribesmen who were paid fifty dollars to go out and shoot rhino and elephants. They were the pawns, desperately poor rural people driven to poaching by hunger. Their employers were middlemen with connections either to the organized-crime networks headquartered around Johannesburg and Pretoria or to the independent operators like Basil Steyn, Hans Beck, and the former Selous Scout Ant White. These were the men the police and the conservationists knew they had to get. And they were not short of proof.

Basil Steyn, for example, ran a curio shop cum import-export business in Bulawayo called Sondela Exports. Although he was licensed to trade legal, certified ivory within the country, he was known to both Ian Crooke and Piet Lategan as one of the major movers of poached ivory through the subcontinent. In November 1980, Kathi Austin, an American undercover investigator, arrived at Steyn's shop posing as a prospective buyer. Steyn was expansive, allowing Austin and her companion to photograph the shop and the carving factory, and told her he could provide her with seven tons of raw ivory, delivered as requested to Texas, at fifty dollars per pound. Later Steyn's driver described in detail how the ivory was carried by truck across into Botswana on back roads, then concealed in containers by Steyn's partner in Gaborone and shipped to America as curios.

But for all the proof, for all of Operation Lock's surveillance and infiltration, nothing ever happened to the smugglers. Basil Steyn carried on running Sondela, even bought his own wildlife conservancy in the lowveld; A. H. Pong's sons took over the family transport business, and nothing more was said; Ant White ran his businesses out of Beira, Mozambique, and to everyone's amazement was granted citizenship in Zimbabwe. There was still a constant flow of smuggled ivory and rhino horn out of Africa to the Far East. NGOs, nongovernment organizations, continued to raise funds in Western capitals, run projects, and underwrite investigations, but if you asked anyone who had worked on the Africa beat for any length of time whether there was hope for the continent's wildlife, he would give you a litany of troubles—government cor-

ruption, organized crime, internecine wars, and economic anarchy—then tell you it didn't look good.

In the face of all the grim prognostications, I found myself predictably and instinctively taking the African Position, a stubborn,
arrogant belief that only Africans understand Africa and that outsiders misinterpret almost everything. While conceding that the
continent is riven with civil wars, paralyzed by corruption, stricken
with famines, and economically on the way to the knacker's yard—
all of this is documented—the African Position insists that when
you are on the ground, feet planted firmly on the veld, you will realize that there is much to celebrate and much to be optimistic
about. Finally, the African Position holds that once the physical
beauty of the place has seduced you and the spontaneous friendli-
ness of the people has charmed you, you will look out on the endless, peaceful bushveld and begin to wonder where the hell all these
stories of collapse and anarchy came from in the first place.

What in fact really sticks in the craw of the white Africans is that
most of the revelations about corruption have been coming from
environmental activists based in London and Washington. Groups
like the EIA, which was founded in 1984 by two Greenpeace executives, have consistently exposed poaching and smuggling networks
throughout the continent in their excellent reports. The EIA runs a
staff of twenty-five on an annual budget of $1.25 million, figures
that suggest its employees are driven more by purity and good intentions than by ambition and greed. Their mission is to facilitate
the preservation of endangered species by exposing their exploitation, and thus far they seem to have made a significant contribution.

But a burning enmity exists between southern African conservationists and the Western activists, and there is a gap in conservation
philosophies as wide as the Rift Valley. The African Position is that
for wildlife to survive, it must be managed and have a commercial
value. Thus the reintroduction of the ivory and rhino-horn trade is
advocated. The position of the Western NGOs is that the bans must
stay and that control methods such as culling should be stopped.
Even with these measures, they say, there is little hope.

But the rift is more than philosophical. Western NGOs seemed to regard all white conservationists operating in southern Africa with deep suspicion. The white Africans express the same misgivings about the NGOs, accusing organizations like the EIA of ignoring the needs of the African people while favoring grandstanding policies devised to raise funds to keep the organizations in business. Every two years at the international CITES (Convention on the Illegal Trade in Endangered Species) conventions, these two forces collide over the cornerstone issue—the continued listing of the African elephant as an endangered species and the ban on trading ivory. The white Africans want the ban lifted and the profits from a regulated trade plowed back into conservation. The Western NGOs say the ban must stay because the white Africans cannot regulate the trade and the elephants will be wiped out.

Mindful of all this bickering and ego wrestling, I arrived in Johannesburg determined at least to establish some credibility on behalf of the African Position. I had hardly set foot on the continent when Colonel Lategan offered me some advice, a slice of bushveld sagacity. It was, he said, advice he had offered others who had come from the West and attempted to understand African ways. "Time is on Africa's side," he said. "You are in Africa now, and if you don't work the way Africa works, it will destroy you."

A FEW DAYS LATER, AS I SAT IN A LAND ROVER SIPPING A COLD CAStle lager and staring out over the green patch of floodplain running alongside the Save River on Zimbabwe's southeastern border with Mozambique, Colonel Lategan's words came back to me. The powerful tranquillity of the African landscape was something natives like the colonel understood. It struck me that it was this intimacy with, and reverence for, the forces of nature that allowed the Africans the shards of optimism so notably absent in Western NGO circles.

There were four of us in the Land Rover, and for fifteen minutes we sat in silence, watching the long grasses change from cream to yellow to gold as the sun went down. A herd of impalas was grazing under the acacia albida trees to our left, and some zebras and a couple of giraffes were feeding farther along. Two vultures circled on the currents high above, scanning the thick foliage for an abandoned kill. My companions were three key players in a development program aimed at returning this wilderness area to its former glory and using wildlife tourism to fund it. Clive Stockil, a white Shona-speaking local, born and bred in the lowveld, is the driving force behind the Mahenya Campfire Project, a sustainable-utilization program that is a model for the rest of Africa. (Sustainable utilization is a conservation philosophy built on the premise that wildlife must have economic value and that the rural people living beside the wild animals must benefit from them. Thus, a percentage of tourism and hunting revenues is allocated to the local communities.) Mick Townsend, a prominent farmer and former chairman of the Wildlife Society, is a member of the president's commission on land use. Alistair Wright, a Harare hotel executive, persuaded his company, Zimbabwe Sun, to invest three million Zimbabwe dollars ($400,000) in an upmarket tourist lodge here and then launched a share issue that was intended to fund the transfer of seventeen thousand wild animals into the area. As we sat watching the serene transition from day to dusk, they explained why their mission to restore and sustain this abundant sprawl of African bushveld had become necessary in the first place.

This was the northeastern corner of Zimbabwe's second largest national park, Gonarezhou, a nineteen-hundred-square-mile reserve that lies against Mozambique's border. Gonarezhou is an infamous name in wildlife circles, for it was here in the 1980s that some of the most cynical and calamitous poaching campaigns of modern times took place, campaigns that wiped out almost all the rhino in the park and more than one thousand elephants, mostly young male bulls upon whom the herds depended for successful breeding.

The poaching operations were organized with military precision and brought together an unholy alliance of Mozambican FRELIMO soldiers, Zimbabwe National Army soldiers, corrupt National Parks officials, former Selous Scout commandos who had fought for the white minority in the Rhodesian bush war, military intelligence agents from the then Afrikaner-ruled South Africa, and Zimbabwean government ministers. The Selous Scouts had perfected the technique in the late 1970s. They would cordon off an area in the park, declare it off-limits to civilians, and move in on the elephant herds with automatic weapons. Trucks then moved the tusks across the border into South Africa, where the contact men were waiting to take them on to Johannesburg.

The 1989 slaughter in Gonarezhou, when between eight hundred and one thousand bull elephants and all of the two hundred black rhinos were killed, was known to local conservationists but consistently denied by Zimbabwean government officials. The park had been closed to tourists since 1986 because gangs of RENAMO (resistance-movement) guerrillas armed to the teeth were slipping over the border from neighboring Mozambique. This made it easier for the poaching syndicates to operate undisturbed. While officials turned a blind eye, the warden of the southern sector of Gonarezhou, a dedicated young man named Gordon Putterill, undertook an investigation on his own and came up with a list of people involved in the poaching, a syndicate that included senior National Parks officers and government ministers. In 1991, he handed the list and his evidence to a government commission of inquiry.

Far from welcoming Putterill's information and acting on it, the Zimbabwe government's officers mounted a campaign of harassment against him. He'd had to shoot an elephant in Gonarezhou after it had stepped on a land mine, and while his rangers were guarding the fallen animal, a group of poachers attacked, chased them off, and stole the tusks. An inquiry was conducted by the head of the National Parks' investigation branch, Graham Nott, and an astonished Putterill found himself accused of stealing the ivory. Soon after, while Putterill was on leave, Nott sent two of his men to interrogate Putterill's assistant, Salani Jack. They wanted him to change his statement and indict his boss, and in broad daylight, in government offices, they beat Salani Jack to within an inch of his life. Even so he would not betray Putterill.

Some months later, after Nott's department had conducted another investigation, Putterill was suspended without pay and accused of misusing German aid money and of illegally translocating elephants to a game park in South Africa. For knowing too much and saying too much, the young idealist was now plunged into Kafkaland. It mattered not that the German embassy official who had administered and overseen the aid package publicly stated that no irregularities had taken place and that all the money was accounted for. Neither did it matter that the elephant relocation operation was conducted with all the appropriate permits and government documentation. What mattered was that yet another highly skilled conservationist had been removed from Zimbabwe's National Parks Service.

Putterill was the latest in a long line of Zimbabwean conservationists who since independence in 1980 have been harassed and hassled by Graham Nott's department. In 1988, after twenty-four years of service, the legendary Clem Coetsee quit as warden of Hwange National Park, the country's biggest game reserve, when his staff warned him that Nott's people were out to get him. "I was always being investigated and accused of stupid things," he told me. "Then I was warned that they would find something to put me in jail, and I decided to pack it up. We all left because of harassment."

Nott's harassment of the parks staff was not confined to the worthy conservationists on the ground, however. In the early 1990s, he went after Zimbabwe's most famous wildlife official, Dr. Rowan Martin, dragging him through the courts for several years on charges of corruption. Dr. Martin, it seems, had accepted a Land Rover donated by the New York rhino-conservation group SAVE, a routine matter among Africa's financially beleaguered wildlife departments. The charges were thrown out of court.

Although Nott retired a few years ago, his malign legacy remains. There is a great deal of speculation about his motives, but everyone agrees that his actions were devastating. The removal of conservationists of the caliber of Putterill and Coetsee from the National

Parks system accelerated a collapse that was already in progress. In the space of a decade, what was once the finest wildlife department on the continent was reduced to an underfunded, ill-equipped, ill-disciplined shambles. And when the thin khaki line formed by Putterill, Coetsee, and their ilk was breached, even the optimistic standard-bearers of the African Position, the white Africans who had told the world to butt out and leave them to solve their problems the African way, found themselves fearing the worst.

They did not have to wait long for their misgivings to be realized. One winter's morning a group of white conservationists conducting a game count of Zimbabwe's flagship reserve, the fifty-six-hundred-square-mile Hwange National Park, discovered that only four of the forty-six diesel pumps installed to keep the water holes filled were functioning. As they drove from one dried-up water hole to the next, watching in horror as thousands of animals died of thirst around them, they realized that Hwange was on the cusp of becoming an extinct ecosystem.

"We had known there were problems," said Colin Gillies, local chairman of the privately funded Wildlife Society and leader of the group, "but we had no idea of the magnitude. It was terrible. The plains game—kudu, roan antelope, giraffe—would stand for hours in the queue and never get to the little water there was. We saw elephant stuck in the mud, too weak to get out and then finally collapsing and suffocating to death."

Gillies and his colleagues immediately called up local businesses and asked for help getting at least some of the pumps working again; in some cases they had simply run out of fuel. But so indifferent was the National Parks staff to the problem that the provincial warden at the time, one Claudius Hove, did not even know that the famous Nyamandhlovu Pan, only a few miles from his offices, had dried up.

The Zimbabwe government's commitment to nature conservation has, since independence, been all but nonexistent, and as the real value of the treasury's annual allocation has declined, the private sector has been forced to make ever larger contributions of money and expertise just to keep the national parks functioning.

Add this indifference at the government level to the cynical exploitation by the white destabilizers and get-rich-quick merchants,
the slick modus operandi of the crime syndicates, and the seemingly
insatiable appetite for ivory and rhino horn in the Far East, and you
can hear the clock ticking very loudly for Zimbabwe's wildlife. And
yet in the midst of all this chaos and destruction, there are beacons
of light, albeit scattered thinly across the sprawling bushveld: Clive
Stockil, for example, whose family settled here after World War II
and who grew up in Africa.

As we sat in the Land Rover and the sun went down over the
Save River that afternoon, Stockil began a dissertation that would
continue almost uninterrupted for two days. It was an infinitely detailed explanation of a conservation philosophy he has put into
practice here, in this ravaged corner of Zimbabwe's wilderness. We
would visit the conservancy in the morning, Stockil said, "and even
if I say it myself, this is the greatest conservation story to hit Africa.
It is the only project that is re-creating the elephant habitats, the
only area expanding its elephant habitat. That's elephant conservation. The bottom line. Survival in Africa has to be sustainable, and
unless it's sustainable, we're on a shortcut to disaster."

On cue, as we were driving back to the camp, we passed through
a heavy thicket and suddenly smelled elephant. With an expert eye
Stockil spotted their dark outlines in the half-light some fifty yards
away. We edged toward them gingerly, but they knew we were coming. At twenty yards the matriarch stirred and gracefully strode
across our path without a sideways look, signaling for the others to
follow. Ten more elephants emerged from the thick, tangled
bushveld, following her toward the river. The last, a young bull,
paused and gave us a halfhearted mock charge before trumpeting
off into the bushes.

That night around the Mahenya campfire, Stockil explained how
the Shangaans, the original inhabitants of this area, had for centuries lived among the wild animals and incorporated basic conservation principles into their tribal culture. Only a few were allowed
to hunt the animals, and the hunting campaigns were directed by
the chief, who distributed the spoils among his subjects. Their sur-

vival depended on the wildlife flourishing. Then, at the turn of the century, the white colonials changed all that by ruling that the wildlife belonged to the Crown. At the stroke of a pen, these people who had been living in perfect harmony with the wildlife were transformed into poachers.

With the coming of independence and black majority rule in 1980, the Shangaan expected their land to be returned to them. The government, however, demurred, explaining that the young country needed the foreign exchange from tourism and that tourists wanted to visit the national parks. The angry Shangaan concluded that if there were no animals, there would be no tourists, and if there were no tourists, then the government might as well give them their land back. So they went on a poaching campaign to rid their land of the animals they had once shared it with.

For a time in the early 1980s, this northern sector of Gonarezhou was a battle zone, with shooting wars between National Parks rangers and the fleet-footed Shangaan hunters and a trail of rhino and elephant carcasses scattered in their wake. Then, in February 1982, with the anarchy at a high point, Clive Stockil was called in to mediate between the Shangaan and the National Parks. He called a meeting, which was attended by seventy tribal elders, and he sat patiently under a Natal mahogany tree as they complained bitterly of their treatment at the hands of white and black governments. For the three hours, Stockil and the elders talked about their history and agreed that the Shangaan should be allowed to participate in the management of the wildlife again, that the wildlife would be returned to the people with whom it shared the land.

The Shangaan gave Stockil a mandate to negotiate a deal with the National Parks on their behalf, and he managed to wrestle an agreement out of some very skeptical government officials in Harare. The disputed area had been among the most heavily poached in the country, and they found it hard to believe that the belligerent Shangaan would suddenly start protecting the game they'd been killing. Stockil had no such doubts and organized an exercise that would illustrate to the local tribespeople the benefits of sustainable utilization. Two Americans were invited on an elephant-hunting sa-

fari and duly bagged their two bulls. The tribeswomen, who traditionally provide the food for the community, were invited to take
part in the skinning and cutting up of the animals, and Stockil later
arrived with a briefcase full of cash, the community's share of the
trophy-hunting fees. Each villager was handed a small pile of notes,
and then, one by one, they handed back a small percentage, which
would go into a fund for building a school.

Now, a decade later, the school is flourishing, attended by some
forty children from the surrounding area; a grinding mill has been
built, and another is planned; construction has begun on a model
village that will accommodate small groups of foreign visitors; and
poaching is almost nonexistent. With the revenues from upmarket
foreign tourists expected to fly into this smart new camp at Mahenya, the community is very optimistic about the future.

"This community has the potential over the next five years to
start generating a million dollars annually," Stockil was saying as the
last flames flickered in the campfire. He had been complaining
about Western conservation organizations failing to understand the
needs of the African people and refusing to accept that projects like
Mahenya Campfire depend on the management of wilderness resources, management that entails shooting animals. "We have a big
job to do, but we have no alternative. And the wildlife has to pay its
way. We must not be distracted by emotion. For example, we have
forced elephants into confined areas and stood by watching as they
ate themselves out of house and home, then died of starvation. We
have to get into managing habitats. Let's look at the survival of the
species, not at the individual animals."

To an outsider, Stockil may sound somewhat unsentimental
about the animals he professes to protect, but this is a misconcep-
tion. He told one story of an encounter with elephants that, for all
his years in the bush in the company of animals, left him breathless.
It happened at the end of a three-month elephant relocation operation in which four hundred animals were released in Stockil's
SAVE Conservancy some fifty miles northwest of the Mahenya
camp. The last two trucks, carrying eleven elephants between them,
arrived at the release pens in midafternoon after a six-hour drive.

Some American visitors had flown in to watch the release, and Stockil wanted to impress them with a smooth and efficient exercise—good PR, he thought.

The trucks backed up to the stockade, and slowly nine of the animals disembarked, leaving a reluctant mother and calf in one truck. For two hours Stockil and his frustrated staffers prodded and cajoled the pair, but they would not budge. "Suddenly a big bull elephant emerged from the bushes and began walking toward the truck. I recognized him as one we had translocated three months before. He stopped at the gate and began that low rumbling noise. Within five minutes the mother and calf had moved into the stockade with the other nine."

The bull moved off, but the disoriented, nervous elephants wouldn't make the final move from the stockade to freedom and followed one another round in circles like sheep. Stockil sent the vehicles and the workers away, hoping the bull would return, and as silence descended, he appeared again out of the bushes. This time he pushed almost his entire body through the stockade gate, leaving one massive foot firmly planted in the wild, then wrapped his trunk around the nearest female and pulled her to the exit. Once out, he led her away from the stockade and stood beside her for a while, patting her down reassuringly with his trunk.

"You could actually see her gradually relaxing. And when she was calm, he went back to the stockade, climbed right in, and went through a greeting ritual, starting with the matriarch. All this time there was the low rumbling sound. He began pushing them toward the exit, and one by one they came out and joined the waiting female. When they were all gathered, the matriarch led them away. The bull was the last to leave, and as he did, he turned toward us, flapped his ears, bellowed, and shook his trunk at us, as if to say, 'Well, that's taken care of, then.'

"We were dumbfounded," said Stockil.

We stared at the stars for a bit after he'd finished the story. The Southern Cross had come up, Orion's Belt glistened brightly against an inky backdrop, and a luminous moon threw a soft light over the canopy of Natal mahogany trees set back from the riverbank. Conversation seemed unnecessary. Clive Stockil was right when he said that this was the greatest conservation story to hit Africa. The problem, of course, was that hardly anybody had been listening.

After Stockil and the others shambled off to their thatched huts, I sat alone for a while, listening to the barks and grunts and calls of the animals across the river in the park and staring fixedly at the gray embers of the fire. I wanted the good men to prevail—the Stockils, Putterills, and Coetsees—but I found it hard to believe they would. Theirs may be the only sensible course to follow, but there are too many forces working against them, too many agendas being proffered, too much greed and corruption washing over them. As I wandered glumly back to my thatched hut, I thought that the dedicated southern African wildlife conservationist, like the wild animals he is protecting, is fast becoming an endangered species.

A WEEK LATER I FOUND MYSELF STARING OUT ON ANOTHER OF Africa's wilderness areas, this time under a full moon on a calm and clear night. The Hluhluwe-Umfolozi Park is 750 miles south of Mahenya, cradled between the foothills of the Drakensberg Mountains and the ragged Zululand coastline. This park, according to the conservationists, police investigators, and informants I had been talking to, was to be the next target of the rhino poachers.

Under the heavy cloak of acacia trees, some two thousand rhinos were browsing and grazing, the last wild population left. I peered into the darkness, looking for a flash of light and listening for an echoed report that would confirm that poachers were in the park. I saw nothing, but I knew that shadowy figures were out there, running crouched through the tangled thickets, closing in on their prey, raising their weapons to their shoulders and leveling their sights at the spot just below and behind the huge animals' ears, the site of their tennis-ball-sized brain.

The undercover investigations of poaching in the Natal parks was headed by a somewhat melodramatically secretive man named Simon Pillinger, whose skill in running a network of agents and informers had contributed greatly to Natal's enviably low poaching statistics. Pillinger knew who the main smugglers were—he repeated the five or six names I had been hearing but would do so only off the record—and conceded that the Natal parks were without doubt the next target of the rhino poachers. "There are a lot of weapons in the area, there is widespread unemployment, rhino are very easy to kill, and we have a lot of them."

Unlike the national parks in Zimbabwe and most other African countries to the north, Hluhluwe-Umfolozi and the other Natal reserves were extremely well funded and extremely well run. The parks had an annual operating budget of one hundred million rand (twenty-two thousand dollars), half of which came from revenues earned from tourism and sales of game and curios. Dr. George Hughes, the head of the Natal Parks Board, told me that more money was spent here than in any other wildlife conservancy in the world. "Two hundred dollars per square kilometer is the accepted standard; we spend eight hundred dollars," he said triumphantly.

The Natal park system was one of the few unqualified successes in Africa, a controlled, well-managed group of more than sixty protected areas from the Drakensberg Mountains to the Zululand coast. The Hluhluwe and Umfolozi reserves were designated protected areas in 1897, making them the oldest in Africa, and at the time there were no more than fifty white rhino in the area. With careful management the population grew slowly until it numbered three hundred in 1962, after which it exploded. In the thirty years that followed, Natal exported more than four thousand white rhino to game reserves, zoos, and private reserves throughout the world, some as gifts but most for hard cash. Sales of live rhino continue to bring in 3.5 million rand ($800,000) a year, and with the population growing at the rate of one hundred a year in good years, this steady income should roll in ad infinitum.

The other—more controversial—source of revenue lay in a series of secret vaults scattered through the province. In those vaults were an estimated six hundred rhino horns, collected over the years from animals that had been poached and from those that had died natural deaths and were worth anywhere from twenty million to thirty million rand. It was said that only one man, Dr. George Hughes, knew where all the horns were stored—he refused to comment on the matter. Hughes and his Natal Parks colleagues wanted to put these horns on the market, arguing that the revenue would help protect living animals, but the rhino's status as an Appendix I protected species forbade the trading of its horn.

There had been a growing call to farm rhino as one does cattle. The proponents of this plan argued that the demand for rhino horn would cease only when there was none left and that it was logical to satisfy the demand in an orderly, controlled manner by creating viable herds large enough to sustain culling.

On my last day at Hluhluwe, I visited the translocation pens on the edge of the wilderness area in southern Umfolozi. It was too early in the year for the main capture operation, and there was only one rhino in the compound, a huge white female that was waiting to be tranquilized and moved to a European zoo. I stood beside the stockade for a while and then gingerly extended my hand between the wooden poles and began scratching the rhino behind her ear. She raised her massive, prehistoric head toward me and cocked her ear, and I swear if rhinos could purr, she would have purred. My instinct to get closer was suppressed only by the sight of her outsize horns and the vivid memory of a film clip that showed the Kenyan hunter-artist Terry Mathews being sliced open by a charging rhino in the Nairobi National Park. The beast had hit the retreating Mathews at around thirty miles an hour and with a startlingly economic upward flick of its head had thrown him into the air like a rag doll. The horn had cut him open from his thigh up through to his chest.

So I backed off. It was enough just to gawp at this exquisitely designed animal, its formidable appearance little changed in the million and a half years it has roamed the planet. In nature, design perfection is measured by the longevity of the species, and until *Homo sapiens* arrived with his shooting sticks in the last century, the species *Diceros bicornis* was about as successful as you could get.

I turned away from the rhino's gaze and felt ashamed.

• • •

AFTER HAVING SPENT SOME TIME IN THE CALM BEAUTY OF HLU-
hluwe, Johannesburg seemed like Gomorrah, a gathering place for
all the hustlers, dealers, and smugglers operating on the African
continent. If there was a fast buck to be made, then this was the
place to make it, and the ivory and rhino-horn operators were in
here with the gem smugglers and drug traffickers and counterfeit-
currency hoods.

Colonel Lategan said that to give me an idea of how widespread
the ivory and horn trade was, he wanted me to meet a recently recruited informer. Back at Vlakplaas again he introduced me to Hendrik, a minister in the Zion Christian Church, the largest black
church in South Africa. Hendrik was a jovial, perspiring man in his
early fifties, and he explained that he was at Vlakplaas because he'd
been arrested in Johannesburg attempting to sell a rhino horn, and
in exchange for the leniency of the court he had turned informer.
He had been involved in the illegal wildlife trade since 1969, operating in Namibia, Zambia, Botswana, Zimbabwe, and of course
South Africa. In Zambia, he said, you could buy a rhino horn for a
case of .375-millimeter bullets, because the poachers couldn't get
their hands on ammunition: "In Zimbabwe it is more expensive,
maybe four thousand rand [$1,150] for five-kilo horn." The price
in South Africa was ten thousand rand ($2,900) and, in the Far
East, ten times that.

He said he could introduce me to a woman in Messina, a small
northern Transvaal town, who would take me straight to a rhino-
horn dealer in Mutare, across the Zimbabwe border. And he admitted with a smile that he had contacts in most of the game parks,
in Zimbabwe, in Botswana, even in Natal, but he had been shot "in
the political troubles." It was a Damascene revelation, helped on no
doubt by the threat of a jail sentence, that changed his mind about
aiding and abetting the plunder of game. He had come to understand the value of wildlife, he explained, and then, wringing his
hands and offering a sly sideways grin, he said, "For money's sake
you always fall into temptation, especially when you are a Christian."

This certainly appeared to be a common failing among African church people, for soon after my meeting with the Zionist minister I found myself leafing through a document headed *"Association pour l'unification du christianisme mondial,"* which detailed a smuggling operation that ran from Zaire through Zambia to South Africa. Colonel Lategan's men had arrested six members of the AUCM with 250 pounds of carved ivory. Then they'd swooped down on an apartment in the Johannesburg suburb of Hillbrow and picked up an AUCM minister, Joseph Mbayi, who was in possession of five hundred carved ivory blocks.

A further raid on the Hillbrow apartment had netted another clergyman, Pastor Bosco Murayire from Zambia, and a pile of documents linking the AUCM in Zaire with the smuggling network. Pastor Mbayi escaped from prison and has not been seen since, but Pastor Murayire eventually appeared in court and admitted that the smuggling operation "was part of a fund-raising campaign for the church." He had a detailed ledger recording each transaction and a contact book listing a network of connections from Nigeria and Zaire through to Japan and Korea. The judge took pity on the contrite and ailing Pastor Mbayi and fined him three thousand rand ($880), but stiff jail sentences were handed down to his accomplices, one man getting six years in prison.

Colonel Lategan laughed when I expressed dismay at discovering that even the church was partaking of the rape of the continent. The corrupt government ministers I understood, so too the old white security establishment, the ex–Selous Scouts, the organized-crime syndicates—but the church? "This is Africa," he said. "It's tough. People do what they can to survive."

Lategan insisted that the trade would go on as long as there was demand for ivory and rhino horn in the Far East, which meant forever. The bans on the trade and the animals' listings by international forums as endangered species had done little to stop it thus far. "In the last EIA report they said there was no elephant poaching as a result of the ban. It's a lie; there is still a lot of poaching. They say the ivory price has collapsed, but how do they know the black market price? We don't even know. One guy wants one thousand rand a kilo and another wants ten rand. There is a trade. There is demand. That is the story."

Like most southern Africans, Lategan favored a return to legal trade in wildlife products. "I don't think the elephant is endangered," he said. "If we could use the money from ivory to protect species that are really endangered—beetles, pythons, birds, cycads—then we would be getting somewhere."

The colonel had one more thing to say: "When you go back to America, ask some of those people who've been criticizing us to come out on a small operation. Then if they don't wet their pants, we'll take them on a big one."

SHOULD THE IVORY BAN BE LIFTED? SHOULD THE FENCES COME down and the wildlife cohabit the land with people and cattle? Would breeding farms save the rhino as they have that other prehistoric survivor, the crocodile? If these wildlife habitats and their occupants are the treasures of all mankind, would it not be appropriate for the international community to take responsibility for their protection before it is too late?

I listened to the disparate views of the Western conservationists with growing impatience. It was not that I doubted their sincerity or their commitment to their cause, nor indeed their broad understanding of the issues at hand. It was that, without exception, their views seemed to patronize Africans. One Zimbabwean conservationist's ideas were dismissed because the man was allegedly a serial adulterer, and a prominent Kenyan was villified as a money launderer and "one of the biggest thieves in Africa." Everyone else's positions on the big issues were suspect because most of them were on the take. Every name I mentioned—every African game warden, biologist, conservationist, investigator, fund-raiser—was greeted with skepticism and contempt.

Then one afternoon I received a telephone call from a conservationist in Natal. He told me that the wardens at the Hluhluwe-Umfolozi Park had just admitted that they were now losing a rhino to poachers every seventeen days. There, in a single sentence, lay the cold, hard truth. The dark forces were indeed gathering around the borders of Africa's last wild rhino sanctuary. One rhino kill every seventeen days was three times the previous year's rate, and pretty soon it would be one every ten days. There were some twenty-five hundred rhino in the area, and a quick calculation, even assuming a modest exponential growth of poaching, suggested they would be gone by the end of the decade. And once the rhino was gone, then the cheetah, the African wild dog, the silver-backed jackal, even one day the African elephant, would be gone.

Of all the acts of destruction the white man's colonization has visited upon this blighted continent, this must surely be among the most devastating. When we arrived, there was abundance and variety beyond our blinkered European imaginings, a riot of extravagance and exotica that nature had created in another, distant age. Then, just as we had laid waste Europe and most of North America, so we set about this place, blithely, ignorantly trampling it into the dust. Now we find ourselves poised to extinguish the last scattered outposts of wild Africa and to render its animals extinct.

I had set out believing that good men like Stockil and Putterill and Lategan would prevail and had ended up an environmental atheist, a nonbeliever. I'd even honed my nonfaith to an aphorism: If the poachers don't get the animals, then the black population, upon whom we have bestowed "culture," "civilization," and inordinate longevity, will surely outbreed them and crowd them into extinction.

While I had been out in the bushveld, South Africa had been negotiating itself toward elections that would wrest power from the last white tribe, the Afrikaners. In the comparatively sane world of people's politics, one was under no illusions about the men spouting rhetoric and making promises on public platforms. Nobody expected them to tell the truth. One didn't expect idealism or integrity. This was about cutting the best deal you could.

THIRTEEN

The Search for the Man in a Brown Suit

Afrikaners have a word for the English-speakers who live in Africa. The word is *soutpiel,* and literally translated it means "salt penis." They say that the English have one foot in Europe, the other in Africa, and their genitalia hang in the ocean.

It is a most appropriate epithet. The British, like the other European colonials—the French, the Portuguese, the Belgians—had always been somewhat disconnected, somehow a step removed from the heat and dust of the African drama. They came to Africa as empire builders and profiteers, and they had motherlands to go back to when things got rough. In the '60s, the Congo refugees fled to Belgium; in the '70s, tens of thousands of Rhodesians resettled in Britain and its more stable colonies; and in the '80s and '90s, more than 1.5 million white South Africans held foreign passports and were also ready to run.

For the Afrikaners, Africa was the final destination. For almost 350 years, they had forged their culture and beliefs in a harsh landscape, and they had learned quite early on that to survive, they had to adhere to the first law of frontier society: you keep your heel firmly on your enemy's neck, or he will rise up and consume you.

At the height of Afrikaner power—in the '60s and '70s—most *soutpiels* saw them as a fierce, impenetrable force, a nation that would keep its grip on government whatever the cost. Conversely, most Afrikaners perceived the *soutpiels* as corrupt opportunists who happily rode on the coattails of apartheid, making wishy-washy liberal noises about equality and integration while they stuffed their profits into foreign bank accounts. The *soutpiels* could not be relied upon to stand by the Boer when the crunch came.

This kind of skepticism is in every Boer's blood. I remember a day in 1989 I spent with Jan Boland Coetzee, the famous Springbok rugby player and now equally famous wine maker, just before Mandela was released from Pollsmoer Prison. I remember it because as hospitable and friendly and generous as Jan Boland was that day, I left feeling that there was an intractable gulf between us, that all we had in common was an accident of pigmentation. I had visited his Stellenbosch farm with an English wine writer to talk about wine and also to find out about a labor scheme Coetzee had devised that sounded suspiciously socialist. When he greeted us, he was polite, but I could see what he was thinking—What do these pink Engelsmanne want with me? He was too honest a man to conceal it.

Coetzee looked and sounded like a Boer should. A descendant of Huguenots who landed on the Cape in the seventeenth and eighteenth centuries, he spoke with what is called a Malmesbury bray, a gutteral flattening of the *r* that has its roots in the French language. He is six feet tall and built like a brick outhouse. He wore tight khaki shorts from which bulged the muscular legs of one of rugby's great flank forwards, a short-sleeved shirt that revealed forearms the size of most people's thighs, and regulation khaki socks and veldschoens. A graduate of Stellenbosch University, the cradle of Afrikaner intellectual culture, a Springbok, and now a wine maker, Coetzee was a true hero of the *volk*.

Coetzee took the two pink Engelsmanne on a tour of his estate, proudly describing how he was applying to the African soil the knowledge he had gleaned from two years at the feet of the great vintners of Burgundy and patiently explaining along the way the profit-sharing scheme he had set up for his Coloured workers. By the time we had returned to the cellars, my companion was talking

Jan Boland Coetzee, South African rugby hero and
celebrated winemaker.

about "malolactic fermentation" and "maceration *carbonique*," and Coetzee started bringing out some of his good wines for us to taste.

We spent the afternoon sitting at an old oak table in the cool darkness of his cellar talking wine making and politics, and as time passed, Coetzee loosened up a little. He told us he was a reformist and had hitched his colors to a breakaway movement in the Nationalist Party that felt that President Botha, de Klerk's predecessor, was moving too slowly. He didn't know where the country was going, but he did know the blacks had to have a say in it.

Then Coetzee sighed. For a moment the skepticism left his face and was replaced by a look of uncertainty. "We are on our own, you know. The Afrikaner and the Afrikaner alone will have to solve this problem. No one else can help us. We must change, but if it doesn't work out and we have to fight, then we will fight." Then he said gravely, "And believe me, we can fucking fight."

I made some asinine remark about let's hope it doesn't come to that, and he looked at me, and again I could see what he was thinking, What does this *soutpiel* know about any of this? And what does he care?

Melancholy and mistrust. The cornerstones of the Boer psyche. It was in their religion, it permeated their literature; the somber Boer monuments reflect it. That day in Stellenbosch, I was reminded that the Afrikaners really are an African tribe, like the Zulus and the Xhosas. Their ancestors had set them on their course in another age, and unlike the feckless, rootless *soutpiels,* they were destined to play it out in Africa among the other tribes.

The early Boers were an odd mix of French Huguenot, Dutch Calvinist, and German outcast, religious dissidents who left Europe before the Enlightenment. They were not cold, stoic Calvinists but fiery and emotional people prone to fighting among themselves. The deep and bitter divisions that tore the Afrikaner tribe apart right up to the very end can be ascribed in part to the strong influence of Scottish pietism on the early Boers.

Through the nineteenth century the Boers trekked away from the *soutpiels* and the long arm of British imperial rule. Endless ox-wagon trains trudged into the interior, through uncharted bushveld at a mile an hour, to establish Boer republics anywhere the British weren't. Along the way they fought heroic battles against the Zulus and two terrible wars against the British army and established a tribal mythology built on the heroes and martyrs of these wars.

While British colonial historians were celebrating explorers like Frederick Selous and David Livingstone and empire builders like Cecil Rhodes, Boer history was filled with generals, war heroes, and martyrs who had fallen along their freedom road. Among their martyrs are the twenty-six thousand Boer women and children who died in British concentration camps during the Second Boer War, from 1900 to 1902. It is said that an Englishman cannot understand South African history until he has seen the Vrouemonument outside Bloemfontein, the shrine to these women and children. At the base of the monument, sculpted in stone by Anton Van Wouw, is a scene depicting life and death inside a concentration camp. Above a tableau of two little Boer children watching their mother die are written the words *Ik zal u niet begeven, Ik zal u niet verlaten,* "I shall not fail thee, I shall not forsake thee." That is the promise the descendants of the Afrikaners who fought in the Boer War solemnly swore to keep.

After the British won the war in 1902, they set about containing and subjugating the Afrikaners. Under the British high commissioner, Lord Milner, English was made the country's official language (even though Afrikaners outnumbered the British), and British immigration was encouraged. "If ten years hence," Milner said, "there are three men of British race and two of Dutch, the country will be safe. If there are three of Dutch and two of British, we shall have perpetual difficulty."

Far from containing the Boers, Milner's Anglicization policy stiffened their resolve. They were dirt-poor, on the fringes of white society and white business, but they were fiercely proud of their culture and not about to give it all up and become quasi-British. They started their own Afrikaans-language schools founded on the rock of "Christian-National education," and they formed the Broederbond, a secret society that would eventually guide the Afrikaner people to power. Central to all of this was the Dutch Reformed

Church, which, like the German Christian churches that supported Hitler, was strongly influenced by the early-nineteenth-century German theologian Friedrich Schleiermacher.

It was the Federal Mission Council, the missionary arm of the Dutch Reformed Church, that was at the forefront of the move to introduce apartheid. In 1942, the council's leaders approached the South African prime minister, Jan Smuts, with a prototype apartheid plan and told him it was the only Christian policy to pursue. General Smuts, a religious man but not a churchgoer, thanked them for their views and then said, "It is not for me to tell you as churchmen that apartheid will not be the final solution to the human problem of this country."

Smuts, of course, was a traitor to the hard-line Afrikaners. He was an empire loyalist, an international statesman who wanted South Africa to take its place among the great Western nations. The hard-liners, many of whom had been jailed during World War II for refusing to fight alongside the British against Hitler, wanted isolation and ethnic purity. But Smuts was one of many traitors, a long line of Judases that led all the way through to F. W. de Klerk, now perceived as the greatest traitor of them all.

While most of South Africa's three million Afrikaners finally accepted the inevitability of black majority rule, a vociferous minority stood back, unable to reconcile it with their religion, their culture, their history. Some said that God would stop the election from taking place in 1994; others foretold a civil war that would win for the Boers a *volkstaat*, or homeland. A man called Jannie told me in a bush bar one night that there was nothing to worry about, that it had all been prophesied by his forefathers: very soon the savior of the Boers would rise up from within the Afrikaner community. No foreign governments. No United Nations missions. No Vance-Owen or Kissinger-Carrington peacekeeping sortie. No *soutpiels*. A Boer would sort it all out.

Jannie told me about a Boer at the turn of the century named Nicolaas "Siener" van Rensburg. *Siener* means "seer," and he was a man who had strange visions, many of which even he did not understand. A close friend and adviser to the legendary Afrikaner generals Koos De la Rey and Jan Kemp, Siener performed as a kind of Boer witch doctor on the battlefield, his dreams and hallucinations guiding the tactics of the generals and the movements of the troops. When Siener said he had seen a sea of army blankets rising in the west, the soldiers marched westward; once when he dreamed of the Boers' escaping across a particular spot on the Orange River, General Kemp led his men there, successfully crossed the flooded river, then watched as the pursuing enemy soldiers were consumed by raging waters. Siener had even foreseen the death of his friend De la Rey, shot down by government troops who mistook him for a member of a notorious criminal outfit, the Forster gang.

Siener's visions were at their most vivid and their most powerful when they portrayed the final destiny of his people. He saw a black snake crawling down from the north and engaging the Boers in an epic battle in the Transvaal. He said there would be a massive drought, and when the fields turned white and the yellow cling peaches opened, the final onslaught would begin. And he said that a Boer with a white beard and a brown suit would lead the people to victory and to everlasting peace in their own land. Siener said this would happen at a time when all seemed lost for the Boer. "So you see," said Jannie, "everything will be fine."

It was unusual to find an optimistic Afrikaner. Most were engulfed in melancholy, as if the weight of all the martyrs, all the humiliations at the hands of the British, the leaden quality of their religion, and now the loss of political power were pressing down on them. I wondered how the Boer *bittereinders* were going to handle the final reversal of fortune, the apparent snub from the God they had made a pact with 150 years ago. My people—the British colonials—had always taken for granted that the Afrikaners would fight rather than submit to black rule. But even the Boers could not stop Africa from being reclaimed by its own.

FOURTEEN

The Hawk, the Dove, and
the Designer Boer

Early in March 1994, General Constand Viljoen stood ramrod straight on a podium, his pale blue eyes staring out on ten thousand Afrikaners who had assembled before him. "God helped us at Blood River," he intoned. "Having God on our side, we can face any enemy. Nothing can stand between the Afrikaner and freedom."

South Africa was at that moment only a few weeks away from its first democratic elections, and freedom for General Viljoen and his audience meant one thing—a *volkstaat,* a people's state, a white homeland where the Afrikaners could govern themselves. This was their demand to Mandela, de Klerk, and the other reformists. Anything less, they said, and they would declare war.

Although the general was being hailed as the Afrikaners' new messiah and the Vaclav Havel of the white right, he was clearly not Siener van Rensburg's man in a brown suit who would lead his people to victory. For in spite of his ringing words about facing the enemy, he had been drawn into negotiations with the government and the ANC, and he was beginning to see virtue in compromise.

General Viljoen had retired as the head of the South African Defence Force in the mid-1980s and was happily running his farm in the northern Transvaal when the call came to lead his people. Their

General Constand Viljoen and his wife, Risti, at an Afrikaner rally in
Pretoria just before the 1994 elections.

country was about to be swallowed up by the Communists, and they needed someone to take them through the darkness to the other side. Who better than this model Boer: deeply religious, a heroic military leader in the image of Christiaan de Wet and Koos De la Rey—calm, intelligent, a strategist, a man of the *volk*. And so early in 1993, he was elected head of the Afrikaner Volksfront.

Viljoen's AVF—an umbrella organization for the seventy or eighty disparate groups that made up the white right—claimed to represent some two million people, and the government and the ANC immediately lured him into talks. The general demanded that an Afrikaner state be declared before the April election, and they said that if he brought the AVF into the election, they would be able to prove the extent of their support, and a *volkstaat* would be negotiated with the new government. The negotiations had been dragging on for months and seemed to be going nowhere.

Now General Viljoen had come back to his people for a mandate, but as he stared out from the podium, he realized how difficult it would be to get them to agree on anything. He saw row after row of uniformed Afrikaner Resistance Movement (AWB) commandos snorting and pawing at the ground; he saw church leaders, farmers, businessmen in suits with their families, university professors, members of parliament; and more than anything else he saw fear and confusion in every corner of the hall. He told them that if they wanted a *volkstaat* by election day, they would have to take it by force. The second option would be to go into the election and prove that the AVF was a meaningful political force. "Now you must indicate to me whether you are prepared to walk the path of violence," he said.

The response was deafening. Urged on by the AWB commandos in the front rows, the crowd began chanting, "Now. Now. Now." "We have links with Germany," shouted one. "We can call people up from there." Then a huge bearded Afrikaner in camouflage gear—a man I later discovered was Alwyn Wolfaardt from Naboomspruit—began yelling "Traitor!" at the general.

A scuffle broke out beside the podium as a group of uniformed Boere Kommandos seized a press photographer and ripped the film from his camera. A black reporter from *The Washington Post* was hustled out of the building by armed Boers, and some women shouted after him, "Go tell your newspaper we don't want any kaffirs in here."

Meanwhile the general was trying to make himself heard above the chaos. He implored his audience to consider very carefully the option of violence, "for it is a terrible choice to have to make." Now the AWB commandos were chanting "Coup d'état! Coup d'état," and the general flinched.

More scuffles were breaking out, more shouts of war, more chaos, and the general stepped down from the podium with a look of weary resignation and walked slowly across to his seat. His wife, Risti, who had not moved during the pandemonium, patted his hand. He looked up at her and saw she had begun to cry.

A burly figure dressed in a snappy camouflage outfit and wearing a matching peaked cap took the microphone. This was Eugene Terre Blanche, leader of the AWB. He was South Africa's most vocal advocate of an armed uprising. In a thundering speech Terre Blanche evoked the spirits of past Boer heroes who had fought the British and the Zulus through the centuries for their place under the African sun. He spoke of Afrikaner bodies spread over the bushveld like a shroud and once again evoked the bitter memory of the twenty-six thousand women and children who died in the British concentration camps. He said his people were not prepared to take part in elections where "the ANC is counting the heads of Boers. We are on our way to our own free republic, the new republic, the third republic, the Boer Republic—God's Promised Land."

With that the fifteen thousand Boers stood at attention and, with hands on hearts, began singing "Kent Gij dat Volk?" "Do You Know the People," the plaintive, doom-laden national anthem of the old Transvaal Boer republic, taken from the hymn the Russian Decembrists sang on their march to Siberia in 1825.

SOME SIXTY MILES AWAY, IN RUST DER WINTER, GENERAL CONstand Viljoen's twin brother, Braam, was attending to farm business and taking a day off from the political maelstrom. He looked a little more road worn than his brother—the face more lined, the hair longer and shaggier, the stance less upright, the clothes more rumpled. He was a retired professor of theology and an active supporter of the liberalization process. He said he would be voting for the ANC.

Braam Viljoen's opposition to the apartheid system had, over the years, driven him into head-on conflict with the government. His links with an anti-homelands underground organization in the mid-1980s led to a warrant for his arrest, and years later he discovered that his name had been on the same death-squad hit list as that of David Webster, the Johannesburg academic assassinated in May 1989. It was his work with the homelands' War Against Independence campaign that first brought him to politics and made him realize just how untrustworthy and underhanded the government really was.

In the eyes of the Afrikaners assembled at the Pretoria rally, Braam Viljoen was a traitor, but to the majority of South Africans he represented conciliation and hope for the future. After several years as head of the Northern Transvaal Peace Commission, he had started the Conservative Dialogue Project, a group dedicated to bringing nervous conservatives into the fold. Although adamantly against the idea of an Afrikaner *volkstaat,* he brokered the first secret meetings in September 1993 between his brother and the ANC.

There was something rather Zen-like about Braam Viljoen, a calm quality shared with his twin. One could easily see why soldiers wouldn't hesitate to go to war with the general and why friends and associates of the academic twin revered him for his rational intellect. Until recently Braam had seen his brother rarely, and although they always got along, they seldom discussed politics. "We talked about farming and our families," he said. "Constand wasn't interested in politics." He was surprised when the general was declared leader of the Volksfront, but in the months that followed, their paths began to cross with some frequency. The secret meetings he brokered

Professor Braam Viljoen, the general's twin.

were a breakthrough for both sides. "The exposure the ANC and the Volksfront had to one another during those meetings generated a lot of mutual respect," he said.

Deep divisions have plagued the Afrikaners throughout their history. By the end of the Boer War, more than a fifth of the Afrikaner fighting force had changed sides and joined the British army. Piet de Wet, brother of the great Boer general Christiaan de Wet, was a *hensopper,* "hands upper," and turned sides in 1901. Another Boer hero, and the country's first Nationalist prime minister, Barry Hertzog, was horrified when his son became a pro-Nazi Purified Nationalist in the late 1930s. More recently, the Breytenbach brothers—Breyten, the poet and artist who served seven years in a South African jail for revolutionary activities, and Jan, who was the colonel responsible for creating the army's feared special units—have maintained the tradition. Most dramatically, the grandson of Hendrik Verwoerd, the architect of apartheid, had joined the ANC, and his wife was standing for parliament on an ANC ticket.

The Viljoen brothers were born in 1933 in the eastern Transvaal at a time of great hardship for Afrikaners. Their father was a farmer and their mother a teacher; their upbringing was strict and austere. They were Smuts Afrikaners, supporters of the great statesman's more liberal policies. The boys were fifteen in 1948, when the Afrikaner National Party finally defeated Smuts's party, and soon after, their lives took diametrically opposed courses. Constand joined the military and rose rapidly through the ranks to become head of the South African Defence Force in 1980. Braam studied philosophy and theology, traveled widely, lectured, farmed on the side, and became involved in liberal politics.

The general was a soldier's soldier, a true and honest man who led his troops into battle with, some say, reckless bravery. On several occasions during the civil war in Angola, he parachuted into the heart of the battle to direct operations. This was at the time when the Cubans were in Angola, and the general's army, with a covert nod from South Africa's Western allies, was fighting for Jonas Savimbi's wanna-be capitalists against José Dos Santos's Marxist government. The Rhodesians had just lost their war, and another

Marxist, Robert Mugabe, was in power there; on South Africa's eastern border, Mozambique was being run into the ground by Samora Machel's beleaguered socialist government, and a civil war was tearing that country apart. The "total onslaught," the final overwhelming attack on Afrikaner values by the forces of communism, seemed imminent.

Avowedly apolitical though he was, the general became increasingly aware that unless the South African government abandoned apartheid, the liberation war would go on forever. As early as 1969, he sat down on the banks of the Zambezi River with three prominent Nationalist members of parliament and told them they had to find a political solution to the country's problems. "I said we can carry on fighting indefinitely, but we can never win," the general remembered. "I suggested we form a federation of states based on the Swiss canton system. They said I was talking heresy. Today they would give half of what they own for that solution."

When the general retired to his farm in the northeastern Transvaal in 1985, South Africa's political problems were in an even more parlous state. The Soweto uprising of 1976 had changed everything, giving young black people confidence. Civil disobedience, sabotage, mass strike actions—the revolution was under way. While the general despaired on his cattle farm, his twin was becoming increasingly involved in prodding the country toward a negotiated solution. In July 1987, he flew to Dakar with fifty influential Afrikaner "rebels" to meet the then banned ANC. The trip was condemned by the government and cries of "traitors" once more resounded through the conservative Afrikaner movement.

It was a nervous, tentative meeting, the first time the Afrikaners had had serious talks with the opposition in exile. But like many of his fellow delegates, Braam came away with changed perceptions about the quality of the ANC leaders and their seriousness about finding a solution to South Africa's problems.

When the returning rebels landed at Johannesburg's Jan Smuts Airport, they were greeted with a ferocious demonstration by Terre Blanche's AWB. They were ushered through a side entrance, Braam remembered, "and as we moved into the hall, there were all sorts of big shots—generals and brigadiers—waiting. They thought I was the general, and they gave me VIP treatment—it was the only time I didn't correct them." He said he still wondered what these military men made of their general going off to Dakar with traitors.

By the time F. W. de Klerk became president, in 1989, dialogue with the ANC was frequent and out in the open, and with the freeing of Mandela and his fellow political detainees and the lifting of bans on all political parties, the country began rumbling toward democracy. An enormous negotiating chamber was set up in Johannesburg at the World Trade Centre, a squat and unattractive conference complex next to the airport, and delegations from most of South Africa's political interest groups gathered to argue over the constitution for the new South Africa. Four groups boycotted the constitutional talks—representatives from Lucas Mangope's corrupt Bophuthatswana homeland, representatives of the Ciskei homeland, Chief Gatcha Buthelezi's Zulu Inkatha Freedom Party, and the white right represented by the Conservative Party.

Terrible altercations occurred in the townships between Buthelezi's Inkatha members and the ANC comrades, leaving more than three thousand dead; politically motivated attacks on church gatherings and crowded pubs and a spate of bombings sent shivers down the spines of the middle classes, both black and white; and murderous attacks on farmers and their families in the northern Transvaal had Afrikaners reaching for their weapons. Then, on April 10, 1993, Chris Hani, the head of Umkhonto we Sizwe (Spear of the Nation), the ANC's guerrilla movement, was assassinated, and the tension rose a few more notches. Hani was second only to Nelson Mandela in popularity and had a big following among the radical youth of the townships. There were fears of mass reprisals against whites, fears that were stoked by black youths chanting "Kill the Boer, kill the farmer" on national television. Even by South African standards, the country was a tinderbox.

It was in this hothouse of passion and fear that the Afrikaner right finally found its leader. On Tuesday, April 20, a group of retired generals gathered in Pretoria to watch the television broadcast of Hani's funeral. What the military men saw was an outpouring of grief and anger and a terrible potential for violent reaction. What they imagined was a tide of black anarchy finally overwhelming the whites. They needed to unite the fragmented Afrikaners and make a case for an independent Boer state, away from all this madness. That evening the generals formed the Afrikaner Volksfront, and they chose as their leader and spokesman the most reluctant general of all, Constand Viljoen.

"I SUPPOSE BRAAM GOT THE BRAINS AND I GOT THE BRUTE FORCE and ignorance," said the general. We were sitting in his sparsely furnished office at Afrikaner Volksfront headquarters in Pretoria just days after the tumultuous rally. He was dressed in the same neat gray two-piece suit with matching shoes, white shirt, and dark tie; his white hair was neatly clipped, and his face was tanned and unlined. For the past two days he had been locked in talks with the government, the ANC, and his partners in the Freedom Alliance— Buthelezi's Inkatha Freedom Party and Lucas Mangope's Bophuthatswana homeland régime. Their common bond was their loathing of the ANC.

Aware of the dangers that the white right and the Zulus posed to peace, the major parties had been working hard at trying to draw them into the process—even to the point of agreeing to change the ballot system in favor of the Alliance. But the talks were not going well, and time was running out. The general worried that the country was being held hostage by an election date and that the prevailing levels of violence—political and criminal—indicated incipient anarchy. He had a point. The township wars were claiming more than one hundred lives a week.

Just as the general was warming to the subject, the telephone rang. It was P. W. Botha, President de Klerk's predecessor, the man who had taken the first hesitant steps toward political reform in the mid-'80s but then lost his nerve and retreated to the laager. He was prone to wagging his finger at people who disagreed with him and was called the *Groot Krokodil,* the Big Crocodile.

Before taking the call, the general leaned over and fiddled around with the telephone wires. "I do this because we are usually bugged," he explained. Then he began a long exchange in Afrikaans with the *Groot Krokodil.* The former president explained why he thought the elections should be called off. The general agreed and said something about Afrikaner disunity. It seemed that factions of the right had branded him a traitor because the "Communist" Braam had helped arrange the talks. Word had been going around that the general was either a government agent or an ANC agent. When the general put down the phone, he laughed ruefully. "Braam is not a Communist," he said. "I chose him because he was the most honest and reliable person around. And he is a farmer and part of the Afrikaner nation."

The general was now certain the de Klerk government's undercover operatives had been acting as agents provocateurs at the rowdy Pretoria rally. "It is quite possible that the security establishment and especially the intelligence people, through their clandestine operatives, orchestrated that meeting to discredit me as a leader," he said, "to cause division between me and my people."

AUTOMATIC-RIFLE FIRE ECHOED THROUGH THE HILLS AROUND Donkerhoek, where one of the crucial battles of the Boer War was fought. General Koos De la Rey, Siener van Rensburg's friend, had almost overcome the British army here with a ragged band of Boer commandos. Donkerhoek means Dark Place, and now, ninety years on, it had again become a focal point of Afrikaner resistance. Farmers had set up a pirate radio station in Donkerhoek, and their broadcasts were transmitting traditional Afrikaner values to the highveld on FM. When the government threatened to close the station down, a call for help was sent out, and overnight more than a thousand armed Boers turned up. They built lookout towers, dug trenches, piled up sandbags, surrounded the place with razor wire, and mounted round-the-clock armed patrols.

This Saturday a traditional Afrikaner *braaivleis* and fair were in full swing around the station. Massive speakers had been set up and were providing a sound track of Afrikaner polka music and hyperclean popular folk songs mixed in with right-wing news bulletins and religious programs. Wouter Botes was the DJ, and in between takes he told me that if the government tried to take the station by force, they would have to kill him. He called his former employer, the government-run South African Broadcasting Corporation, "Radio Black Man."

A motley collection of white separatists were in attendance at Donkerhoek that day. A seventy-year-old retired university professor told me how his great-grandfather, a Prussian officer, had fled to South Africa to escape execution and how his grandfather had fought right here during the Boer War. His eyes filled with tears when I told him I had grown up in Bulawayo. "On behalf of my people," he said solemnly, grabbing my hand, "may I apologize for South Africa selling Rhodesia down the river." I accepted on behalf of the Rhodesian people. He was right, of course. The Vorster régime did rat on the Smith régime in the mid-'70s, but it helped shorten the war, which for most people was a good thing.

The man in charge of security at the station was Commandant Willem Ratte, a tall, wiry, former soldier of some notoriety. During the Angolan civil war he had been a fearless and wild special-operations commando fighting against what his government told him was communism's total onslaught. Now his government was telling him it was all right to have Communists in the government, and he didn't get it at all.

A few months earlier he'd caused a stir by leading an armed band of seventeen AWB members in the occupation of a historic Boer monument called Fort Schanskop. The South African Army was deployed to take back the fort, and as its soldiers were moving in, Ratte told journalists he would not be taken from the fort alive. He was heavily armed—with explosives, grenades, automatic weapons—and for a moment it seemed a terrible firefight would take place. Then General Viljoen stepped in and managed to talk Ratte and his men out of a confrontation. In the early hours of the morning, the seventeen AWB members gave themselves up, but Ratte had slipped off through the bushveld and escaped. There was still a warrant out for his arrest, for trespassing, but the government did not seem inclined to come and fetch him here in his high-profile bunker.

I expected Ratte to be quite mad, but he was nothing of the kind. He talked quietly, reasonably, and quite chillingly about refusing to take part in the "Azanian" elections, using a revolutionary name for post-apartheid South Africa, and about creating an independent state before the elections. He seemed deadly serious.

IN A SMALL FIELD HALF A MILE TO THE EAST OF THE RADIO STATION, shielded by a thick clump of woodland, a weapons training course was in session. This too was deadly serious. I'd been given permission to visit the camp by Eugene Terre Blanche, and I was welcomed warmly by the camp commandant, "Colonel" Charles Nelson, who despite his ancestral British surname was an unreconstructed Boer.

I watched as uniformed instructors conducted target practice, teaching accountants, laborers, and housewives how to use everything from a nine-millimeter handgun to a semiautomatic LM-5. Colonel Nelson's twelve-year-old son, Étienne, a leader in the AWB youth league, was one of several young kids wielding handguns. A farmer's wife tried to explain why she was here. "This is the war," she said, "between the light of Christianity and the darkness of Lucifer. My worst nightmare is that we should live under a Communist régime."

Out here, among the simple foot soldiers of the militant right, the inherent right-wing fear of communism was transformed into a duck soup of mad fundamentalism expressed in an ungainly, faltering English. "With de Klerk's Communist government handing over to Mandela's Communist government, I can only see black days for this country," said General Chris van der Heever without a trace of irony. "We feel we shouldn't mix with blacks—the Bible tells you so. A lot of blacks want to marry whites to spite us. Why do they come and live amongst us when there is so much empty land? To spite us.

"The time will come," he said more ominously, "when we bring the country to a standstill. We're waiting for God to make the decisions; when the time is right, God will tell the *volk*. There can't be peace unless we pay with blood. Our forefathers paid with blood for their freedom, and we will have to do the same."

Even right-wing *volkstaaters* like General Viljoen found the muddled, bellicose fringe unpalatable, but for all that the AWB appeared to have pretty solid support. The farmers' wives, the computer analyst, the businessmen at Donkerhoek—all were behind Terre Blanche.

THE NEXT DAY I HURTLED THROUGH A MASSIVE TRANSVAAL THUNderstorm, windshield wipers thrashing hopelessly at the torrents of water and the wheels of my car sometimes aquaplaning across rivers of rain. I was headed for Ventersdorp, a tiny two-bit farming town in the middle of the western Transvaal, where I had an appointment with Eugene Terre Blanche himself. He was a notoriously volatile man and sometimes pathological about promptness, particularly when it involved members of the much-loathed liberal press.

As it happened, I pulled into the colorless little farming town with five minutes to spare and soon found the colorless single-story building that was AWB headquarters. Everyone was dressed in full camouflage gear, and all the men carried nine-millimeter pistols, either slung in a holster at the hip or upside down in the small of the back. A uniformed foot soldier told me that "the General" was on his way. (In fact Terre Blanche's only legitimate rank was lance corporal in the commandos, the South African citizens' force.) Fifteen minutes later he pulled up in his *bakkie*—no armed bodyguards, no outriders, no fanfair, just a Transvaal Boer driving his *bakkie* to the office.

A big man with the rich, tanned skin of a farmer, a handsome white beard, and piercing blue eyes like those of the Viljoen twins, Terre Blanche had led the extreme right of the Afrikaner tribe for twenty-one years. He was a former policeman and had been Prime Minister John Vorster's bodyguard. He started the AWB in a garage in July 1973 with six like-minded Afrikaners. They claimed to stand for white supremacy and resistance to the imminent Communist invasion, and they modeled their insignia on the Nazi flag—three sevens arranged like a swastika on a white circle with a red background.

Eugene Terre Blanche, leader of the Afrikaner Resistance Movement.

For the first few years they operated covertly but broke into the public domain in 1979 when they tarred and feathered the historian Professor Floors van Jaarsveld while he was delivering a speech on the desanctification of the Boer holy day, December 16. Terre Blanche and thirteen other AWB members were prosecuted for the assault.

Over the years the AWB had played an incendiary role on the fringes of South African politics. On the surface it appeared to be rather silly and antediluvian—all daft hats, funny secret handshakes, and nineteenth-century folklore—but underneath it harbored and supported sinister characters who could not be taken lightly. Barend Strydom, who in 1988 went on a shooting spree in Pretoria, killing eight blacks, had deep AWB connections, as did Janusz Waluz, the man who cut down Chris Hani. Leonard Veenendaal, who killed a man while attacking a United Nations base in Namibia was also AWB and a particular favorite of Terre Blanche, who called him "my little fanatic." It was Veenendaal who told a Johannesburg newspaper that the AWB had secret suicide squads in place and that even Terre Blanche had no idea who or where they were.

Like most Afrikaner organizations, the AWB was constantly in a state of argument and division, with sections regularly falling off the main body and forming into splinter organizations, usually even more fanatical than the AWB. Thus the emergence of the Wit Wolwe (White Wolves), who carried out a number of fatal attacks on blacks through the late 1980s; Eddie van Maltitz's Resistance Against Communism group, which maintained that the United States was conducting a weather war against the whites of South Africa; and the Church of the Creator, which was the home of maniacal racist fundamentalists like Cornelius Lottering and Barend Strydom. (At Strydom's murder trial his father was asked by the prosecuting counsel whether he regarded blacks as people. He answered, after some deliberation, that there was a great deal of debate on the subject and his belief was that "the whites are the descendants of Israel and the blacks the descendants of animals.")

A most significant rift occurred in the late 1980s, when the AWB suffered a serious crisis of confidence in its leader. Far from behaving like the God-fearing defender of Christian morality he claimed to be, Terre Blanche was leading a rather debauched, fast-lane lifestyle. In December 1988, he was arrested at one of the sacred Boer monuments in the company of a peroxide-blond gossip hackette called Jani Allen, and it was not long before their wild, high-octane encounters were all over the newspapers. The public announcement disclosing that the feared AWB leader wore green underpants with holes in them was too much for the organization's diehards, and many—including Terre Blanche's deputy, Jan Groenewald, and his old friend Manie Maritz—left in disgust. Manie wanted to press charges against Terre Blanche for besmirching the good name of the Afrikaner *volk*.

Although Jani Allen was instrumental in causing a split in the far right, she was also enormously influential in determining the Boer-resistance-army look that the AWB took up in the late '80s. Terre Blanche had traditionally favored the '50s Afrikaner look—a black ill-fitting boxlike, time-to-shine business suit—for public appearances. Jani, a fashion-conscious northern-suburbs yuppie, told him he looked like a Bryanston Jew and suggested he try designer camo. And it was Jani who dubbed him Ramboer.

Gradually the Jani Allen scandal died, and Terre Blanche managed to reestablish his position, but only with the agreement of a group of AWB "generals" who would run the serious business. In the early '90s, the organization became increasingly militarized and, under the umbrella of the Wenkommandos (Winning Commandos), created structured fighting battalions in the elite Ystergarde (Iron Guard) and in the Witkruisarende (Black Eagles) and its female equivalent, the Rooivalke (Red Falcons). The responsibility for these fighting units lay increasingly with the "generals," while Terre Blanche handled the ceremonials and public performances.

RAMBOER'S OFFICE WAS A TABLEAU OF AFRIKANER SYMBOLS. Behind his desk was a full-size ox wagon, the kind that carried the rebel Afrikaners away from British rule on their Great Trek in the 1830s. Beneath the ox wagon was a World War II Browning machine gun with ammunition belt in place. A stuffed eagle sat in the far corner, and on the wall, portraits of the great Boer generals stared sullenly out on the man who claimed to hold their legacy in his large, calloused hands. Terre Blanche stared right back at them. Then he said with great relish that if he had to die for his beliefs, "in heaven, at least, I shall meet these great fighters. Isn't it wonderful? Even Paul Kruger. I would meet him in our *volkstaat* in heaven."

His *volkstaat* on earth was becoming a rather more elusive prospect. The negotiations between General Viljoen, the ANC, and the government had all but broken down, and as Terre Blanche had pointed out at the Pretoria rally, that chapter appeared to be closed. The white right was on its own, outside the constitutional process and talking a good war. But would the farmers with families and mortgaged homesteads really put it all on the line for an idea that few people outside their constituency took at all seriously?

Terre Blanche was quite emphatic. "There is no force on earth," he said, "that will stop the right wing going to war if these insane people try to create a unitary state." Over the past weeks I'd heard Afrikaners say they would take up arms only under General Viljoen. Terre Blanche roared at that suggestion. "Nonsense. We can raise more than sixty thousand AWB commandos overnight." He thought that General Viljoen, while an honest and committed man, was out of his depth. "I couldn't believe he brought the idea [of taking part in the elections] to the Pretoria rally; he was trying to put us on Mandela's payroll."

In Terre Blanche's view, President de Klerk—"the biggest traitor South Africa has known"—had conspired with his fellow Communists in the ANC to hand over the country. "How could he reject those things his father believed . . . ," Terre Blanche said in horror, "those things for which our people fought and died and paid for in installments of blood, . . . the mothers' tears. How could he?" The way Terre Blanche saw it, Zulus and Xhosas would start the war off, the white right would be drawn in on the Zulu side, a state of emergency would be declared, large sections of the army would defect to the right wing, and the government would fall.

I asked him whether that meant Boer would fight Boer and what would happen to the liberal Afrikaners like Braam Viljoen who had fraternized with the Communists. "We would have to kill him," he said. "In the Boer War, General de Wet said of his own brother [who had surrendered and then joined the British forces], 'I will hunt him like a dog. I will shoot him like a dog.' "

IN EARLY MARCH THE TOWNSHIPS AROUND JOHANNESBURG WERE war zones, with daily street battles erupting between ANC supporters and Inkatha supporters. Atrocities were being reported in Natal every week. The Zulus, Lucas Mangope's Bophuthatswana homeland, and the white right would still not come into the election, and there was war talk everywhere. Mandela, de Klerk, and the election executives were insisting that the election would take place on April 27 come hell or high water. As affirmation of this, international peace monitors and election observers began flying in in droves. To ensure the peace, two armies of former foes—ANC guerrillas and white South African soldiers—had been suddenly lashed together by the chains of expedience and called a peacekeeping force. There were so many damned peace people that you wondered whether there was anyone left out there to disturb the peace. There was. Thousands and thousands of fanatics, black and white, who cared little for the electoral process.

A guy I sat next to in the bar in Johannesburg's Rosebank Hotel was watching President de Klerk's platitudes on television. He'd seen it all before. He had been in Zambia in the 1950s, Rhodesia in the '60s and '70s, Namibia in the '80s—and now here. He said it was all over. The white extremists hadn't got a prayer. Look at Rhodesia; there was supposed to have been a coup if the Marxist Mugabe won the election—it was all planned, only that telephone call just didn't go through. The fellow's name was Dennis and he had traded all over Africa, legitimate goods like ball bearings, mining equipment, plant machinery—import, export. The only thing that would stop the process, he said, was if Mandela or de Klerk were assassinated.

The eight-o'clock news told us that five right-wingers had been arrested in the western Transvaal in connection with the bombing campaign that had destroyed ANC and government offices over the past two months. "Mickey Mouse," said Dennis. Then the grave countenance of Constand Viljoen appeared on the screen as the general emerged from yet another day of negotiating. He didn't seem very warlike, just weary and concerned. The ANC had made serious concessions to the white right and the Zulus in a last-ditch attempt to bring them into the elections, and the general had to return once more to his divided people for a mandate.

It was just six weeks away from the election, and Viljoen's Freedom Alliance partner, Lucas Mangope, was struggling to suppress a popular uprising in Bophuthatswana. There were riots in the streets of Mmabatho, the civil service was out on strike, and the university students were in pitched street battles with the police. Mangope and the general were in telephone contact regularly, and as the situation deteriorated, Viljoen began planning military action.

The scene was set for the Boers' last trek.

FIFTEEN

Alwyn's Last Trek

The story of Alwyn Wolfaardt's last trek is not an easy one to tell. It made news around the world, and right-thinking people clucked, and newspaper headlines said things like THE ROUT OF FRANKEN-STEIN'S MONSTER and BLOODY DAWN OF A NEW ERA. But it was more complicated than that. When Alwyn embarked on his last journey, he was not going out on a "kaffir-shooting expedition," as some newspapers claimed. He was going out to defend his people, his family, and his eight-year-old daughter against communism, anarchy, and the forces of evil.

Alwyn was born in 1949, the year after apartheid formally took root. For his whole life he was among people whose social system was predicated on the belief that they were the people God had chosen to rule the land. His church told him this, his government created a political system based on it, and his family and friends lived it.

As a boy in the '50s, Alwyn heard Afrikaner leaders say that black people were inferior and that they would never rule South Africa; in the '60s, he was warned that encroaching communism was the greatest threat to his white tribe, and he spent much of the next decade fighting in the bush war on his country's borders; in the

Alwyn Wolfaardt moments before he was killed in March 1994.
His colleague in the AWB, Nick Fourie, lies dead in the dirt.

early '80s, he was assured that white rule would prevail in South Africa even though black-run countries lay right against its borders.

Now the same leaders, the same churchmen, even some of his friends, were telling him all that had changed. Everything that he had lived by and held sacred for the past forty years had to be shelved. He had watched in genuine horror in 1990 as people he'd been told were terrorists, the enemies of his beloved country, were let out of jail and the banned Communist organizations he'd fought against in the bush had been declared perfectly acceptable. That messed up Alwyn's head.

In some ways it was easier to be a white liberal in South Africa in the '70s and '80s than to be a supporter of apartheid. The tide of history was on the liberals' side, and their awareness of world events constantly reinforced the rightness of their cause. By contrast, the ordinary Boer, commanded by successive Afrikaner governments to avoid contact with any kind of "progressive-liberal-leftist thinking," a dictate reinforced by a battery of censorship laws, looked inward and lost contact with a changing world.

Alwyn's last trek began at that Pretoria rally in March 1994, when ten thousand Boers gathered to argue yet again about their future. He was not more than a few rows away from his friend and leader Eugene Terre Blanche, shouting down Constand Viljoen. He'd had to borrow money for petrol to drive there, but it didn't matter. This was more important than money. This was about the future of the Boer people.

I saw Alwyn there that day. He looked magnificent. Six feet five inches tall, weighing around 250 pounds. Even for a Boer he had a splendid beard, a dark mattress of hair exploding from his face. He was a "colonel" in the AWB and was dressed in regulation AWB khaki, with the black and red insignia of the Wenkommandos on his epaulets and the AWB's three-sevens insignia on his shirtsleeve. As he bellowed at the stage, the veins in his forehead stood out like electric cables. He was chanting along with the other hard-liners, "We want war now. Now, now, now."

After the rally broke up, the Boer families stood around in groups, arguing, gesticulating, desperately looking for something that wasn't there. Alwyn and a couple of friends got a barbeque going and were soon eating *boerewors* and drinking cold Castle lagers out of cans. There would be no elections. They were going to war. From where? Against whom? When? They agreed it wasn't for them to decide. All of this would surely come from their leaders in good time. And when the call-up came, they would be there.

As he prepared to drive back to his home in Naboomspruit, Alwyn shook his fellow Boers' hands. More firmly than usual. A final show of brotherhood before Armageddon.

"Now we must pray," he said.

They all agreed.

THE PEOPLE OF NABOOMSPRUIT HAD A SAYING. IT WAS THAT THEIR town was the last place in South Africa "where the air is still clean and sex is still dirty." It wasn't very witty, but the sentiment was quite clear. In a town with only one hotel, two schools, a hamburger bar, a scattering of gas stations and car-repair shops, and a total population of some four thousand whites, there are six churches. Three of them are mainstream Afrikaner Dutch Reformed churches, one is the more radical Afrikaans Baptist Church, one is Presbyterian, and one Apostolic. On Sunday mornings Naboomspruit looked like a scene out of *Invasion of the Body Snatchers,* with large groups of identically dressed people moving slowly toward the six churches as if in a trance. The men were dressed in dark suits and the women in gaily printed frocks that were too bright in the sharp northern Transvaal sunlight. Once they were all inside their respective churches, the town went silent.

Not much had changed in Naboomspruit in forty years. The white population had grown slowly, a few more small businesses had started up, but it remained the kind of tidy, orderly little white Christian town that you found all over Africa in the 1950s. All but a handful of the citizens were Afrikaners. On the other side of the freeway, beyond the cemetery and the railway tracks, was the black township of Mokgopong, where some seven thousand people live in varying degrees of squalor. Those who worked were employed either in the town or on the neighboring farms, but most were unemployed. They were mainly northern Sotho people, although some were Matabele and some Shangaan.

The town is located midway between Pretoria and Pietersburg, just north of Nyl (Nile River), so called because when the first Boer trekkers came through here in the middle of the nineteenth century, they thought they had reached Egypt. (This wild miscalculation is somewhat explained by the fact that they had been traveling from the Cape across uncharted bushveld at about one mile an hour for over a year.) It lies at the foot of the Waterburg Mountains on the seam of the Springbok Flats, a hard brown landscape that is unforgiving of the weak. The most prevalent indigenous plant is the naboom, a large, prickly, poisonous euphorbia after which the town was named. Not far from Naboomspruit is a graveyard containing the bodies of five hundred Boer women and children who were among the twenty-six thousand who died in the British concentration camps during the Boer War.

The town began as a refueling station for ox-wagon trains carrying passengers north to Pietersburg and across the Limpopo River into Rhodesia at the turn of the century. As the wagons gave way to horse-drawn coaches and then to motor vehicles, Naboomspruit was declared a town and began to prosper. Like the rest of the northern Transvaal, it attracted conservative Afrikaners keen to escape the urban moral decline of modernity. The town's officials boasted that they had the lowest crime rate in the country and put it down to the low ratio of blacks to whites, also the lowest in the country.

At the beginning of 1990, Alwyn brought his wife, Esther, and four-year-old daughter, Annalise, to Naboomspruit. He'd been working as a diesel mechanic in Pretoria, but he needed to get away from the madness he saw all around him.

With the little cash that he had, Alwyn opened a car-repair shop that he called Wolf Trekkers and Motors and began servicing the farmers' vehicles and scratching out a living. Esther, a nurse, took a job at the old people's home, and the family soon settled into a modest bungalow on a thirty-acre smallholding outside town. They kept a couple of sheep and some chickens and grew corn, not for profit, just to be close to the land. Alwyn was born not far from here and had grown up on a farm. His father, Phil, was a foreman at ISCOR, the state-owned iron and steel corporation, where so many working-class Afrikaners found sheltered employment. He was a die-hard Boer who had served a jail sentence during World War II for refusing to serve alongside the British. The Wolfaardts were poor and proud, and Phil raised his three sons on a diet of Boer history, Dutch Reformed religion, and Afrikaner Nationalist politics.

Modest though his upbringing was, Alwyn could nevertheless claim heroic Afrikaner ancestry. One of his ancestors, Pieter Jordaan, was one of the seventy-nine Boers under Piet Retief who were lured into the kraal of the Zulu king Dingane in 1837 and slaughtered in the most hideous fashion. Whenever Alwyn needed to justify his mistrust of "the kaffirs" he would raise the specters of Retief, his great-uncle Pieter, and all those other Afrikaners who had been impaled on stakes pushed up their anuses, dying in agony under the African sun at the whim of a savage. You could never trust a kaffir. That was Alwyn's most unshakable belief.

Although he enjoyed the tranquillity and solitude and the Christian way of life of Naboomspruit, Alwyn could not distance himself from the political storm that was brewing. He and Esther had joined the AWB in the early 1980s, and he had become a firm friend of Eugene Terre Blanche's, with whom he shared the belief that true Afrikaners could never live under black rule. He would sit around the public bar with his friends François Du Toit and Fanie Uys and berate them for not taking a more active part in the AWB. "You know where to find me when you really need me," Fanie said. "But don't ask me to go to all those meetings and those parades. They're a waste of time."

Alwyn was at all the meetings and all the parades. He was there in Pretoria in May 1993 when five thousand people marched on the Union Buildings and Terre Blanche delivered a petition demanding the immediate recognition of an Afrikaner homeland. (It was there, more poignantly, that the AWB revealed its Underwater Commando Unit to the public for the first time—it comprised two

Boers in full wet suits and flippers marching abreast.) Alwyn was also at the World Trade Centre invasion a month later—he was one of the first to pass through the smashed plate-glass doors and enter the government's chamber for debating South Africa's new constitution—and would recall with relish "the look of fear on those kaffirs' faces when we broke in."

Alwyn told his friends he wanted a peaceful life, but he was convinced that Afrikaners would have to fight—and be prepared to die—for it. His friend François agreed. He had seen the results of black rule in Zimbabwe. "The kaffirs have fucked it up for everyone," he said. "Their own people were better off under the whites." So François brought his wife and children to Naboomspruit. But that was before they let Mandela out. Now he agreed with Alwyn that they would have to make a last stand.

The problem was that none of their leaders could agree on what form the last stand would take. General Viljoen continued to argue that participation in the election was the best tactical option.

Alwyn, François, and Fanie knew where they stood. Foursquare behind Terre Blanche.

ALWYN, FRANÇOIS, AND THE MEN WHO LIVED AROUND NABOOM-spruit had never questioned the fundamental principals of separate development. In recent years they had come to use the word *apartheid* less, at the request of their government, but they had always believed in the idea. It seemed so logical. All these different and diverse tribes of people clearly preferred living among their own, so what was the problem with giving them their own areas and their own government and letting them get on with it? Even the white right admitted that the land had not really been distributed fairly, given that the whites, who made up 14 percent of the population, had awarded themselves 86 percent of the country—not only 86 percent, but the most arable, productive, beautiful, and developed 86 percent. But with some redistribution and investment surely the idea would work.

Of course, the homelands policy was apartheid's greatest folly. The 1970 Bantu Homelands Citizenship Act made every black

South African a citizen of a tribal homeland and thus a noncitizen of South Africa. In a wave of forced removals that uprooted millions of people from their long-established communities and deposited them in distant dumping grounds, the government's social engineers created a patchwork quilt of supposedly self-governing territories. The first was the Transkei for the Xhosas; then through the early '70s, nine more were declared self-governing, including Bophuthatswana for the Tswana and KwaZulu for the Zulu.

They were but fragments of land—KwaZulu was in forty-eight pieces and Bophuthatswana in nineteen—with no core, no industry, no nothing. By coercing the tribal chiefs and luring acquiescent community leaders into a series of meaningless elections, however, the South African government pressed ahead, pouring in billions of rand to establish parliamentary buildings, civil services, infrastructures—whole new countries.

Rather hopelessly but with grim determination, the government tried to sell the homelands to a skeptical world. Take Bophuthatswana, they would say. It remained unrecognized "despite the fact that in both democratic and economic performance it outranks many Third World States with seats at the U.N." It wasn't true. Millions of rand a year were being poured into Bophuthatswana to keep it afloat. Its two genuine sources of revenue—the platinum mines and the Las Vegas–style Sun City casino resort—were bringing in only a quarter of its annual requirements, and the South Africans provided the rest.

Bophuthatswana was located quite near Naboomspruit, at least some bits of it were. It was called Bop by the South Africans and comprised seven fragments of land, six north and northwest of the Transvaal and the seventh some two hundred miles farther south, near the Lesotho border. Most of the two million Tswanas who were reluctant citizens of this patchwork country scratched a meager existence out of the land and felt no loyalty to the puppet government.

Lucas Mangope, a schoolteacher by profession, was the president, and like most African dictators, he ran his fiefdom as if it were a private company. He established "embassies" in Western European capitals that were little more than private hotels set in expensive suburbs for the use of friends and connections. And whenever he did manage to lure right-wing parliamentarians or businessmen to the homeland, he'd lavish vast amounts of taxpayer money on entertaining them at Sun City. Occasionally a backbench Tory MP would stand up in Britain's Parliament and make some wishy-washy statement about Mangope's being a legitimate African leader, but hardly anyone took any notice.

But as the wind of change blew through South Africa, Mangope's grip on his homeland became increasingly tenuous. In 1988, an attempted coup was quelled only when South African tanks rumbled into the capital, Mmabatho, and the rebel troops were locked up in Independence Stadium. P. W. Botha flew in and reassured Mangope, "You can sleep soundly now, Mr. President; we are back in control" before correcting himself and saying; "That is, the government of Botswana is back in control." By the time Mandela was released from prison, the Bop government was holding almost a thousand political prisoners without trial.

That Mangope joined the Freedom Alliance in 1993 alongside the white right and the other beleaguered homeland leader, Buthelezi, surprised no one. The one obsession they had in common—to prevent Mandela from taking over the government of the country—far outweighed the innumerable ideological and political differences the Alliance's members brought with them. Mangope embraced General Viljoen and Chief Buthelezi as his last allies and even went so far as to make a secret pact with Eugene Terre Blanche.

MANGOPE'S DARK DAYS WERE NOT FAR OFF. IN EARLY MARCH 1994, the Bop civil service, backed by students at Mmabatho University, began striking and demanding free elections in the territory. Mangope had banned the ANC from political activity, and the civil servants feared their exclusion from the election would jeopardize their jobs. The still-loyal police put down the demonstrations with their usual ferocity, clubbing, teargasing, and jailing all in their path. That is, until someone put out the word that their salaries and pensions might not be secure if they persisted in backing the old régime.

On Wednesday, March 9, the police were talking of changing sides and joining the protests in downtown Mmabatho. By then the whole town was in chaos. Looters ran through the Megacity shopping mall (partly owned by the Mangope family) like locusts, carrying away refrigerators, entire suites of furniture, emptying the stores like this was some gigantic liberation-day sale. Elsewhere the Bop Broadcasting Corporation had been seized by staff members, and its chairman, President Mangope's son Eddie, was being held hostage.

Throughout the morning Mangope had been closeted in the legislative buildings with Judge Johann Kriegler, head of South Africa's Independent Electoral Commission. Kriegler told him that he had no choice but to come into the elections. But soon after Kriegler left, Mangope called General Viljoen, who immediately took a helicopter to Mmabatho. The following morning the Bop minister of Defence, Rowan Cronjé, sent a formal request for help to AVF headquarters in Pretoria, where a meeting of the Volksfront's executives committed the organization to going into Bop. Viljoen had promised Mangope that the reinforcements would be disciplined commandos from the Boere-Krisisaksie (the Boer Crisis Front, or BKA) under the command of Colonel Jan Breytenbach. The deal was that BKA commandos would be issued automatic R-4 rifles by the Bophuthatswana Defence Force. There were not to be any AWB men among the Afrikaner Volksfront forces, since the presense of politically unacceptable racists would threaten the loyalty of Mangope's troops.

But even as the executive was instructing Terre Blanche to keep his men out of Bop, the AWB leader's call to arms was being broadcast across the platteland by Radio Pretoria.

It was midmorning on March 10 when Esther Wolfaardt got the call. She had come off the night shift, and the ringing telephone woke her. It was Whitey Austin, AWB commandant for the region. Instructions had come through from AWB headquarters in

Ventersdorp to assemble that night at various farms in the northern Transvaal. She must contact Alwyn immediately. Whitey didn't say where they were going, because the phones were probably bugged, but Esther knew. It was Bop.

Alwyn was at his repair shop, and he asked Esther to pack him enough clothes for a weekend and specifically instructed that she not pack his AWB uniforms. Then he jumped into his blue Mercedes-Benz and drove around to the town's small businesses and work-shops, rousing his AWB colleagues. They had been instructed not to take weapons and were told they would be issued the appropriate equipment at their destination. Still, Alwyn decided he would take his thirty-eight-millimeter pistol and Fanie would take his nine-millimeter weapon. François would come, but he didn't like the sound of it. Whom were they defending? And against whom? It didn't matter, said Alwyn, the call-up had come from Ventersdorp, and they would be briefed when they arrived at their meeting place, a farm outside Lichtenburg.

As the day wore on, Alwyn got involved in longer, more convo-luted arguments with his fellow Boers, and by the time he arrived home in the late afternoon, he was furious. He told Esther that half the AWB had backed out. "They talk big, but when the call comes, they've got excuses," he said. "This one's wife was threatening to divorce him; another one's child has got a pain in its ear." Then there was a whole group who'd been drinking it up at lunchtime and who'd fallen into a vehicle and driven off to Lichtenburg in midafternoon, drunk and dressed in AWB uniforms. It was a sham-bles. He had a truck waiting at the farm, all fueled up and ready to go, but his unit of Naboomspruit commandos was down to him, Fanie, and François. As he drove Esther to work in the early evening, Alwyn said he was thinking maybe it wasn't worth going. Esther responded that of course he had to go. He had been called up. As an AWB colonel, he had no choice. He agreed, they kissed good-bye, and he returned home to gather his things and take his daughter to stay with friends.

There was no point now in taking the truck, so after dropping off Annalise, Alwyn headed off to pick up his two friends in the blue

Mercedes. Fanie was ready and packed, but when they arrived at François's workshop, he was busy talking to a customer. He told Alwyn he needed twenty minutes to sort out some business problem, but Alwyn was now sick of all the procrastination and messing about. "You either come right now, or you don't come at all," Alwyn said. François shrugged, and the blue Mercedes took off in a cloud of dust.

The two lone AWB Naboomspruit commandos drove for four hours through the African night, a hard drive on roads Alwyn was unfamiliar with, skirting Sun City, passing by Brits and Rustenberg, like Naboomspruit, among the last outposts of Boer resistance. At the Lichtenburg farm, they were given directions to the Bop Air Force base on the outskirts of Mmabatho, where they were told the main body of men was gathering. By the time they arrived at the base, sometime after two in the morning, Alwyn and Fanie were exhausted. They reclined the Mercedes' seats and went to sleep. They had to be alert for the battle that lay ahead.

Unbeknownst to Alwyn and Fanie, there had been a flurry of diplomatic activity over the previous twelve hours in an attempt to avert the battle they had come to fight. South African government negotiators were holed up with President Mangope, trying to persuade him to come into the election, and General Viljoen was asked to get the AWB out of Bophuthatswana. They'd been careening through the streets of the town, taking potshots at black civilians.

As dawn broke on Friday, Alwyn and Fanie clambered stiffly from the blue Mercedes and quickly realized that chaos had become anarchy. They noticed groups of Bophuthatswana Defence Force soldiers, who when they'd arrived a few hours earlier had been their allies, changing out of their army uniforms and hopping onto vehicles headed for town. In the officers' mess at the air force base, Colonel Jan Breytenbach was engaged in a ferocious argument with Eugene Terre Blanche, who accused Viljoen and Breytenbach of being traitors. Terre Blanche agreed to leave, but his top general, Alec Cruywagen, insisted that he and his 350 men were staying on. Breytenbach exploded. Pointing at the four stars on Cruywagen's epaulets, he thundered, "I don't know where you got that shit on your shoulders from, and I am just a colonel, but I am ordering you to take your men out of Bophuthatswana or else."

Cruywagen had no choice, and he told his followers that they should begin preparations to evacuate. As the morning went on, convoys of AWB spread out from the base, some clearly determined to engage in one last fight before their retreat was over. On the Mafikeng Road a group of some twenty AWB came across two journalists, John Battersby of *The Christian Science Monitor* and Paul Taylor from *The Washington Post,* and proceeded to beat them up. Battersby was dragged from the car by his hair and kicked and punched till he was almost senseless. A little later, at a gas station in Mafikeng, another AWB group fired on journalists and then stole tape recorders and cameras from them. Independent Television News reporter Mark Austin and his black cameraman were marched off into the veld at gunpoint.

At the base around noon, an AWB general from Pietermaritzburg, Nick Fourie, asked Alwyn for a lift out of town and hopped into the passenger seat beside him. Fanie was happy to take the backseat. Maybe he could get some sleep on the long ride home. The blue Mercedes pulled out of the base at the tail of an eighteen-car convoy and was soon passing soldiers, policemen, and ordinary citizens, all waving their fists and cursing at the retreating Boers. Then gunshots started going off and the AWB began hitting their accelerator pedals. As they sped past the Mafikeng Police Station, they came under a blast of automatic fire, and although some returned the fire, the point now was to get the hell out of there. The convoy was fast disappearing in a cloud of dust when the blue Mercedes bringing up the rear suddenly veered off the road onto the dirt and came to a halt.

The front passenger door opened, and Nick Fourie's body fell to the ground. He had been shot through the neck, and his severed artery continued to pump blood onto the dry, brown earth. Fanie was ominously still on the backseat. As a crowd began running toward the stricken vehicle, Alwyn edged across to the passenger seat, crouching, his thirty-eight-millimeter pistol in his right hand.

A BDF soldier pointed his R-4 at Alwyn and ordered him to drop the thirty-eight and lie on his stomach beside the Mercedes with his hands spread. Then Fanie slid painfully off the backseat, feet first, onto the road. He had been shot in the hip and was in terrible pain.

For the next fifteen minutes the blue Mercedes was surrounded by chaos. A crowd of cheering, jeering Bop civilians was chanting "*Bulala Amabhulu! Bulala Amabhulu!*" (Kill the Boers!). BDF soldiers and Bop police, all bristling with weapons, were running this way and that, and the press—reporters, photographers, and TV crews—were beginning to arrive. As the wounded Boer lay helpless in the dirt, someone shouted at Alwyn, "What's your name? They will kill you, and no one will know who died." Alwyn groaned, "It doesn't matter. They will know who I am." Then he turned on the hovering journalists: "Can you call an ambulance, please. That man is wounded. Are you finished with your fucking photographs? Now please get a fucking ambulance."

Fanie was propped up against the back wheel, his arms raised in surrender, his face grimacing in pain. "Please, please, get me help. I'm bleeding. I've already been lying here for ten minutes." A black reporter replied, "They've called an ambulance. It's coming. Now, baas, please tell us what you were doing here? Who are you?"

"I'm Fanie Uys from Naboomspruit," he said.

"What are you doing here, Fanie?"

"We've come to help the people here."

"Which people are you coming to help?"

"We were ordered to come here and help Mangope," said Fanie.

Alwyn lay silent, facedown in the Bophuthatswana dirt, cursing the black bastards who were putting him through this. Police vehicles flashed by, sirens wailing. Armed soldiers ran this way and that. There were still shouts of "*Bulala Amabhula*" from the crowd, and there was no sign of an ambulance.

Then, without warning, a young Bop policeman stepped from the melee, pointed his rifle at Fanie, and shot him in the head. While everyone looked on in horror, so frozen by this shocking moment that when the spent cartridge hit the road, it clanged like a church bell, he took three paces across to Alwyn and shot him

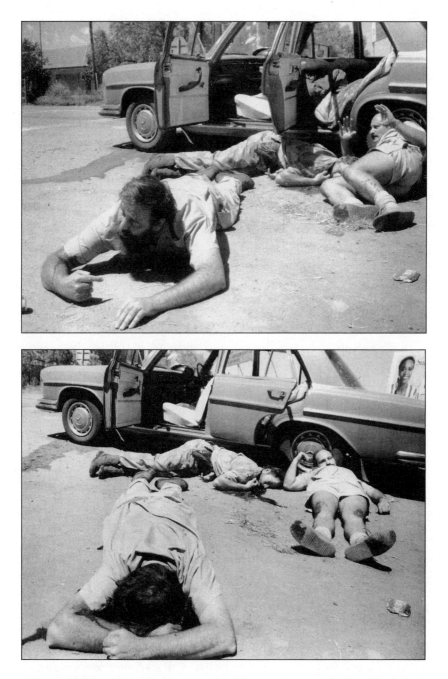

Alwyn Wolfaardt lay in the street for fifteen minutes, pleading for help, surrounded by a crowd of policemen and civilians and reporters, before he and his friend Fanie Uys were shot in the head and killed.

twice in the back of the head. Then he held his rifle aloft in triumph and took a couple of kicks at the dead bodies.

The Boer invaders were dead.

FRANÇOIS DU TOIT HAD LEFT NABOOMSPRUIT ON FRIDAY MORNing to join Alwyn in Bop. He had met with five fellow AWBs in Nylstroom and driven up through Hammanskraal toward Mmabatho. But by the time they'd reached Babaleki, they realized there was no point in going on. They'd seen vehicles packed with cheering black passengers careering all over the homeland, and the news reports over the car radio said the right-wingers were pulling out of town. They decided to turn around. On the way back home François stopped off at a café in Pienaarsrivier to buy a pack of cigarettes. While he was waiting for his change, he noticed a news flash on the television above the counter. There he saw the bodies of his two friends slumped in the dirt beside the familiar Mercedes.

François jumped into his car and gunned it toward Naboomspruit to break the news to Esther and to Fanie's wife, Amelia. But they already knew. Amelia had brought her two daughters home after school, and when she walked into the house, she switched on the television without even thinking. And there it was on the screen. She couldn't see the face of the man lying slumped against the Mercedes' back wheel, but she recognized his legs and his veldschoens. It was Fanie.

At the same time, Esther Wolfaardt had just woken from her morning sleep and was being called into her living room by Annalise. She too saw the terrible picture of the three bodies motionless beside the road. She recognized the blue Mercedes immediately, but before she could focus on the bodies, the image was whipped off the screen, replaced by another news item. Esther thought she had seen AWB uniforms on the three bodies, and she knew Alwyn wasn't in uniform. So she and Annalise sat quietly in front of the TV screen waiting for the two-thirty bulletin. This time she recognized Alwyn right away. They were quiet at first, then mother and daughter began sobbing bitterly.

• • •

THREE HUNDRED MILES AWAY, IN MMABATHO, THE MAIN GROUP of BKA commandos was still hanging around the air force base waiting for orders when the news came through that the three AWB men had been executed. They had suspected there had been AWB casualties—they'd heard garbled reports over their two-way radios that there had been shoot-outs—but they were shocked by the cold-blooded executions. However much they disapproved of the AWB's cowboy actions and general disorderliness, they were still Boers. And the sight of their fellows lying at the feet of a black policeman was hard to take.

General Viljoen arrived by helicopter at around three-thirty. He had come from talks with President Mangope and General George Meiring, commander of the South African Army. Mangope had finally backed down and agreed to free elections in Bop, and two thousand crack South African Defence Force troops were moving in to restore order. The game was up. The defense of the tin-pot dictator was all over. The commandos of the white right listened in silence as the general told them that South African troops would soon arrive to take over the air force base. He ordered all but 150 of them to begin withdrawing immediately and the other 150 to hold the base until the South African Defence Force arrived and then to hand it over.

And so began the final retreat of the white commandos from Bophuthatswana, long trains of BMWs, Audis, and Toyota *bakkies* ignominiously slipping their occupants back to their farms and small businesses by side roads. South African troops arrived soon after and formally took possession of the base.

The convoy of remaining white commandos got halfway through downtown Mmabatho before it hit the first ambush. Unlike the potbellied cowboys of the AWB, Colonel Breytenbach's BKA volunteers had had decent military training and were well prepared for combat. Instead of trying to rush blindly through the ambush in thin-skinned civilian cars, as the AWB had in the afternoon, the BKA stopped their vehicles, dismounted, and returned fire, catching their ambushers out in the open. It was pitch-dark, but the BDF soldiers were too close to the road, and after taking several casualties, they withdrew.

The second ambush came just five hundred yards farther down the road, just as the BKA men hit an area with streetlights, and it turned into a fierce firefight. Again the BKA dismounted, but this time there was a machine gun firing down from a water tower and several others firing from armored Mambas down the side streets. They were pinned down for some ten minutes, and one volunteer was killed and three wounded before the South African Defence Force armored vehicles returned from the head of the convoy to give them some cover. The BKA men lifted their three wounded comrades into a Casspir, then clambered back into their cars, many now riddled with bullet holes, to continue their run down hell alley. They passed through two more smaller ambushes and after some confusion finally found themselves out in the darkness of the African bushveld. They secured their weapons and then stood there shoulder to shoulder and prayed. It was so dark the men couldn't see who was standing next to them. Then they shook hands and drove home.

At a press conference the next morning, General Viljoen announced he had registered his new party, the Freedom Front, before the midnight deadline, and he urged all right-wingers to follow him and take part in the democratic process. He had a handwritten letter from Mandela that supported the principle of self-determination, and he assured the press and his followers that he was to sign an agreement with Mandela and de Klerk that would commit the new government to exploring the idea of an Afrikaner homeland.

After the Bop disaster the white right was more divided and dissonant than it had ever been. The Conservative Party leader, Ferdie Hartzenburg, remained resolutely opposed to the election and continued to dissuade his followers from voting, and Terre Blanche's AWB skulked silently and ominously behind closed doors in their western Transvaal dorps. They blamed Viljoen for the catastrophe at Bop and blamed the press for the deaths of Alwyn, Fanie, and Nick Fourie. They even went so far as to have a photograph of the trio's death scene blown up and circulated among AWB members in an attempt to identify the journalists who had stood by while the men were killed.

With typically eccentric logic, Terre Blanche announced that the Bop incursion had been a great success for the AWB and that the election would not go ahead. The rest of the country, the rest of the watching world, knew otherwise, and as South Africa geared up for its great moment of liberation, everyone sighed with relief. It was all over. All the threats of Armageddon, all the talk of the Third Boer War, had been smashed into the dust of Bophuthatswana. This fictitious country created by the social engineers of apartheid had become the final battleground of the white right. In Alwyn Wolfaardt, the great bearded bully who had believed all the lies of racial superiority spoon-fed him by a succession of Boer ancestors and political leaders, they had a final martyr.

Almost two weeks after he died, Alwyn was given a hero's funeral in Naboomspruit. Fanie had been buried four days earlier in a quiet family ceremony, and Amelia had asked the AWB to stay away, to leave her grieving family in peace. But for Alwyn, the people of Naboomspruit made a last defiant gesture. More than a hundred AWB commandos in full uniform lined the dusty road to the cemetery. The black residents of Mokgopong stayed far out of sight. The day after the executions someone had daubed WOLF IS DEAD—VIVA ANC on the walls of Wolf Trekkers and Motors, and a black man would have been torn limb from limb had he been even near the place. Eugene Terre Blanche attended the service at the Afrikaans Baptist Church, but he was too upset to go on to the cemetery.

Esther said that Alwyn and Fanie were martyrs, that they had gone into Bop to help people and make a future for their own children. But as Annalise stood at her father's graveside, touching the coffin absentmindedly, not quite comprehending what had happened to her father, Alwyn's widow seemed to be having second thoughts.

EPILOGUE

The Last White Man

The image of the three Boers lying dead on a dusty African street is as vivid to me now as it was that day in 1994—a single picture that signifies the end of white resistance, the end of white rule, on the African continent. It is a small and pathetic vignette to mark so momentous an event, and yet it is perfectly appropriate—a dramatic and pointless flourish that will be remembered more for its symbolism than for its real significance. By the time Alwyn and his friends had sacrificed themselves, the new South Africa was already in place.

Relief and optimism were the prevailing sentiments in the ensuing years, not only within South Africa's borders but throughout the subcontinent—relief because for a time in the 1970s and '80s it had seemed unlikely that the Afrikaners would hand over power without going to war, and were going to plunge the whole region into further chaos; optimism because South Africa was led by a great black statesman, Nelson Mandela.

Blacks extended the hand of friendship and reconciliation to whites who had never shown the same magnanimity, and a miracle was taking place. Or at any rate that is how it seemed to the rest of the world. To people like David Dodds and the other besieged white professionals living behind razor wire in Johannesburg's northern suburbs, the "miracle" was something they read about in the newspapers. Their day-to-day reality included carjackings, armed incursions into their homes, and endless debates about whether there was a future for their children in South Africa.

What these people saw when they looked north confirmed their skepticism. Throughout the second half of the century, as one by one the African nations launched into independence, there had been similar surges of optimism, and—without exception—hopes and expectations were dashed as the new democracies succumbed to military coups, corrupt leadership, economic decline, and despair. The new leaders had, like Mandela, promised reconciliation, development, and progress, and then they presided over governments that dragged their people into an abyss. Whatever the moral imperatives of Africa's emancipation, the realities of the liberation era seemed to suggest that Africa was unable to govern itself. What Ian Smith believed in the 1960s, and doggedly reiterated when I visited him thirty years later, was that no matter what the shortcomings of colonial rule, black rule had been even worse for the ordinary African. Even the liberal Garfield Todd seemed depressed and disappointed by what transpired in Zimbabwe after independence in 1980, although he would never advocate a return to white rule, as his old nemesis did.

Africa's decline has been staggering. Returns on investment, which were around 30 percent in the 1960s, were less than 3 percent by the 1990s. In 1991, the total gross product of sub-Saharan Africa, forty-eight countries that support five hundred million people, was $205 million, almost the same as the gross national product of Belgium, a country of ten million people. Eighteen of the world's twenty poorest countries were African, and while the population was growing at 3.2 percent a year (in the next quarter of a century, thirty countries would double their populations), per capita income was declining at 2 percent a year. An addiction to loans and foreign aid didn't help: Africa's debt grew to $180 billion in the early 1990s—the service charges alone were $10 billion a year—and although Africa received more aid per capita than any other region in the world, there were no signs that the aid was being put to good use. "Everywhere in Africa the evidence is of dereliction and decay," observed General Olusegon Obasanjo, the former president of Nigeria. "We are rapidly becoming the Third World's Third World."

So dramatic was the decline that in the early 1990s some Western observers began to entertain the idea of recolonization. The conservative British historian Paul Johnson made the case rather vociferously in 1993. "Some states are not yet fit to govern themselves," he wrote. "Their continued existence, and the violence and human degradation they breed, is a threat to the stability of their neighbours as well as an affront to our consciences. There is a moral issue here: the civilized world has a mission to go out to these desperate places and govern."

There was little likelihood that Johnson's florid rhetoric would win support from African leaders, and the idea of jumbo jets full of civil servants from Brussels, Paris, and London flying into crumbling African capitals like bowler-hatted supermen lends itself more to a William Boyd novel than to real life. Nonetheless, a negotiated arrangement whereby European managers and bureaucrats would run the business end and the blacks would retain political power sounded mildly feasible. Would the expats do a better job? They could not do any worse than the black governments have done.

There is, indeed, evidence of dereliction and decay everywhere. Take Nairobi, for example. In the late 1970s, when I started traveling there, Kenya was in its second decade of independence. It had not taken the socialist path of its emergent neighbors, and remained a stable Western ally. Nairobi was clean, not antiseptic like Salisbury and Johannesburg and Durban, the white cities down south, but neat and well maintained. The roads, the infrastructure, the mechanics of the city—the legacy of the colonial settlers—were in good working order, and for a time it was the best city on the subcontinent.

In the intervening years, Nairobi disintegrated, in uneven fits and starts, like a stop-motion movie. Now it is just another of those broken African cities where nothing works very well and nothing is ever fixed. The city streets are in ruin, with potholes the size of craters; the sidewalks are cracked and smashed; there are heaps of garbage on street corners, rendered all the more pungent by the hot African sun; refugees in rags from various neighbors' civil wars and gangs of thieves and muggers are everywhere. The air is so thick with pollution you can almost grab it in your hand. Nairobi is not the bustling, throbbing cultural crossroads of the travel guides. It reeks of poverty and despair.

The same thing has happened in Zimbabwe, only at a slower pace. Bits of the infrastructure are falling off: the public transportation system, for example, is in such ill repair that workers living in the townships around Harare have to get to a bus stop at three in the morning in order to arrive at their jobs at eight o'clock. Most of the five hours are spent standing in line waiting for a bus. The actual journey takes half an hour. The return trip at night usually takes longer, so the workers rarely arrive home before midnight. For these people, liberation from the Smith régime has meant a harder life.

While aware of the high-minded theories about the benefits of decolonization, development, self-determination, and the rest, the ordinary citizens of Africa continue to experience hardship and disappointment.

MY VICTORIAN ANTECEDENTS BROUGHT WITH THEM TO AFRICA the benefits of industrial progress, modern medicine, and a new god—and in the process of imposing these benefits on African society, they turned the place upside down. In the late 1920s, the South African leader Jan Christian Smuts warned that "no flash in the pan of tropical exploitation will really help the cause of African civilization. It will be a slow, gradual schooling of peoples who have slumbered and stagnated since the dawn of time. . . ." When the Congo erupted in 1960, everyone agreed that it had been folly for the Belgian government to hand the country over to an uneducated, inexperienced people, but white Africans in Rhodesia and South Africa chose not to see this as a sign that they should advance the education of their own subjects. Rather, they decided that the lesson to be learned from the Congo debacle was that you could not entrust power or responsibility to black Africans and, consequently, that there was little point in encouraging them to get an education. The colonials simply ignored the matter and left it to the missionaries. Afrikaners actually went to the trouble of creating a distinctly inferior education system for their black citizens, an act of madness for which the new democratic South Africa will pay dearly well into the twenty-first century.

But it was up to the new South Africa, liberation's final frontier, to prove there was life after the white man and that Africa could rule itself. With its muscular economy, its First World roads, harbors, airports, and communications systems, its modern cities and sophisticated leaders, South Africa was the country most likely to succeed, the one that had the potential to kick-start the whole subcontinent and lead an African renaissance. Despite serious social and economic problems inherited from the apartheid era, South Africa emerged from its first years of democracy in reasonably good shape. In 1996, it recorded a trade surplus of $2.5 billion, growth was at a steady 3 percent, and the rand stabilized at around 4.5 to the dollar. The massive state industries that were the heart of apartheid's siege economy were being dismantled and privatized, and the government was fulfilling some of its promises to bring electricity and water to the squatter townships that now surround all the major cities.

On the downside, economists said the country had to grow at 6 percent—twice the current rate—to sustain meaningful development, and with a labor force that was poorly skilled, notoriously underproductive, and highly unionized, this seemed a tall order. Crime remained an intractable problem, although there was now strong evidence that most of it was caused by organized-crime syndicates and not by anarchic have-nots with AK-47s. Money was still leaving the country, but a significant relaxation of currency controls was expected to slow that down. (South Africa is believed to have lost a hundred billion rand in flight capital over the last thirty-five years.)

If South Africa's future was more promising than that of the rest of post-colonial Africa, this was in some part due to the presence of a large and highly productive white community. President Mandela, the master conciliator, was unequivocal on the subject, and early in his term drew whites into key political and administrative positions. Many of these people did not, however, expect Mandela's successors to be as altruistic, and believed they'd be looking for work in the private sector when the great man retired. Whether they would stay or follow the well-trod path of previous generations into exile in Australia, Canada, or the United States remained an open question.

I remember similar promises of inclusion being made in Zimbabwe in 1980. Robert Mugabe's friend and comrade-in-arms, Mozambique's president Samora Machel, had warned him to hang on to the whites "whatever you do. You will need them." Machel spoke from bitter experience, for the sudden exodus of almost the entire white population of Mozambique had left him with a country that no one knew how to operate. But Mugabe was unable to persuade the Rhodesians to stay, and during the following years the white population shrank from 230,000 to 80,000. Runaway Rhodesians followed white Kenyans, Zambians, South Africans, and the rest to less volatile recesses of the old empire.

South Africa's last whites would for the most part prefer not to take the exile option. They know from family and friends living abroad that expatriation is an alienating and unsettling experience. Like me, these exiles wake up every day and think of Africa and remember a time when they were Africans. They daydream about the exuberance and spontaneous warmth of the African people, the unquenchable optimism that resonates in the towns and countryside, through wars and famines and economic catastrophes. They recall the clear sunlit mornings, the explosive highveld thunderstorms, the sly, snaky rhythms of township jazz, the serenity of an African sunset, and they invariably wonder whether abandoning Africa was the right decision.

For the moment the key players in my African drama were staying put. The Good Family Todd was living quietly in Bulawayo, and Ian Smith was still in Harare. The old vultures were still drinking their Saturdays away at the Old Miltonians bar and complaining about the government, and the government continued to give them a great deal to complain about. For the wildlife conservationists, whose lives were as inextricably bound to the ancient African order as any of today's black occupants, the very thought of migration to a foreign land was too far-fetched to contemplate seriously.

In South Africa the poor whites of Piet and Charmaine's twilight world had long since been swept aside and were making do as best they could in a country that no longer provided them with a safety net. Rick Turner's graduates from the Durban Moment were beginning to find themselves in positions of influence: Alec Erwin was the deputy minister of Finance, Nicholas Haysom was President Mandela's legal counsel; Halton Cheadle was one of the co-authors of the new constitution, Charles Nupen was a UN representative and the country's leading labor mediator. They were so heavily engaged in the process of building a new democracy that they had no time for pessimism.

The Good Cop, Ivor Human, had risen to the rank of colonel and spent his first year in the new South Africa heading the investigation into the apartheid assassination squads led by Colonel Eugene de Kock, the man known as Prime Evil. When we last met at his office in Pretoria, Human seemed a much-chastened man, grim faced and reflective. "Murder is murder," he said, "but de Kock was terrible. If you could see what happened. . . . This is the worst thing I have come across in my career. I cannot believe it. And it was going on under our noses." De Kock was later sentenced to two life terms in prison.

The northern Transvaal farmers, the white Boers like Manie Maritz, had resumed the rhythms of a normal life and were beginning to resemble the old Rhodesian vultures, sitting around at bush bars drinking brandy and Cokes and complaining about the government. Their leaders had gone in different directions—General Viljoen was a member of parliament, and Eugene Terre Blanche had returned to his farm. Esther Wolfaardt had stayed on in Naboomspruit. When I last visited her, a carload of Security policemen was circling her block, monitoring her movements. And her phone was tapped. She assumed they thought she was planning a white uprising in the name of Alwyn. But she was not. She was just a sad widow who'd lost a husband to a lost cause.

There was, however, one last twist to my story, one final flurry of unfinished business. It concerned the murder of Rick Turner.

Around the time of the 1994 election, I was traveling through Durban when I learned that the police had reopened the Turner murder docket. New evidence had come to hand fifteen years on. They were back on the case. I dropped everything and arranged to meet with the policeman in charge, one Jurie Prinsloo.

I always seemed to be meeting policemen in hamburger bars, and this one was in a shopping mall that nestled under a concrete freeway system. Somewhere out there was the lush subtropical flora that distinguishes this from other African cities, but it was left to my imagination. This particular mall could have been in L.A.

The election results were being announced over TV sets bolted to the walls of the bar, and I wondered what Rick Turner would have made of the scene. He would probably have been part of the new government himself, and he would certainly have been proud of the graduates of the Durban Moment. But I doubt he would have approved of the shopping malls.

I was meeting Detective Prinsloo because he seemed to think he knew who killed Turner. After nine months of chasing a new set of leads, he had almost convinced himself he had the right man.

I liked Prinsloo as soon as I met him. He had a pleasant, open face, a regulation police mustache, and I thought I recognized him from my newspaper days. As it happened, he had worked under Ivor Human in the early '80s and had even escorted the murderess Charmaine Phillips to psychiatric examinations at Natal University.

Prinsloo told me he had reopened the docket after he had met with Turner's daughter Jann while she was making a documentary for British television. At the time of Rick's murder, Prinsloo, like most other government employees, had been persuaded that Turner was a dangerous revolutionary, and he'd taken little notice of the case. Now, he said, he had come to realize that Turner had been a pacifist and a man of some substance, so he had decided to go off in search of the killer.

"I don't think it was a political murder," he said finally. "I think a man named Ronald Slugget did it."

Ronald Slugget? His name hadn't been mentioned by any of the theorists, the private investigators, the colleagues, the BOSS agents, the journalists who'd followed the case over the years. What deep and secret organization had he come out of?

"He was an old recluse who traded in engineering equipment," said Prinsloo. "He had no interest in politics."

The story according to Prinsloo went like this. One morning in July 1985, Ronald Slugget stopped off at the home of his neighbor Patricia Nicholson for a cup of tea, something he had done regularly for twenty years. While they were eating biscuits around the dining room table, Slugget asked Mrs. Nicholson whether she remembered the murdered lecturer Rick Turner. When she nodded, he said, "I killed him." At first she didn't believe that her old friend, strange and quick-tempered though he was, could have done anything of the kind. But as he explained in fine detail what had happened, she became certain he was telling the truth.

Slugget said that when he and his brother Desmond, who for some reason was known as Stan, inherited a house in Durban's Glenwood suburb from an aunt, they decided to put it on the market. It was bought by a Durban architect and his wife, who rented it out to university students. The house, at 72 Marist Road in Glenwood, had a garage, and the Slugget brothers had left some engineering equipment in it. They promised to move the stuff out, but a year went by, and the equipment was still cluttering up the garage, preventing the students from parking a car in it. Slugget said that by the time he came to move it, thirty-seven thousand rand in damage had been done.

Slugget said he confronted Rick Turner, who he claimed was using 72 Marist Road at the time, asking for compensation, but Turner told him to get lost. He said he then went to Kings Sports Shop in the center of Durban, bought a box of bullets, and returned to Turner to threaten him. Still Turner refused to pay for the damage. Slugget said that on the night of January 7, 1978, he and a black servant who had worked for his aunt drove to 32 Dalton Avenue, Turner's Bellair house, and Slugget shot Turner dead.

Slugget died of cancer three months after he made his confession to Mrs. Nicholson. She had lived with her secret for eight years when, in 1993, she read a story in the local newspaper once again describing Turner's murder as a politically motivated assassination. This ticked her off, and she made an anonymous call to the newspaper, claiming to know for a fact that the murder was not political. It wasn't long before the determined Detective Prinsloo had tracked down the caller and was interviewing Mrs. Nicholson in her Durban North home.

He also interviewed a neighbor of Turner's in Bellair who claimed that on the evening prior to the murder a man in a brown Cortina had pulled up to his house and asked for directions to "the doctor's house." The neighbor remembered that there was a black male passenger in the car. Prinsloo established that the Slugget brothers had indeed owned a mid-'60s brown Cortina.

Over the coming months, Prinsloo and I talked regularly, jawing over old facts, trying out new leads, and never really coming up with anything. Turner's daughter Jann was still convinced that the sinister David Beelders, whom she had interviewed rather unsuccessfully in Cape Town, was involved in some way, despite his denial and his alibi. Turner's ex-wife and his widow, Barbara and Foszia, could hardly believe it was anything but a political hit. Only Prinsloo held fast to the possibility that an apolitical madman like Slugget could have done it.

Then one day Jurie Prinsloo disappeared. His phone went dead. His office told me he'd been transferred, but they could not say where to. It was while I was trying to track down Prinsloo that I had a vivid dream. I dreamed that Prinsloo had been co-opted by the authorities to concoct the Slugget theory so as to take the heat off apartheid's assassins. Then, weighed down by guilt and the fear that his life was in danger because he knew too much, he'd fled and had disappeared into the heart of Africa. For forty years he lived in a cave in the Drakensberg Mountains, surviving by foraging and hunting, and having no contact with the outside world. Finally he was spotted by some passing soldiers, taken into custody, and transferred to Durban. Like those Japanese soldiers who emerged decades after the end of World War II, the Prinsloo of my dreams was astonished at the world he had reentered.

There was not a single white face on the streets of Durban.

They had all gone.

He was the last white man in Africa.

SELECTED BIBLIOGRAPHY

Beard, Peter. *The End of the Game*. San Francisco: Chronicle Books, 1988.

Blake, Robert. *A History of Rhodesia*. New York: Alfred A. Knopf, 1978.

Bonner, Ray. *At the Hand of Man*. New York: Alfred A. Knopf, 1993.

Caute, David. *Under the Skin*. Middlesex, England: Penguin, 1983.

Churchill, Winston. *The Boer War*. New York: Dorset Press, 1991.

Cole, Barbara. *The Elite: The Story of the Rhodesian SAS*. Amanzim-toti: Three Knights, 1984.

Cooper-Chadwick, John. *Three Years with Lobengula*. Bulawayo: Books of Rhodesia, 1975.

Crocker, Chester. *High Noon in Southern Africa*. New York: W. W. Norton, 1992.

Davidson, Basil. *The Black Man's Burden*. New York: Times Books, 1992.

Driver, C. J. *Elegy for a Revolutionary*. London: Faber and Faber, 1969.

du Buisson, Louis. *The White Man Cometh*. Johannesburg: Jonathan Ball, 1987.

Eppel, John. *DGG Berry's the Great North Road*. Cape Town: Carrefour Press, 1992.

Farwell, Byron. *The Great Anglo-Boer War*. New York: W. W. Norton, 1976.

Finnegan, William. *A Complicated War*. University of California Press, 1992.

Flower, Ken. *Serving Secretly*. Alberton, South Africa: Galago, 1987.

Gelfand, Michael. *Gubulawayo and Beyond*. London: Geoffrey Chapman, 1968.

Godwin, Peter, and Ian Hancock. *Rhodesians Never Die*. Oxford: Oxford University Press, 1993.

Hancock, Graham. *Lords of Poverty*. New York: Atlantic Monthly Press, 1989.

Hancock, Ian. *White Liberals, Moderates, and Radicals in Rhodesia*. London: St. Martin's Press, 1984.

Harden, Blaine. *Despatches from a Fragile Continent*. New York: W. W. Norton, 1990.

Harrison, David. *The White Tribe of Africa*. South Africa: Macmillan, 1983.

Hoare, Mike. *Congo Mercenary*. London: Robert Hale, 1967.

Holderness, Hardwicke. *Lost Chance: Southern Rhodesia, 1945–58*. Harare: Zimbabwe Publishing House, 1985.

Jack, Alex, and Louis Bolze. *Bulawayo's Changing Skyline*. Bulawayo: Books of Zimbabwe Rhodesia, 1979.

Joyce, Peter. *Anatomy of a Rebel*. New York: Graham Publishing, 1974.

Lamb, David. *The Africans*. New York: Vintage, 1987.

Leach, Graham. *The Afrikaners—Their Last Great Trek*. Macmillan London, 1989.

Lelyveld, Joseph. *Move Your Shadow*. New York: Times Books, 1985.

Lessing, Doris. *Under My Skin*. New York: HarperCollins, 1994.

Malan, Rian. *My Traitor's Heart*. New York: Atlantic Monthly Press, 1990.

Mallaby, Sebastian. *After Apartheid*. New York: Times Books, 1992.

Mandela, Nelson. *Long Walk to Freedom*. New York: Little, Brown, 1994.

Marnham, Patrick. *Fantastic Invasion*. London: Jonathan Cape, 1980.

Meredith, Martin. *The Past Is Another Country*. London: Andre Deutsch, 1979.

———. *The First Dance of Freedom*. London: Hamish Hamilton, 1984.

———. *In the Name of Apartheid*. London: Hamish Hamilton, 1988.

Millin, S. G. *Rhodes*. London: Chatto and Windus, 1933.

Moorcraft, Paul. *A Short Thousand Years*. Salisbury (now Harare): Galaxy Press, 1979.

Moore-King, Bruce. *White Man Black War*. Harare: Baobab Books, 1987.

Morris, Donald. *The Washing of the Spears*. New York: Simon and Schuster, 1965.

Naipaul, Shiva. *North of South*. London: Penguin, 1980.

Nkomo, Joshua. *The Story of My Life*. London: Methuen, 1984.

Packenham, Thomas. *The Boer War*. London: George Weidenfeld and Nicolson, 1979.

———. *The Scramble for Africa*. New York: Random House, 1991.

Pauw, Jacques. *In the Heart of the Whore*. Halfway House, South Africa: Southern Book Publishers, 1991.

Pogrund, Benjamin. *Sobukwe and Apartheid*. New Jersey: Rutgers University Press, 1991.

Potgeiter, De Wet. *Contraband*. Cape Town: Queillerie, 1995.

Reed, Douglas. *The Battle for Rhodesia*. Cape Town: Haum, 1966.

Reid Daley, Ron. *Selous Scouts Top Secret War*. Alberton, South Africa: Galago, 1982.

Ritter, E. A. *Shaka Zulu*. London: Longmans, 1955.

Sparks, Allister. *The Mind of South Africa*. New York: Alfred A. Knopf, 1990.

Stengel, Richard. *January Sun*. New York: Simon & Schuster, 1990.

Stiff, Peter. *See You in November.* Alberton, South Africa: Galago, 1985.

Taylor, Stephen. *The Mighty Nimrod.* London: Collins, 1989.

Todd, Judith. *The Right to Say No.* London: Sidgwick and Jackson, 1972.

———. *An Act of Terrorism: Rhodesia 1965.* London: Longman, 1982.

Turner, Richard. *The Eye of the Needle.* Johannesburg: Ravan Press, 1980.

Welensky, Sir Roy. *Welensky's 4000 Days.* London: Collins, 1964.

West, Richard. *White Tribes of Africa.* London: Macmillan, 1965.

Wheatcroft, Geoffrey. *The Randlords.* London: Weidenfeld, 1993.

Woods, Donald. *Biko.* Middlesex, England: Penguin, 1979.

———. *South African Despatches.* Middlesex, England: Penguin, 1987.

ACKNOWLEDGMENTS

This book would not have been possible without the generosity of friends and colleagues in Africa, Britain, and the United States. Above all, my thanks go to two women: my wife, Adriaane Pielou, for her eternal patience and unflagging encouragement, and my editor at Random House, Sharon DeLano, for applying her cool intellect to my sometimes fevered thoughts and for being persistent to the end. This book is also for my brother, David, his wife, Judith, and Colleen Ellis, who shared the last days of empire with me.

In Africa, Martin King and Ellen McDermott allowed me to use their Johannesburg home as my African office for three years. Franco and Debbie Esposito and Nigel Morris provided good companionship and insider aperçus on current affairs. Charles Nupen kept me honest at the gym and helped me understand the political changes more clearly. He and Fink Haysom read the manuscript, made invaluable observations, and conducted memorable briefings at late-night bars in Melville. Jan Taljaard, the unassailable expert on South Africa's white right, was always available to answer questions. The two Good Cops, Colonels Piet Lategan and Ivor Human, were mines of information. And the two pillars of the Endangered Wildlife Trust, Dr. John Ledger and his Moneypenny,

Marilyn Dougal, spent years sharing their knowledge of Africa's wildlife crisis with me.

In Bulawayo, Lu and Sheila Corbi were indefatigable hosts, and every time I returned to my old hometown, the legendary Bulawayo hospitality was rolled out—by Merve and Shuna, Bucky and Lydia, Fred and Maureen, Fats, Arthur and Louise—all Trojans of the Saturday-night razzle. The Todd family, whose collective knowledge of Rhodesian and Zimbabwean history is awesome, were infinitely patient teachers. Judy Todd's help with research and her painstaking examination of the manuscript underpinned large sections of this book. In Harare, Alistair and Tamara Wright opened their home to me, and Nigel Prior provided a constant flow of ironic sagacity. The iron man, Simon Metcalf, was a valuable adviser on conservation politics.

In Nairobi, the Winter family was always welcoming. On those evenings out on the veranda, watching the sun set over the Rift Valley, Bill told some of the most memorable African tales I have ever heard. Long nights and long stories around the campfire at Peter Beard's Hog Ranch were also a welcome relief from Nairobi's grim hustle.

Through the winter of '95 in Sag Harbor, New York, Cheryl Merser served meals of Michelin quality night after night while her husband, Michael Schnayerson, kept pouring the Cabernet and assuring me that one day this book would be finished. Jason Epstein and Judy Miller, Clive and Mimi Irving, Karen Lerner, and the late Joe Fox were kind hosts and marvelous company.

In New York, Linda Perney read early drafts with a critical and compassionate eye, as did my fellow African exile, Maria Mathiessen, and Abigail Winograd's copy editing of a ragged manuscript pulled it into shape. Many thanks to Tom Wallace, the editor-in-chief of *Condé Nast Traveler,* for his generosity and support.

In Washington, Jann Turner not only opened her family archives to me but bravely relived the days surrounding her father's assassination. And Kathi Austin, fearless and relentless human rights detective, was equally generous with her hard-won intelligence reports.

In London, Barbara Follett and Foszia Turner-Styleanou also re-lived the Turner assassination for my benefit and scrambled through boxes of old files to dig out long-forgotten documents. Chris and Margaret Morris, Richard Dawood and Gillian Whitby, and the Groucho Club provided homes away from home.

These are but a few. Throughout my African journey, I was received with kindness and understanding by almost everyone I met. I hope this book adequately reflects my great affection for Africa and its people.

INDEX

PHOTOGRAPHY CREDITS

About the Author

GRAHAM BOYNTON was raised in Bulawayo, Rhodesia, and later emigrated to South Africa, where he attended Natal University and worked as a journalist. In 1975 he was expelled from South Africa because of his opposition to apartheid. He worked for many years as a journalist in London and now lives in New York with his wife and two children.

About the Type

This book was set in Galliard, a typeface designed by Matthew Carter for the Merganthaler Linotype Company in 1978. Galliard is based on the sixteenth-century typefaces of Robert Granjon.